SOCIAL AND CULTURAL HISTORY OF INDIA SINCE 1556

SOCIAL AND CULTURAL HISTORY OF INDIA SINCE 1556

N. JAYAPALAN

ATLANTIC
PUBLISHERS & DISTRIBUTORS (P) LTD

Published by

ATLANTIC

PUBLISHERS & DISTRIBUTORS (P) LTD

7/22, Ansari Road, Darya Ganj, New Delhi-110002
Phones : +91-11-40775252, 23273880, 23275880, 23280451
Fax : +91-11-23285873
Web : www.atlanticbooks.com
E-mail : orders@atlanticbooks.com
Branch Office
5, Nallathambi Street, Wallajah Road, Chennai-600002
Phones : +91-44-64611085
E-mail : chennai@atlanticbooks.com

Printed in India at Nice Printing Press, A-33/3A, Site-IV, Industrial Area, Sahibabad, Ghaziabad, U.P.

Preface

It gives me great pleasure to place this book in the hands of the readers. The book is quite comprehensive and covers all aspects. It covers the entire syllabes prescribed by several universities. I have narrated all the events chronologically from the beginning to the end. I have also made a serious attempt to present the matter in a lucid and simple manner.

There is a plethora of books of the "Social and Cultural History of India since 1556." Most of them are bulky. Hence, I have written this book in a sizable volume *i.e.*, neither too small nor too big. In addition to this, I have given importance to the history of our Freedom Struggle and March of Free India so as to give a clear picture about the Social and Cultural History of India.

My experience of teaching the subject at the college level for several years has prompted me to write this book for the students of our universities mainly to fulfil their requirements. In addition to this, it has been designed to meet the requirements of the examinees of Civil Services Examination in History and Political Science. I hope that the present book will prove to be more useful to the students than any other book on the subject available in the market.

I am thankful to the M/s Atlantic Publishers and Distributors, New Delhi for readily agreeing to publish this book and bringing it out expeditiously and efficiently.

Suggestions, if any, for the improvement of the book in the subsequent editions will be highly appreciated.

N. JAYAPALAN

Contents

1

Mughal India (1556-1707)

(i) Social Structure under the Mughals. The social and economic conditions of Mughal India are important like political history of Mughals. "The real history of the people in Mughal India that is of their social life and economic condition is of greater interest and important for us today than mere catalogues of political events or military campaigns". V. Smith.

Social Conditions

The foreign travellers who came to India during Mughal reign have given a vast account of the social condition of the people.

The society was divided into nobility, middle class and lower class of people. There were also the ruling class, mansabdars jagirdars, zamindars and peasants. King was the head of the society. The Emperors, his courtiers and high officials belonged to privileged class and they enjoyed all the comforts and luxuries. The Mughal Emperors were very particular about their dress and spent lavishly over it. Akbar was more fond of clothes than even of food. He wore dress everyday according to stars. Jahangir adopted for himself certain special clothes. They were called "Nadir's coat" Shahjahan was most fond of splendour. He loved gorgeous and flowery dresses with delicate embroidery. Nurjahan introduced new sartorial fashions. The royal ladies were also fond of wearing saris. They used beautiful silk petticoat. They used beautiful ornaments. Women of wealth and position wore gold ornaments. Abul Fazal gives a list of 37 ornaments worn by a lady from head to foot.

Meat was an important item of food with the Muslims. Abul Fazal's list includes about twenty different kinds of meat dishes prepared in the imperial kitchen. Akbar took a keen interest in the success of imperial kitchen known as Matbakh. A sincere man was appointed to the post of Mir Bakawal (Master of the kitchen). According to pelsaert emperors were fond of khichri dish. Fruits were also used by the Mughal Emperors. Jahangir liked grapes, figs, oranges, apples and mangoes. Drinking of wine by the members of the royal family was common. Jahangir himself was a well known addict to wine. Aurangzeb prohibited wine drinking.

Mughal Emperors patronised music the most popular and artistic entertainment of the time. Aurangzeb forbade the court musicians to sing in the court.

Akbar introduced Mansabdari system in the army. The members of this corp received land from the monarch or fixed salaries for their military service. According to Irvin, "Mansabdar was that measure of status under the Mughal government which determined a Mansabdari (a) rank, (b) his salary and (c) his office of the royal court. Abul Fazal has stated that there were 66 grades of Mansabdars. Every Mansabar was fixed the number of troops to be maintained and in addition to the prescribed troops he had to maintain horsemen, elephants, carts carnels etc. They were given flat salaries. They were not duty conscious and led a life of pleasure. The properties of the Mansabdars were not given to the children after his death. The entire movable and immovable property would be confiscated by the government.

Since the Jagirdari system was abolished by Akbar they were not in a position to take part in the administration. The Jagirdari were corruptive and so the Sultanate period witnessed disaster. Instead of Jagirdari system Akbar organised the whole army on the basis as Mansabdari system.

Akbar introduced excellent land revenue system under Todarmal. During this period the Zamindars were relegated to the background. Their position and possessions were greatly affected. Their life was not so happy as that of the ruling class.

Agriculturists were the first and foremost producing class during this period. Agriculture was the main profession of the people. Bumper crops of grains were grown. During this period they produced wheat, barley, pulses, sugarcane, indigo, vegetables and fruits. Wheat was the main produce of Northern India. Rice was staple crop in Bengal, Orissa and Thatta, Indigo was grown on such a large scale that Sir Thomas Roe called it the prime commodity of India.

Akbar did a lot to the peasants. The advancing of Taqavi loans to the peasants was another important method of encouraging cultivation.

Peasants, weavers, factory and mill owners came under the category of producers and the rest under consumers. Peasants led a miserable life.

Their condition became worse after the death of Akbar. During the time of Aurangzeb agriculture received a great setback, due to the constant war.

In the Mughal Age, the Hindus formed the vast majority of the country's population and included the Jains, the Buddhists and the Sikhs. The upper class consisted of Brahmins, Rajputs, Kayasthas and Vaisyas and they did not inter-marry among themselves. The Brahmins were in priestly and teaching professions and many of them were doing agriculture. The Rajputs were military men and their tribal chiefs were rulers of extensive territories and held ranks as Mansabdars in the Mughal imperial services. Vaisyas were traders. The Kayasthas were largely as clerks, munshifs and revenue officers. Many lower caste Hindus changed their religion and accepted Islam.

The caste system of the Hindus had some influence on the Muslims too. Like the Hindus they also came to be divided into four classes—Sayyed, Sheikh, Mughal and Pathon.

Position of Women

One of the immediate impact of Islam on the condition of women was the introduction of Purdah system. Purdah or veiling of women was a common practice among the Muslims and it was adopted by the Hindu women also under the stress of circumstances. This system was particularly prevalent among high class families of both communities. But there are instances of queens like Nurjahan not observing purdah and going out in public without purdah. Muslim women of middle class families also observed purdah.

The Muslims believed in polygamy and could keep four wives at a time. The nobles could marry as many as they liked besides keeping many concubines.

Among the Hindus marriage was sacred tie for the whole of life. Hence, there was no question of divorce. Hindus mostly believed in one wife but Hindu rulers were exceptions to this rule.

As a general rule girls were married at an early date in both the communities. Girls were married at an early age of 7 or 8 years *viz.*, even before the age of puberty. The girls of the Rajput families enjoyed greater freedom in matters regarding the selection of their husbands. The selection of bridegroom was made on the basis of gallantry.

Divorce was not a common practice among the Hindus although it was an important social feature of Islam.

Widow remarriage was permitted amongst the Muslims but the widows were given the status of the second rate wife. Amongst the Hindus widow remarriage was almost non-existent.

The practice of sati was in full swing. Steps were taken during the Mughal period to curb this evil practice.

Another evil practice prevalent amongst the Hindus particularly the Rajputs was Jauhar. It was performed by the Rajput ladies when attacked by the foreigners and there was no hope of victory. According to this practice the Rajput ladies would apply tilak on the foreheads of their husbands, touched their feet and burnt themselves. This was done primarily to escape from dishonour at the hands of the enemy in case of defeats.

Right from the time of her birth a girl was considered to be a liability. The custom of infanticide viz., killing the girls at the time of their birth was in practice. Todd also mentioned about this evil practice.

As a child much attention was not paid to the education of the girls and they were given some training of the household activities like cooking, needle work etc. Girls of the higher families were however given education. As a wife also the women was supposed to work according to the commands and directions of the mother-in-law. The position of women in relation to her husband was one of honourable subordination.

Economically the position of Muslim women was much better than that of the Hindu women. The Muslim ladies are entitled to a definite share in the inheritance and were free to dispose of the same as they liked. Hindu ladies did not have any share in the property although they possessed movable property like ornaments, jewellery etc.

Certain talented women made good contribution in different spheres, Nurjahan and Zeb-un-Nisa, daughter of Aurangzeb were literary figures, who produced works of distinction. Even in the administration women like Maham Anaga (the chief nurse of Akbar) exercised great influence. It is well known that Nurjahan was the real power behind the throne of Jahangir. Nurjahan also discovered rose essence. She was very brave and once she killed two lions with one stroke of the sword.

The women usually used two types of garments *viz.*, chadar and cholas; cosmetics were used by them. The ornaments were used both by men and women, Abul Fazal has mentioned thirty seven kinds of different ornaments used by the women in India. These ornaments were made either of plain metal such as gold or silver or studded with jewels. Abul Fazal has also mentioned sixteen items of female cosmetics which were considered a must for the ladies of responsible families. These included a bath, an oil massage, dressing of loin putting an ornament on forehead together with sandalwood pastes, a suitable dress, a cast mark, antimony for the eyes, pendants for the ears, a pearl of gold nose ring, some ornaments for neck, bangles for the hands, girdle for waist, some ornaments for feet, chewing of betal-leaf, and grace of manners.

Dress and food habits

Dress varied from region to region and people to people. The lower status of men wore simple dress. The richer section of the people ware embroidered robe. Fine dhotis were used by well to do Hindus.

People in general were vegetarians, meat diet was not forbidden and the drinking of liquor too was fairly common. But drinking was forbidden to women of the Brahmin, Kshatriya and Vaishya castes. The normal food of the masters was 'Khichri' prepared with rice and pulses. The people of the south were mainly rice eaters.

Recreations

Abul Fazal has given us some details about the games in his Akbarnama. Hunting was a favourite pastime of the Mughals. Jahangir was especially fond of it. The tiger and lion hunting was the privilege of the royalty. Akbar took great interest in the hunting and training of wild elephants. The common people delighted in hunting of hare, deer or other wild beasts. Nearly all Mughal Emperors were fond of witnessing animal fights. Elephant combat was the most favourite pastime. Shooting and catching or birds was very common among people of all ranks. Pigeon-fighting was common entertainment for ordinary people as well as the nobility. Mughal kings were very fond of rearing in tanks and ponds various types of coloured and shining fish.

As regards indoor games, the most popular one was chess. Chanper, playing cards, jugglery and dancing were other entertainments of people.

Festivals and fairs

The festivals and fairs were the most common means of amusement for the common village people. The most popular Hindu festivals were those of Basant Panchami, Holi, Diwali, Sivaratri and others connected with the various incidents of the life of Krishna. Dashara festival was also very popular. The most popular Muslim festivals were Nawroz, Muharram, Rabi, Shabi, Barat, Id, Id-ul-Azha and ceremonies connected with the birth of Prophet.

Jahangir followed Akbar and celebrated Hindu festivals as Rakhi, Dashara and Dewali. This they did in order to establish good relations between both the communities. The Muslims participated in Hindu festivals and fairs without prejudices.

Life in Towns, Cities and Villages

Village was the basic unit of economic organisation. Agriculture was the main profession of the people. Bumper crops of grains were grown, Cash crops, such as cotton, sugarcane, lintels, oilseeds, poppy, indigo etc. were produced on large scale. Fruits of various varieties were produced in many parts of the country. Vegetables were grown in abundance in the country.

Facilities for irrigation were made to the farmers. Mughal Emperors followed the policy of trying to relieve the distress of the people as much as they could.

A number of crafts and industries were carried on a small scale in the villages. Among the home industries the most important were those of weaving and spinning of cotton. The villagers were not only economically self-sufficient but also fed a number of rural industries *viz.*, making of ropes and baskets and manufacture of sugar, scents, oils etc. Certain craftsmen like weavers, leather workers, dyers, wood workers etc., were also found in such villages. Usually every village possessed a small market where necessities of life were sold by petty shopkeepers. Every village had its own blacksmith and they manufactured various agricultural implements and arms for home use.

A large share of the produce of land went to the state, in the form of land tax. Of the remainder, a customary share was fixed for various classes of domestic and other labourers.

In the cities and towns there were many silk industries, textile industry and metal industry and other industries. Silk industrial centres were Lahore, Agra, Fatehpur and Ahmadabad. The manufacture of textiles was the biggest industry of Hindustan. It included the manufacture of cotton cloth and silk. Abul Fazal also writes that Malwa produced its best cotton textile. The other centres in the field were Banares, Jalalabad and Meerut. Bengal and Gujarat led the whole of India in the manufacture and export of textile goods. Expert stone workers lived in many towns, during this period. Travernier has given a vivid account of the diamond mines and their working. Silver, paper, sugar and leather works were largely undertaken in many cities and towns. Akbar encouraged perfumery industry in his reign.

India traded with Ceylon, Burma, Japan, China, Indo-China and many European countries. Portuguese, Dutch and English people used to sell Indian goods in the European markets. Besides cloth, indigo, sugar, salt, spices, alum, sealing wax, beeds etc., were also exported in large quantity. In return India would get gold, diamond, pearls, velvet, medicines, wine and also slaves from Africa. Glass ariticles were mainly imported from Venice.

Agra was well connected by the roads to different parts of the empire. Boats, carts, animals, elephants and horses were used for transportation of goods. A foreign traveller wrote in 1685 that Agra and Sikri were two big cities and both of them were more prosperous than the city of London.

There was wide gulf, between the producers and consumers.

During the Mughal rule the things of daily use like corn, vegetables, fruits, milk, ghee etc., were cheap. The people of cities, towns and villages led a comfortable life. In short the economic condition of the people was good and people were happy and prosperous.

(ii) Education. With the coming of the Mughals educational and cultural activities received great fillip. Akbar the great Mughal ruler, showed much greater interest in education. His reign marked the beginning of a new chapter in the history of education for Muslim India. Though Akbar was himself much educated he showed a great love for the scholars and education. Akbar took keen interest in child education and expressed his great love for children. In one of his sayings he expressed his great love he bore for children. Children are the tenderest birds of the Garden of Existence. By loving them we praise the creator. Akbar also took interest to introduce reforms in the curriculum of primary schools. He laid down that every one ought to read books on morals, arithmetic, the notation peculiar to the arithmetic, agriculture, mensuration, geometry, astronomy, physiognomy, household matters, the rules of Government, medicine, logic, the Tabii (Physical Science), Riyazi and Ilahi (theology), science and history; all of which may be gradually acquired.

The Emperor (Akbar) directed that in the schools meant for Sanskrit learning Vyakaran, Nyaya, Vedant and the commentary of Patanjali should be taught. No one should be allowed to neglect the important things of the time. Akbar also tried to simplify the mode of instruction. He realised that much time was wasted by making boys at school to read many books and therefore he ordered that first a boy should learn to write combined words. After this he should commit to memory some verses to the praise of God or moral sentences each written separately.

Care is to be taken that he learnt to understand everything himself, but the teacher may assist him a little. A great change which was made in the time of Sikandar Lodi and it continued during the reign of Akbar. It was that Hindu students began to be admitted into the Muslim Maktabs and Madrasas. The result was that within half a century there was a large number of Hindu scholars, historians and poets of Persian, and some of these excelled in rational sciences and were appointed teachers of the Persian language in the Madrasas. The bias of education in the time of Akbar was more secular than religious.

The syllabus of Madrasas all over the country was called as Dars-e-Nizami consisting of eleven subjects with books prescribed for each. These were (1) Sarf (Declension of conjugation). The books recommended were: Mizan, Munshaib, Sarf-e-Mir, Fusul-e-Akbari, Zubda, Panjganj and Shafia, (2) Nahv (grammar of syntax). The books recommended were: Nahv Mir, Sharh-e-ma-ta, Amil, Hidayatum Nehv, Kafia, Sharh-e-Jami, (3) Mantiq (Logic). The books were: Shughra, Sharh-e-Jahzib, Qulb-e-ma, Kubra Isaghoji Tahzib, Qulb-e-ma-Mir and Sallamut Ulma, (4) Hikma (Philosophy). The books prescribed were : Shams-e-Bazi-gha, Maibazi, Sadra, (5) Raizi (Mathematics). The books were : Tashrihul Aflak, Risala-i-qaush-ajia, Sharhe, Tahrir-e-uqlides Maqalai-ula, Babe-e-Awwal. (6) Balaghar (rhetoric), The books were : Mukhtsir Maani. Mutawwal upto Maani qutlu, (7) Fiqh (Jurisprudence), The books recommended were : Hidaya Akherin, Sharh-e-waqaya Awwalin, (8) Usul-e-Fiqh (Principles of Jurisprudence), The books were: Taudih-i-Talwih, Nurual Anwar, (9) Kalam (Dialectic), The books were: Sharh-e-Aqaid Nasafi, Sharh-e-Aqaide Jalali, (10) Tafsir (Exigencies), The books were : Jalalain and Baizawi, (11) Hadis (Traditions), The book was Almasabih. The other four Subjects were also added to the above syllabus, (1) Adab (Literature) books Nafhatul Yaman, Saba Muallaqa, Diwan-e-Muntannabbi, Mugamat-e-Hanri and Hamasa, (2) Faraiz (Obligations) books; Sharifia, (3) Munazara (Disputation) no books recommeded, (4) Usule Hadis (Principles of Hadis).

The result of the new education policy of Akbar was that many Hindus took to the study of Persian. Della Valle, who visited India at the time of Jahangir tells us that in Madrasas and the Maktabs there was no invidious discrimination between the Hindus and the Muslims. Abul Fazal has given a list of some Hindu scholars in the Ain-i-Akbari, who excelled in rational science (U' aqulat). These names are Narain Madho Bhat, Sir Bhat, Bishan Nath, Ram Kishan, Balbhadra Misra, Vasudeva Misra, Bhan Bhat, Vidya Nivas, Gauri Nath, Gopi Nath, Kishan Pandit,

Bhattacharji, Bhagirath, Kashi Nath, Mahadeo, Bhim Nath and Narain Sivji. The last four scholars were scholars of medicine as well as practising physicians attached to the court. Some of the Hindu physicians wrote books in Persian on the science of medicine. Akbar built a magnificent Madrasa near the royal residence on the hill in the palace city of Fatehpur-Sikri. Abul Fazal also founded a Madrasa at Fatehpur-Sikri which was known as Madrasa Abul Fazal. Akbar founded a Madrasa at Agra and Chalpi Beg a Savar of Shiraz, was appointed as its principal.

Akbar's foster-mother, Maham Anaga, established Madrasa at Delhi, with a mosque attached to it. It was called 'Khairul Manzil.' Akbar and his nobles and successors founded Madrasas and endowed them with funds. Jahangir made a rule that if a noble died without an heir his property should be utilized for the maintenance of Madrasas. Shiekh Husan Ali of Mosul taught Jahangir lessons from Persian and treatise on philosophy. Jahangir encouraged men of learning. The celebrated servant of his time, Shaikh Abdul Haq Muhaddis, was partonized by him. Jahangir has mentioned in Tuzuk that professors of every religion and creed had taken up their abode in Agra, where students thronged from far and near. To such an extent was Jahangir interested in the promotion of education that soon after his accession, he repaired even those Madrasas and Maktabs, which for three decades had been dwelling places of birds and beasts, and filled them with students and learned professors. Shahjahan founded a Madrasa near the Jama-Masjid of Delhi and endowed it with sufficient estates for its maintenance. In his reign Mulla Farid a great Mathematician of the time prepared a new astronomical table and was named 'Ziche Shahjahani' (Amal-i-saleh), Shahjahan partonized men of learning and poets. One of his beneficiaries was Chander Brahman, a writer of distinction whose 'Manshaat-i-Brahman' was a text book in schools for very long time. Abdul Hakim Siakoti, Mulla Muhammad Fazil and Qazi Muhammad Aslam were also learned men of his time. The daughter of Shahjahan, Jahanara Begum founded a Madrasa at Agra, attached to the Jama Masjid.

Aurangzeb founded various Madrasas all over the country and fixed stipends for teachers and students. The Madrasai Rahimiyya was built in his reign. According to Alamgirnama, a considerable amount of money used to be spent annually on the stipends to the students in the Madrasas increased and poor and deserving students could continue their studies without financial difficulties. Assistance was provided to the students according to their proficiency. The students who studied Mizan received one anna daily, and those who studied Munshaib two annas, and upto Sharhe waqayat eight annas daily. Aurangzeb issued a Farman to Makramat Khan, the Diwan of Gujarat with regard to establishment of schools and awards of stipends to students. Maulana Nuzruddin who taught in the Madrasa Hidiyat Buksh did not accept a royal stipend which Aurangzeb wanted to grant him. Akramuddin Khan, Sadar of Gujarat, built a Madrasa at Ahmedabad with a cost of one lakh and twenty four thousand rupees and requested the Emperor to meet its running expenses. The Emperor was pleased to sanction a Jagir the village of Sondrah and the village of Sabilah and granted the stipend of two rupees daily to be distributed to poor and deserving students.

A great achievement of Aurangzeb's time was the compilation of the 'Fatawa-i-Alamgiri' the most comprehensive digest of Muslim Jurisprudence ever compiled.

In the later Mughal period, most of the new Madrasas were founded by the nobles who were also interested in the advancement of learning. The Madrasas of Ghaziuddin Khan, and the Madrasa of Sharfud Daulah and the Madrasa of Raushanud Daulah in Delhi, the Madrasa of Hasan Raza Khan at Farrukhabad and similar Madrasas at Allahabad, Hyderabad, and Kurnool were all founded by nobles.

It may be mentioned that each seat of higher learning specialized in one particular branch. For example, the Delhi School of Shah Waliullah specialized in the Traditions (Hadis) and the exigencies (Tafsir) the Farangimahli school of Luknow specialized in Jurisprudence (Fiqh), and the Sialkot school specialized in grammar.

Students were promoted from a lower to a higher class according to the opinion of the teachers concerned who took into account the total academic career of the students. There was no regular system of annual examinations. One who had excelled in logic and philosophy was awarded the degree of 'Alim' and the expert in literature was awarded the degree of 'Qabil. A ceremony was held at the time of the awarding of the degrees.

Hindu Education

Hindu students rarely attended Muslim educational institutions. However, when Persian became the court language, many, Hindus attended Muslim schools. Similarly some Muslim students also attended Hindu schools to learn subjects like Astronomy, Astrology, Mathematics, Medicine etc.

Hindu education was mainly imparted by Pathshalas or elementary schools, Tols or colleges and private-tutor schools. Besides Brahmins, other persons also imparted education. Regular study of a Hindu child started after the Upanayana ceremony. The courses consisted of instructions in the alphabet, vowels and consonants, combination of words, spellings, grammar, lessons in reading elementary arithmetic.

There were no slates, pencils or black boards in those schools. Great attention was paid to handwriting. A beginner first learnt writing letters in a comparatively bigger size till his hand would be set to write smaller ones. At this stage palm leaves and Bhoj-Patra served the purpose of paper.

Students desirous of getting higher education would continue to learn further from their teacher and join some Tol (college) which was the higher seat of learning. Sanskrit was mainly taught in these Tols. Students were generally taught subject like Kavya, Vyakaran, Jyotis and Astrology, Chhanda (Rhetoric), Nirukta and Philosophy.

There were many centres of higher Hindu learning, and the most famous were Banaras, Mathura, Prayag, Ayodhya, Nadia, Mithila and Srinagar in Kashmir. Abul Fazal says about Banaras "from time immemorial it has been the chief seat of learning in Hindustan. Crowds of people flock to it from the most distant parts for the purpose of instruction, to which they apply themselves with the most devoted assiduity." Here there were many institutions of higher learning and a large number of Brahman teachers devoted their entire lives to the study of the Veda Shastras and the Purans and taught these subjects upto the highest classes. Bernier compares Banaras with Athens of ancient Greece. The towns contain no colleges or regular classes as in our Universities but resembles rather the schools of the ancient days. Though he failed to inform us the existence of colleges, but there is no doubt that there were such institutions of higher learning. Travernier who visited India in 1665 described the working of college established by Raja Jai Singh for the education of youth of well to do families. In Bengal, Nadia or Navdwip was the most famous centre of learning and the city was full of learned professors. In North Bihar, Mithila was also a flourishing centre of learning. Abul Fazal also confirms the importance of Mithila as a great centre of Hindu learning. Two Maithili Brahman scholars and poets of Hindi and Sanskrit had achieved great fame for scholarship and poetic talent.

Female Education

During the Mughal period, there were no separate schools for girls. Sometime boys and girls read together in the same elementary schools.

This stipulates that there was no separate curriculum for boys and girls. The education of women, Hindu and Muslim was mostly confined to rich and well-to-do classes of the society. On account of the marriage of women at an early age and the purdah or seclusion system in vogue, their opportunity of receiving education was greatly restricted. Women belonging to the poorer classes of society had very little chance of getting education.

In Mughal age also women belonging to royalty got education. Gulbadan Begum, Humayun's sister, wrote Humayun Nama. Salima Sultana, Maham Anaga, Nur-Jahan, Chand Sultana and Mumtaz Mahal were all educated women. Jahanara Begum, daughter of Shahjahan, a genius for poetry, Zebunnisa, daughter of Aurangzeb, were highly intellectual women. She established a literary academy and library for the use of scholars. She wrote a poetry of high order. Besides royalty and the nobility, even among the middle classes the education of girls was quite common. There were Maktabs for giving religious education to girls in private houses where elderly ladies taught the Quran, Gulistan, Bustan and books on morality.

(iii) Art and Architecture-Painting and Music. The Mughal age was not only a period of experiment and innovation but of continuation and culmination of the process of fine arts that had their seed sown in the later part of the Turko Afghan rule. Again, The Mughal Emperors being lovers of fine arts had evolved new styles and techniques which indicate a happy mingling of Persian and Indian elements. This synthesis has left a deep impression on painting, architecture, embroidery, jewellery and metal work of the age. All the fine arts of the period breath a spirit of luxury.

Mughal Architecture

The Mughal Emperors took keen interest in the art of architecture. The architecture of the Mughal period presents of fine example of the synthesis of Persian and Indian elements. The Mughal Emperors had enormous wealth. They built many beautiful buildings. According to Fergusson, the Mughal style of architecture was foreign in origin, especially from the point of view of decoration. But E.B. Havel has rejected this view and has remarked that Indian culture had a remarkable power of absorbing foreign elements of art. It has been rightly remarked by Dr. Iswari Prasad that "the Mughal style, which was amalgamation of many influences was more sumptuous and decorative than the style that preceded it, and its delicacy and ornamentation furnished a striking contrast to the massiveness and simplicity of the art of pre-Mughal days."

With the Mughals getting a strong foothold at Delhi, Indo-Islamic architecture entered its most fascinating phase and large number of works of unusual brilliance and splendour were produced. It was purely Indian architecture movement where in both the Hindus and Mohammedan craftsmen joined together their inventive and artistic faculties to create dreams in marble and stone.

Architecture under Babur

Babur, a man of critical taste, did not much appreciate the buildings of the Turkish and Afghan rulers at Delhi and Agra. But he was impressed by the beautiful architecture at Gwalior where he saw all the palaces of Man Singh and Vikrama Jit and pronounced them "Singularly beautiful, though built in different patches and without regular plan." The palaces at Gwalior were a fine example of the Hindu architecture and attracted Babur. He employed many hundreds of workmen on his buildings in Agra, Sikri, Bayana Dholpur, Gwalior and Aligarh (Koil). But ably two of his buildings have survived and these are a large mosque at Panipat and a Jama Masjid at Sambhal in Rohilkhand, both built in 1529. The style of these buildings are purely Indian. The third building of his time was also a mosque, built by Abul Baqi at his orders at Ayodhya. But these buildings have no special architectural significance.

Humayun was also fond of architecture, did not leave behind any permanent architectural monument. His troubled reign does not seem to have been favourable for providing buildings at least on a permanent scale though we learn that he erected a magnificent palace of seven storeys surrounded by gardens and orchards, which is also called as 7 halls of audience.

The building seems to have been splendid but it may have been composed of ephemeral materials. The two mosques built by him, one at Agra and the other at Fatehabad in Hisar, are in ruins and do not possess any originality of design. It has been embellished in Persian style.

Khana-i-Tilism

The most fascinating building which Humayun erected was the famous Khana-i-Tilism (the magic house). It contained a group of buildings constructed at Agra on the bank of river Jamuna. The whole is collectively, known as Khana-i-Tilism or Imarat-i-Tilism.

Qasr-i-Rawan

This was the most novel of all his buildings. It consisted of three storeys, whose separate pieces were most artistically joined, and it was not easy to distinguish them from one another.

The Mausoleum of Shershah

The next example of the Indo-Muslim architecture is the mausoleum of Shershah which was built by him on a high plinth in the centre of a lake at Sahasram in Bihar. The building is Muhammadan in design, but its interior is embellished with Hindu corbelling and horizontal architraves, Havel says that Shershah tomb is as purely Indian in conception as any Hindu temple. Shershah erected another important building, namely, the Purana Qila on the site of Humayun's Din Panah. Only a part of the Purana Qila has escaped the ravages of time. He also built a mosque inside it, known as the Qila-i-Kunhna Masjid.

Akbar's buildings

The style of architecture evolved by Akbar represented a fusion of the Hindu and Muslim styles and may be called the mixed Hindu Muslim style. During the reign of Akbar architecture got much impetus. The emperor's interest and patronage of architecture led to the erection of magnificent monuments. Abul Fazal says that "His Majesty plans splendid edifices and dresses the work of his mind and heart in the garment of stone and clay. In the sphere of the building arts, Akbar found the artisans of India still maintaining the living traditions of their craft. The guilds of workmen merely required organisation to provide the type of structure that be desired. The style of building that evolved under this ruler's patronage was chiefly executed in red sand stone readily available in these parts. Fergusson says that Akbar was one of the greatest builders of his race and left few of his capitals except perhaps Delhi without some fit monuments of his greatness. His buildings are all very similar to one another in style, but very unlike those either before or after his time.

In fact the Mughal architecture begins with Akbar who was without doubt a great and prolific builder. During his reign, many beautiful buildings were built which were later on developed by his successor. Akbar stood and worked sincerely for Hindu-Muslim unity and he was an admirer of Hindu-Muslim arts. He liked the Hindu arts as much as he liked the Muslim arts, and there is a combination of both styles in his monuments. An example of Hindu style of architecture under Akbar may be seen in the Jahangiri Mahal in the Agra Fort. Besides this, the palace of Jodhbai resembles the Jain temples.

Humayun's Tomb

The earliest buildings of Akbar's reign is the tomb of Humayun at Delhi which was built by Haji Begum, the widow of Humayun. This building is Persian in style.

The Agra Fort

The earliest specimen of Akbar's new style of architecture is the Red Fort at Agra. It was begun in 1565 under the supervision of Qasim Khan and it cost thirty five lacks of rupees in the currency of that time. It is nearly 1½ miles in its circuit, and the inner walls, entirely made of bewared sand stone, are nearly 70 feet high. Percy Brown says that these walls "were composed of a massive interior core of rubble and concrete faced with carefully worked block of sand-stone linked together by iron rings". The fort had originally four gates, two of which were later walled up. The other two remain to this day. The main gate on the western side, which was finished in 1566, is known as the Delhi Gate. Passing through this gate one reaches the inner entrance called the Hathi Pole or Elephant gate, because its arch way was flanked by two elephants with their riders in stone. These were raised to the ground by Aurangzeb's order in 1668. Percy Brown says, "This Delhi Gate is undeniably one of the most impressive portals in all India". The other gateway is a smaller one and is known as the Amar Singh gate. It was for private use, and it derived its name from an incident that took place in the time of Shahjahan. Within the Fort Akbar erected more than 500 buildings of red-sand-stone, carved out in the beautiful styles of Bengal and Gujarat. Many of these beautiful edifices were destroyed by Shahjahan who erected white marble structures in their place. According to De Laet, the fort is a wonderful place and is most beautiful to look from all view points.

Jahangiri Mahal

It was built by the Emperor for the residence of his son, Jahangir. This palace is almost a square building, measuring 249 feet by 260 feet, and is surmounted by four large kiosks, one on each of its four corners. The gate of the palace is a pointed archway and simple in design, but is embellished with patterns carried out in white marble in lay. "The small entrance, through a narrow corridor, leads to the inner building, the Jahangiri Mahal, which is built after the plan of a central rectangular courtyard with tiers of double storeyed rooms on each of the four sides. The rooms are built almost entirely of red-sand-stone. The palace is almost wholly Hindu in design and workman-ship, the principle of construction being the 'beam and bracket'. The roofs are flat and not vaulted : the arch too has been avoided as far as possible and used only 'in its ornamental capacity'." The most notable feature of this palace is its carved and ornamental stone brackets which support the stone beams, wide caves and flat ceilings in all part of the building. Jahangiri Mahal is characteristically Hindu and is almost of Gwalior style.

In front of the Jahangiri Mahal lies a stone cistern of Jahangir. It is shaped like a bowl hewn out of single block of greenish black stone, and is 5 feet high, 4 feet deep, 8 feet in diameter and 25 feet in circumference. It was used as a bath tub.

Akbari Mahal

It was one of the earliest buildings of Akbar. Though the main structure of Akbari Mahal is no longer in existence, its general plan is clear enough. It was constructed after same design as Jahangiri Mahal.

The Fort of Lahore

Akbar had to shift his capital from Fatehpur to Lahore in the year 1586. The Uzbek menace had increased. The fort of Lahore was built almost at the same time as the Agra fort and was constructed on the same ground scale.

The Fort of Allahabad

The fort of Allahabad was built by Akbar in November, 1583. The outer walls of the fort have been partly dismantled. This fort too, like the Agra fort, is built after an irregular plan on account of its position at the junction of the Ganga and the Yamuna. One noble pavilion, however, still remains intact, the Zenana palace, from which the character of the whole may be surmised.

The Fort of Attock

The fort of Attock was constructed in 1581 when Akbar went to the north west frontier to suppress the rebellion of his brother Mirza Hakim of Kabul who had invaded the Punjab. It is a massive structure, constructed for the purpose of defence and is not of great architecture value. It is in ruins.

Fatehpur Sikri

The most ambitious architectural project and notable building achievement of Akbar's reign is the new capital city of Fatehpur Sikri and its buildings. Fergusson remarked that Fatehpur Sikri was the reflex of the mind of a great man (Akbar). Fatehpur Sikri is no original and so experimental that every building in it is a variation on a theme and a novel invention. Never before, never since has any one succeeded in blending so admirably structural and stylistic components of Hindu architecture with Islamic motifs. As we know Akbar was a prolific builder, but it was at Fatehpur Sikri his new capital, that he congregated the grandest of his monumental works. He built many fine buildings for his own residence, bath gardens and an arena for elephant fights and a playground.

Abul Fazal writes, "His (Akbar's) exalted sons (Salim and Murad) had taken their birth in Sikri and the God-knowing spirit of Shaikh Salim had taken possession thereof, his holy heart desired to give outward splendour to this spot which possessed spiritual grandeur and order was issued that the superintendents of affairs should erect lofty buildings for the special use of Shahanshah." Jahangir writes in his autobiography, "My revered father, considering the village of Sikri, which was the place of my birth, lucky for him, made it his capital. In the course of 14 of 15 years that hill, full of wild beasts, became a city containing all kinds of gardens and buildings, and lofty, elegant edifices and pleasant palaces, attractive to the heart." After the conquest of Gujarat, this village was named Fatehabad, but in common use it began to be called Fatehpur Sikri.

Diwan-i-Am

The Diwan-i-Am situated on very high plinth is by itself an unpretentious, though richly carved, structure having a single oblong room with a verandah in front, covered by slanting roofs of red-sand-stone and shielded by beautiful stone screens. In this room Akbar used to hold his Darbar.

Diwan-i-Khas

The buildings stands on a high red sand stone terrace. It is the most distinctive among the administrative edifices in the city being most unusual in conception. It is a square edifice measuring 43 feet on each side and containing a single vaulted chamber, 28 feet and 8 inches square. It has a flat terraced roof, each angle of which is surmounted by a pillared kiosk. The vaulted chamber is surrounded by corridors containing staircases that lead to the galleries above. The interior arrangements of the Diwan-i-Khas are unique. Percy Brown says that in Fatehpur Sikri, the Diwan-i-Khas or Hall of private audience, which is undoubtedly most distinctive, is not a large structure but conceived in an unusual manner.

The Treasury

The buildings next to Diwan-i-Khas and just to the North of it is the royal treasury. It consists of a suite of rooms and does not seem to possess any architectural significance.

The Astrologer's Canopy

Adjacent to the treasury on a stone platform to its west, is situated a square canopy called the Astrologer's seat. The canopy is open on all sides and is richly decorated with carvings.

The Panch Mahal

It is a five-storeyed structure raised on elaborate ornamental pillars, each carved in a wholly different design. The ground floor of this five storeyed open pavilion is an extensive hall with 48 pillars, over which are erected the remaining four storeys. All the storeys are connected with one another by suitable stair cases.

Turkish Sultan's Palace

This is the most exquisitely carved building and it is an exquisitely cut structural composition, consisting of a single storeyed pavilion and a pillard verandah. All the walls of this palace are chiselled into a pattern of exquisite delicacy and refinement. This building is remarkable for the application of blue-glazes to its slanting roofs. Percy Brown thinks that this building, on account of its character and the technique of plastic embellishment, suggests a wooden derivation and must have been built by artisans from the Punjab where timber tradition in the building art was in vogue in Akbar's time. He was so much impressed with this building that he called it an architectural gem.

The Khas Mahal

It is a double storeyed building adjoining the Turkish Sultan's palace and consists of a suite of chambers on the ground floor and the upper storey. The building was surmounted by four cupolas arising from its angles. "There was an outer wall with screens of white marble and red granite to provide seclusion for the ladies of imperial seraglio". It is a square room nearly 15 feet on each side, and is simple in design and the room has four doors. On the upper storey of this palace is Jharokha-i-Darshan from where the emperor used to show himself, every morning to the assembled public down below. Facing the Khas Mahal and the Turkish Sultan's palace is a masonry tank with a raised platform in the centre. The tank used to be filled with rose water and the emperor and his queen used to enjoy the cool fragrant breeze.

Jodh Bai's Palace

It is the most elaborate and complete structure among the residential buildings of Fatehpur Sikri. It is a rectangular edifice and measures 230 feet by 215 feet, enclosed by a wall 32 feet high. It has one entrance. On the south of the building are situated service and bathing apartments, and on the North there is a double storeyed pavilion or Hawa Mahal. The enclosing wall is quite plain, but very strongly built. The gateway on the east is decorated with balconies and surmounted by two handsome kiosks. The interior of this palace consists of a series of symmetrically set double-storeyed building on the four sides, all facing in ward on to the quadrangle." The buildings on the first storey are not continuous, for in the corners there are open terraced roofs decorated with coloured tiles, with all the four corners of the palace surmounted by low-pitched domes. The whole structure was so designed that each group of apartments could on occasion be readily divided off from the others, and it was also arranged that the chambers below in cold weather could be heated, those above always remaining airy and cool."

This building is almost completely Hindu in design and workmanship. Havel and Percy Brown say that its construction must have been entrusted to artisans from Gujarat.

House of Mariam

In the same spacious court yard of Jodh Bai's palace is situated the house of Mariam. Akbar's chief Rajput queen and mother of Jahangir. Mariam or Mariam-us-Zamani was the posthumous title of Jahangir's mother. Mariam's house is a small structure meant for the residence of Akbar's principal Rajput queen. It is in two storeys and consists of rooms without any court-yard. Mariam's house is notable for the stone carving on the capitals of its pillars which are beautified with figures of animals. Such as, elephants, tigers, and monkeys. It is also distinguished for its interior decoration. On its wall there are portraits of human beings in gold and red, blue and other colours, which have now disappeared.

Birbal's Palace

Birbal was a court wit and a favourite of Akbar. He became one of the Nau-Ratanas of the imperial court. His palace is one of the most exquisitely carved and embellished building in Fatehpur Sikri. It is a two-storeyed house and consists of four rooms and two porches on the ground floor. The most remarkable thing of the building lies in the exuberance of its carved decoration and in its highly ornate brackets. Its wide caves are supported on elegant brackets which are amazingly embellished with profused carving. In no other building in Fatehpur Sikri has this structural and decorative element been so liberally employed or so elaborately designed and executed as in this relatively small but lavishly devised ministerial abode.

Royal Stables

At a little distance from Birbal's palace are situated the royal stables for elephants, camels and horses.

Hathi Pol Sarai and Hiran Minar

The Hathi pol or the Elephant Gate is a massive structure flanked by two octagonal bastions. Very near the Elephant Gate lies a splendid bastion, called Sangin Burj. Outside, between the Elephant gate and Sangin Burj is situated a vast Caravan sarai which was built by Emperor Akbar for merchants and other travellers from the various parts of the empire as well as from the countries of Central Asia. Here merchants brought costly embroidered silk and woolen fabrics and jewels and articles of silver and gold. There was a splendid gallery screened by a stone lattice connecting the Sarai with the female apartments of the palace, so that the ladies of the harem could visit the place and see the rich merchandise exhibited here. The building is now in a dilapidated condition.

At a corner of this Sarai, on the brink of the lake, there stands a tower known as Hiran Minar. It is a 90 feet high tower, circular in shape, and is surmounted by a domed cupola open on all sides. It is presumed that Akbar used to watch deer bunts from the top of this tower. So it is called Hiran Minar.

Jama Masjid

Akbar wished to make it one of the most splendid mosques of Sikri. It was modelled after the famous mosque at Mecca. The enclosure is a rectangular courtyard, measuring 542 feet by 438 feet, and had originally three identical gates in the centre of each, the north, the south and the east wings. But later on, the northern gate was closed. Akbar, after the return from Deccan campaign, ordered the demolition of the southern gate and built in its place, a more magnificent gateway known as Buland Darwaza. The Jami Mosque was begun in 1571 and was completed in

1575. The mosque is very elaborate in design and measures 288 feet by 66 feet. Jami Mosque being a religious building is also an important building of Fatehpur Sikri. Although the plan of the mosque is based on the Persian model the building is Indian in design. The pillars of this mosque, as well as its roof, are purely Hindu. All the domes have Hindu pinnacles, the brackets in the principal building are of pure Hindu design. The mosque including the nave has decorative murals. This mosque is one of the finest in the country.

The Buland Darwaza

The Buland Darwaza is an imposing structure and 134 feet above the raised plinth upon which it is built. Its southern facade is 130 feet broad and from front to back, 123 feet. The Buland Darwaza is a complete structure. It contains large halls, and a number of smaller rooms which are connected with one another. "Buland Darwaza is built of red sand stone and as there a painted decoration on it, but only carving and discreet inlaying of white marble, the design of the whole structure and its decoration was in the hands of Akbar's Indian Master Builders." It is the highest of the Indian gateways, and among the largest in the world. This Buland Darwaza is much wide and beautiful. It was erected to commemorate the Akbar's victory of Khandesh in 1601. This has been described as the most perfect architectural achievement in the whole of India.

Shaikh Salim Chisti's Mausoleum

The Mausoleum of Shaikh Salim Chisti is a beautiful architectural example of Sikri. It is built of white marble, and it is the only building in Fatehpur Sikri in the construction of which nothing but marble is used. According to V.A. Smith and Percy Brown, it was originally built of red-sand stone like other buildings of Sikri, but either in the time of Jahangir or in the beginning of the reign of Shahjahan the same was changed completely into a marble structure. The tomb is a square in plan, measuring 24 feet on each side. The mausoleum pullars in the portico are embellished by brackets of the most elaborate design and seem to have been the work of the early years of Jahangir's reign. These architectural details were borrowed from Hindu temples. V.A. Smith was surprised to own that the whole structure suggests Hindu feeling. Both Fergusson and Percy Brown are of opinion that the decorative designs of some of the brackets and struts though unique, produce an effect more fantastic than beautiful, suggesting the unrestrained imagination of the temple builders rather than the rationality and reserve of Islam.

Islam Khan's Tomb

Islam Khan's tombs stands to the south of Shaikh Salim Chisti's mausoleum. Islam Khan died in 1613 A.D. and was buried in the courtyard of the Jami Mosque, and a gigantic red sand stone mausoleum was constructed over his tomb. It is a magnificent building "in excellent taste, but quite eclipsed by its surroundings." Fergusson observes, "This place at Fatehpur Sikri is romance in stone, such as few, very few, are to be found any where; and it is a reflex of the mind of the greatman who built it, more distinct than can easily be obtained from any other source".

Jahangir

Fergusson says that Jahangir contributed little to the architectural designs of India. Emperor Jahangir was fond of gardens and paintings, than of buildings. Hence for nearly a quarter of century there was no development in the building activity of the Mughals. But even then, Jahangir took interest in the construction of some remarkable buildings and first of these buildings was Akbar's mausoleum at Sikandra.

Akbar's Tomb

This tomb is in a village known as Sikandra. It is a huge structure planned by Akbar himself during his life time, but it took many years in building and was completed in 1612. This mausoleum is not a conventional Muslim tomb; it is quite unlike any other ever built in this country. In design it is like a Buddhist Vihar. The Akbar's tomb is of a pyramidal form, 100 feet high, and stands on a high terrace in the centre of a very extensive and well-laid out garden. Its beauty is set off by four graceful minarets of white marble, one at each corner. According to Percy Brown no other monument in northern India had an elegant minaret of this type before Akbar's tomb was built at Sikandra. The double arched gateway of this tomb is embellished on both sides with inlay work of exquisite beauty.

The mausoleum itself is a five-storeyed building and looks like "a low truncated pyramid", each storey of which grows smaller than the one below it. It stands on a raised platform 339 square feet. At the head of the tombstone is inscribed in bold relief the expression 'Allah-hu-Akbar' (God is great) and at its foot 'Jall-e-Jalal-Hu'. There is at the head of the tomb-stone, a small half puller with a circular niche. Ninety-nine names of God are inscribed in Arabic around the tomb. According to Fergusson the total height of the building now is a little more than 100 feet to the top of the angle pavilions, and the central dome 30 or 40 feet higher, which is the proportion that the base gives, seems just what is wanted to are this tomb as beautiful in outline and in proportion as it is in detail. Had it been so completed, it certainly would have ranked next to the Taj, among Indian Mausoleums. But Percy Brown says that the monuments, as it is, including its upper storey, is complete. "In many respect", he says, "the unroofed terrace and its refined treatment is an appropriate finish to the building as a whole." Havel says that Akbar's tomb is a worthy monument of one of the greatest of Indian rulers.

The tomb of Itmad-ud-Daulah

The next notable building constructed at Agra during Jahangir's reign is the tomb of Itmad-ud-Daulah, father of Nurjahan. It was built by Nujahan in 1626. It is situated on the lift bank of the Yamuna across the Yamuna bridge and at a distance of nearly two miles from the fort. The mausoleum stands in the midst of parterres tanks and fountains on a sand-stone terrace, 149 feet square and three to four feet high. It is a double storeyed building, the ground floor of which is square in plan, each side of which is 70 feet in length, and consists of a central structure "with broad octagonal towers in the form of minarets thrown out from each angle and a small pavilion." The floor of the hall is built of marble and is richly decorated with mosaic work. In this hall are the tombs of Itmad-ud-Daula and his wife. There are inscriptions on the walls of the hall in Tughra Character from the Quran and other Islamic scriptures. Percy Brown says that "this building with its accessories of garden and gate ways, is one of the most perfect of its kind, while its fineness is enhanced by the exquisite white marble of which the central structure is composed". This is the first Mughal building entirely made of white marble and on this building pietradura inlay was for the first time used. It has supreme triumph of feminine influence on Mughal architecture.

Jahangir Mausoleum

This mausoleum is situated at Shahdara near Lahore. It is presumed that the monument was designed by Jahangir himself, but it was completed under the supervision of his queen Nurjahan. The mausoleum is built somewhat on the same lines as Akbar's tomb at Sikandra. But it is less lofty and lacks the super structure of the Sikandra mausoleum. The building is a single storey and is in the form of a square terrace 22 feet high. The monument is characterised by profuse decoration, particularly by the use of lavish inlaid marbles, glazed tiles and painted patterns.

Tomb of Abdur Rahim Khan Khanna

It is an elegant building and seems to have been built after the style of Humayun's tomb near which it is situated at Delhi. The Khan Khanna's tomb is built on a terrace having 17 arched recesses on each side. It appears from this tomb the Persian influence was still there at the end of Jahangir's reign:

Shahjahan

Akbar's grandson Shahjahan was the greatest builder among the rulers of the Mughal dynasty. He was a great builder of religious as well as secular buildings. He had a passion for architecture and he revolutionalised the Mughal style of architecture. In the history of Indian architecture his age is regarded as golden age. Percy Brown also remarks, "With the reign of Shahjahan, the golden era of Mughal domination, was attained a period which found an expression in style of architecture of exceptional spelendour and carried to the highest degree of perfection. In the sphere of building art it was an age of marble, this material in its most refined form taking the place of sand stone largely employed so that architecture received a new impressiveness during this regime." According to Dr. Charles Fabri, for the emperor Shahjahan building was a passion and it was he who considered white marble, which was expensive, shiny and splendid to look at, the proper building material for an emperor of Hindustan. Under Shahjahan Mughal architecture reached its climax. Dr. Banarsi Prasad Saxena says that the Emperor's entire attention was devoted to the development of architecture and the buildings constructed in his reign stand as a living monument of unsurpassed engineering skill. They breathe sublimity, peace, elegance and grandeur. Even if the entire mass of historical literature had perished and only these buildings had remained to tell the story of Shahjahan's reign, there is little doubt that it would have still been pronounced as the most magnificent in history.

The experts hold divergent opinions on the architectural style of this age. The style is the natural growth and consummation of strictly Indian traditions. Really the style was the product of an impact of one culture and the other. It had steady growth which attained perfection in this period, when it received impetus and patronage. Besides this, "the Emperor himself understood the science of architecture well and possessed a keen sense of distinguishing the impressive and grandios from the ugly and grotesque." Shahjahan erected building at every place. He erected buildings in Kashmir, Lahore, Ambala, Bari, Faizabad, Gwalior and Kabul, but the most representative and the best preserved are those of Agra and Delhi.

Agra

The fort of Agra is a conglomeration of buildings of various types ranging from the time of Akbar to Shahjahan. The following buildings of Agra are remarkable.

Diwan-i-Am

Diwan-i-Am is an open and spacious building erected by Shahjahan in 1628. Of all the buildings, the most elaborate and highly ornamented is Diwan-i-Am and Diwan-i-Khas. The hall of Diwani-i-Am is open on three sides, and is 201 feet long and 67 feet broad, and its roof are supported by three rows of high pillars placed at regular intervals. The pillars are connected by beautiful marble arches so that the final effect is one of sustained grandeur. In the centre of the fourth side of the hall is an elevated long niche built of white marble, richly decorated with petradura work and flowers and foliage in low relief. In this gallery (riche) the emperor sat on a throne, and in the time of Shahjahan the imperial throne was made of pure gold and jewels and was known as the 'Peacock throne'. It was built under the supervision of Bebadal Khan, and was 3½ yards long, 2½ yards broad and 5 yards high.

Machhi Bhawan

It is situated behind the Diwan-i-Am and is an oblong elaborate edifice carved in red sand stone. In the centre of the building is a courtyard, 60 yards broad. There was a golden throne set inside this pavilion. In the courtyard were many tanks and reservoirs of white-marble. These were filled with water from the Yamuna and served as fishing pools for the amusement of members of the royal family. Now, Machhi Bhawan is in a dilapidated condition, and its tanks and reservoirs have been filled up with earth.

Diwan-i-Khas

The Diwan-i-Khas lies to the north-west of the Machhi Bhawan. It is an oblong building of white marble, 64 feet 9 inches long, 34 feet broad and 22 feet high. It consists of two halls which join and open marble gallery of equal size. The halls are an exquisite piece of architecture. "The pillars and arches are beautifully carved an inlaid, and the walls are ornamented with reliefs of rose flowers and foliage. These were originally over laid with fold and adorned with mosaic in precious stones." Bernier remarks, "Khas is really a noble edifice; it consists of a large square court of arcades, a place of audience". The hall is very handsome, spacious, gilt and painted. It is larger than its prototype built by Akbar in Fatehpur.

Shish Mahal

Beneath the Diwan-i-Khas, is situated the Shish Mahal, a delightful chamber, the doors and walls of which were adorned with glass mosaic and in gold and other colours. This chamber had two reservoirs, one of which was filled with water from a canal, ten yards long and one yard broad.

Moti Masjid

Moti Masjid is probably the chastest mosque in Asia. Shajahan built Moti Masjid in 1654 A.D. in the fort of Agra. Its arches reveal the influence of Hindu style. This mosque is significant from the point of view of architecture. The Moti Masjid or Pearl mosque was built in 7 years at a cost of three hundred thousand. It is an instance of supreme perfection of art combined with simplicity. The mosque measures 187 feet by 257 feet. The square court of the mosque is paved with large white flags and is surrounded by an exquisite gallery. In the courtyard, in front of the mosque, stands a beautiful fountain. The mosque is situated on an elevated terrace in a spacious courtyard to the north of the Diwan-i-Am. "Access to the courtyard is obtained through an arched gateway of red sand stone. The mosque is connected with private apartments of the palace by staircases on both sides. It has side rooms, separated by marble lattice work, to enable the ladies of the harem it say their prayers there without being seen by the people in the mosque below. There is Persian inscription in the black marble lettering over the front arch of the mosque giving the date of its construction". The Moti Masjid of Shahjahan inside the fort of Agra is a veritable masterpiece of Indo-Islamic art. In beauty and grace, the mosque is unparalleled in the world.

The Jama Masjid

It was built by Jahanara Begum, the elder daughter of Shahjahan. It is an attractive building, situated on a raised platform and is built of red-sand-stone. The main building is 103 feet long and 100 feet broad. The Masjid is divided into three compartments and is surmounted by three beautiful domes whose exterior is decorated with white marble and red-sand stone inlay work. It is supported by rows of arches. It was built in 1641 AD at a cost of five lacks of rupees. According to Bernier, every part of this Masjid appears well contrived, properly executed and correctly proportioned.

Nagina Masjid

The Masjid is situated in the north-west corner of the Machhi Bhawan which is a small but beautiful mosque built entirely of white marble. It is said to have been erected for the ladies of the harem, and is considered to have been a counter part of the more elegant Moti Masjid of Shahjahan.

Khas Mahal

The Khas Mahal is situated near Divan-i-Khas. It was exclusively for the residence of the emperor and his queen. The sub-structures of the Khas-Mahal are of red-sand-stone and were, at one time, washed by the water of Yamuna. The upper structure of the palace, its chambers, corridors and pavilions are built of white marble. Its roof is surmounted in the river side by two small but extremely lovely golden cupolas. It is enriched with elaborate carving and fine ornamentation of flowers and festoons in relief. The inlay work, painting and exquisite carving give an elegant appearance to this lovely mansion.

The Musamman Burj

It was originally called the Shah Burj. This exquisite structure of white marble built by Shahjahan lies to the north of the Khas Mahal and hangs like a fairy bower over the green rampart of the fort. From the Musamman Burj, ladies of the Mughal harem would watch the animal fights held in the space below. The emperor took his seat on the marble throne on the opposite side. It was in this tower that Shahjahan breathed his last with his eyes turned towards the Taj.

The Red Fort

In 1638, Shahjahan laid the foundation of a new city at Delhi which he named Shahjahanbad after his own name. Within the wall of this city he built a red fort on the right bank of the Yamuna. The fort, known as Red Fort, is a parallelogram running north and south, 1600 feet by 3200 feet. It is enclosed by a wall of same type as the one at the Agra fort, but more delicated and less strong. The fort has three gates of which the main gate is of great architectural value. "Inside the fort are private and public Darbar Hall's private enclosure having residential palaces with ornamental gardens. Royal store rooms, kitchens, horse and elephant stables, regalia chambers, and other minor amenities pertaining to the royal establishment."

Naubatkhan

The next important building is Naubatkhan. In a large rectangular part constituting the official block in the centre of the fort are situated the Diwan-i-Am (the hall of Public-audience) and Diwan-i-Khas (the hall of private audience) The most remarkable palaces are the Moti Mahal, the Hira Mahal and the Rang Mahal which are built of the same style. "The style of each is much the same," says Percy Brown, "although there is a very pleasing variety of plan each consisting of a single storeyed hall usually open on all sides, divided into bays by massive piers and the roofs supported by foliated arches."

Jami Masjid of Delhi

The foundation of Jami Masjid were laid in 1644 and it was completed in 14 years. It is an extremely dignified building and was meant for the ceremonial attendance of Shahjahan and his courtiers. It stands on a high pedestal, built of bed-sand stone and is in complete harmony with the outer walls of the fort. The Masjid has three entrance gates, which are really beautiful parts. The exterior view with the lofty foundational storey, steps and the gateways are full of dignity and impression.

Taj Mahal

The Taj is perhaps the most beautiful building in the world. Rawlinson remarks "The Tajmahal is indeed, the miracles of miracles, the final wonder of the world." The Taj which deservedly ranks among the finest tombs of the world stands on the right bank of Yamuna. Havel calls it a great ideal conception which belongs more to sculpture than to architecture. It is impossible to convey an idea of its extreme delicacy, its architectural grandeur and of the perfect taste and skill of the men who built it. "It is verily a thing of beauty and will remain a joy for ever. There are buildings more massive, there are others which have more elaborations but nowhere have grandeur and simplicity been coordinated in such perfect rhythm and symmetry. It soothes the eye and delights the heart. It is a monument conceived in vanity but marked by tenderness."

It was built by Emperor Shahjahan (1628-1658) as a mausoleum of his most favourite queen, Arjumand Banu Begum, known as Mumtaz Mahal. He decided to build a "Nayab" Kamal, "Lalid and Ajeeb-o-Gharib tomb in memory of his deceased queen. Shanti Swarup writes, "It is a monument erected in memory of an undying love. The Taj Mahal at Agra is the vision beautiful, materialised in marble. But unique in its liveliness as it is the Taj would loose half of its charm if taken out of its beautiful settings. Much of the beauty of the Taj lies in the choice of the materials and the process of decoration. The quality of marble used here is of such a nature that it is extremely susceptible to the slightest changes in the light, thus, all the time picturing the passing colour of the moment." Percy Brown calls it a monument which marks the perfect moment in the evolution of architecture during the Mughal period. The broad conception of the memorial can ably be attributed to the imaginative mind of Shahjahan himself.

"The queen died in 1531, and the grief stricken emperor decided to build over her grave a mausoleum of matchless beauty to immortalise his passionate devotion to the lady who had captivated his heart." The aim of its construction was to convey the romantic sentiments which Shahjahan bore for his queen Mumtaj Mahal. For its construction experts, architects, engineers, master masons, calligraphists, specialists in dome construction, flower carvers, and pietradura, inlayers were called from far and near. They were called to draw up a plan of the proposed mausoleum with a garden and a mosque and an ornamental gate, and work out to the minutest detail a scheme of ornamentation for the edifice.

Sleeman makes the fantastic suggestion of its having been designed by a French engineer Austin de Bourdeaux. V. Smith attributes the origin of the design to Germono Vironeo. Father Marnique also supports Smith's view. But on the basis of contemporary Persian records Indian scholars maintain that no European was employed either as an architect or an engineer or even as a mason. Havel and Percy Brown rightly rejected the theory of the European origin of the Taj, as the entire edifice, in all its aspects was according to their opinion,"the natural evolution of Indian style." According to a contemporary document, named Diwan-i-Mahandis, of Hafiz Luffullah Mahandis, the designer of Taj Mahal was Ustad Ahmad Lahare, who was the Chief Architect of Shahjahan and whom the emperor had honoured by bestowing on him the lofty title of Nadir-ul-Asar. V.A. Smith accept Ustad Isha as a chief architect during later stages of construction.

Rightly speaking the question to who designed the Taj is disputed was Ustad Ahmad Lahare. Ustad Ahmad's eldest son Ataullah Rashidi in his work Khulasatu-Hisab also written during the reign of Shahjahan mentions his father as Mimar-i-Kul Chief architect of Shahjahan. According to 'Diwan-i-Afridi, a Persian manuscript preserved in Khuda Bux Library. Patna, Amanat Khan Shiraji Ustad Isha Khan, Ustad Pira, Bajuhar Jatmal and Zorawar, Ismail Khan Rumi and Ran Mal all worked in the construction of Taj.

The mausoleum was constructed under the superitendence of Makramat Khan and Mir Abdul Karim, the dome being built by Ismail khan of Turkey. The tomb began in 1631 A.D. and completed in 1648 A.D. The white marble so plentifully used were from Makrana, red sand stone from Fatehpur Sikri and jewels and precious stones from Persia and else where. The exact cost of the Taj with its complementary building is not known. Dr. Ishwari Prasad says that in the construction of this world fame mausoleum about 9 crores were spent and it was completed in 22 years. Prof. S.R. Sharma says that Taj was built on a plot of Raja Jaising of Jaipur at the cost of 9 crores 17 lakhs according to Diwan-i-Afridi. Travernier who was present in India in the year 1653 writes that Taj Mahal was constructed in 22 years at the cost of 3 crores. The plan was admirably executed by both Hindu and Muslim artisans and took 22 years to complete it at a cost of fifty lakhs of rupees. The contemporary author Abdul Hamid Lahori writes that Taj was completed in 12 years at the cost of fifty lakhs of rupees. The recorded expenditure of 50 lakhs of rupees is rightly construed to mean that the above amount was expended on miscellaneous *i.e.*, petty charges and the wages of 20,000 workmen etc, who worked for Taj for so many years, but not on the acquisition of marble and semi precious stones and for inlay.

According to Percy Brown the design of the Taj Mahal as finally approved by Shahjahan "was based largely on the recently completed tombs of Khan-i-Khanan at Delhi, which in its turn was a reduced and modified copy of the mausoleum of the Emperor Humayun." "Regarding the choice of material the inspiration seems to have come from Itmad-'ud-Daulah's tomb, which was the first Mughal building made entirely of white marble and in which the pietradura mode of decoration was used for the first time."

The gate way of Taj Mahal is an admirable composition of red sand stone with a lofty pointed arch in the centre, flanked by two handsome kiosks supported on brackets. The facade of the gateway is beautified by calligraphic inscription in Arabic and the spandrels on both the sides of the pointed arch are decorated with inlaid floral patterns. The gate is surmounted by eleven white marble cupolas, on either side of which stand out slender turrets. All these details are repeated on the further side of the gate facing the mausoleum.

The whole building of Taj is in the form of a rectangle with its long axis lying north and measuring 1900 feet by 100 feet. This is enclosed by a high wall which is surmounted by four arcaded marble pavilions, one at each corner . On a plinth of 22 feet high, the pearl white marble tomb of Mumtaz Mahal stands. The main structure of the square mausoleum of 108 feet high with a cupolas at each corner and a bulbous dome of exquisite grace and proportion in the centre rising to a height of 187 feet and towering above the surrounding cupolas. To extent and distribute the architectural effect, a minaret in three stages and crowned by a kiosk rises from each corner of the plinth to a height of 137 feet.

The loveliness of Taj Mahal has been described by Percy Brown and he writes "for every hour of the day and for every atmospheric condition, the Taj has its own colour values, from the soft drowsiness at dawn, and the dazzling whiteness at midday to its gold splendeour in the moonlight, when the dome, thin of substance as the air, hangs among the stars like a great pearl. Yet none of these effects can equal those few fleeting moments when, softly illuminated by the brief Indian afterglow, it assumes the enchanting tint of some pale and lovely rose." A. Yusuf Ali remarks that the most superb monument left by Shahjahan is the Taj, the tomb of his beloved wife, which is unrivalled. So it is dream and poem in marble. It is poem full of grief which Shahjahan personified in stone.

Aurangzeb

Like his ancestors, Aurangzeb did not show any love for fine arts. He constructed only a few buildings but they are not much splendid monuments as his ancestors had erected.

Moti Masjid of Delhi

The only building of note worthy in the city of Delhi, is his Moti Masjid built with the white marble. It is 40' in length, 30' in breath and 25' from floor to roof. Like Shahjahan's work it is wholly built of white marble and contains engrailed arches, though supposed to have been built in 1659.

The Tomb of Rabia-up-Daurani

Aurangzeb planned and designed the tomb of his favourite queen, Rabia-'ud-Daurani at Aurangabad in the Deccan in 1679. In size it is half of the Taj Mahal, and is a medicore production. It is popularly known as second Taj Mahal. It was built by his Chief Architect Ataullah in imitation of Taj Mahal but the copy is poor.

Badshahi Mosque at Lahore

It is the most prominent on account of its sound construction and great size. It was built under the supervision of the emperor's Master of ordinance, Fidiai Khan and it is a stately monument. But it is poorer than the Jama mosques of Agra and Delhi. Another mosque built by Aurangzeb's order is the one at Banaras, erected on the site of the celebrated Vishwanath temple and has lofty minarets towering over the city. The Jami mosque at Banaras was also built by Aurangzeb on the site of the Panchganga Ghat, one of the most sacred spots of Hindus and with the materials of the broken temples. Gayan Bapi Masjid of Banaras is also built on the site of a Hindu temple in the year 1669-70 A.D. A lofty mosque at Mathura is built on the site of the Keshava Deva temple of Bir Singh Deva Bundela. Aurangzeb ordered his Governor Abdur Babi Khan who demolished the temple and raised the present Jama Masjid. It is made of red-sand stone and is a gigantic structure.

The tomb of Jahan Ara (1681) Raudhan Ara (1670-1671) and of Zibunisa (1702) was also built in his reign.

Aurangzeb had built innumerable mosques in the course of his long reign but most of them were devoid of magnificance and grandeour. The Lakshmantila mosque of Lucknow is an apt illustration of their style.

The Aurangzeb's reign marked the decadence of the empire in the domain of art as in so many spheres of human activity.

Painting and Music

Akbar was a great lover of the art of painting and patronised it. Without paying any attention to the Quranic prohibition, Akbar not only introduced painting at his court, but also justified the cultivation of this art and looked upon it as truly religious. He said "there are many who hate painting, but such men I dislike. It appears to me as if a painter had a peculiar means of recognising God; for a painter in sketching any thing that has life, and in devising its limbs, one after the other, must come to feel that he cannot bestow individuality upon his work, and is thus forced to think of God, the giver of life, and will thus increase in knowledge."

Regarding his love and patronage to the art of painting, Abul Fazal writes, "He gives it every encouragement, as he looks upon it as means both of study and amusement. Hence, the art flourished and mangy painters have obtained great reputation. The works of all painters are weekly laid before, His Majesty by the Daroghas and the clerks; he often confers rewards according to excellence or workmanship or increases the monthly salaries. Much progress was made in the commodities required by painters, and correct prices of such articles were carefully ascertained. The mixture of colours has specially been improved. The pictures thus received a hitherto unknown finish. Most excellent painters are now to be found, and the masterpieces worthy of a Bihzad may be placed at the side of wonder works of the European painters who have attained world-wide fame. The minuteness in detail, the general finish, the boldness of execution, etc., now observed in pictures are incomparable; even inanimate object look as if they had life. More than a hundred painters have become famous masters of the art, while a number of those who reached perfection, or those who are middling is very large." The real form of the Mughal painting was evolved during this period. The paintings of the earlier rulers were influenced by Persian style. In the course of time, Indian elements began to predominate.

In the reign of Akbar, Hindu-Muslim school of painting made its appearance and hilly developed. The names of Daswant, Basawan, Keshava Lal, Mukund, Madho, Jagan, Mahesh, Khem Karan, Tara, Sanwala, Haribans and Ram are recorded in the Ain-i-Akbari. 'Tulsi' Surjan, Surdas, Isan, Sankar, Ram, Anand, Nanha, Jagjiwan, Dharamdas, Narayan. Chatarman Suraj, Deojiva Sarn, Ganga Singh, Paras, Dhanna and Bhim were Hindu artists of Gwalior, Gujarat and Kashmir. These three were pre-eminently centres of Hindu culture during the early Medieval period, and the fact that the painters of Akbar came from these places confirms the tradition that the Hindu art continued to flourish after Ajanta; it also clearly establishes the contention that the Mughal art was not altogether an off-shoot of the central Asian and Persian styles but as development of the ancient art under new impulse.

Hindu artists excelled in the art of painting. Regarding the perfection attained by the painters of Akbar's court, Abul Fazal writes, "This is specially true of Hindus. Their pictures surpass our conception of things. Few indeed in the whole world, are found equal to them."

Khwaja Abdus, who had taught Akbar drawing in his childhood enjoyed the title of Shirin Kalam, was ordered by the young Emperor to paint portaits and murals for him. Abdus Samad had no equal in the art of painting. He laid the foundation of the Indo-Persian or Mughal school of pictorial art.

Abul Fazal informs us that the art of painting in its general finish reached its perfection. More than a hundred painters mastered the art. Among them, Mir Sayyid Ali of Tabriz, Khwaja Abdus Samad, Daswant and Basawan were the most famous. Baswant was a Kahar by caste. He was fond of painting pictures on walls. Vincent Smith remarks, "Daswant who disputed with Basawan the first place among the Hindu painters of Akbar's court had devoted his whole life to the art, and used to draw and paint figures even on walls." Daswant was raised to the status of an artist by the Emperor. In a short time he surpassed all the painters and became the first master of the age.

Basawan rivalled Daswant, "In backgrounding, drawing of features, distribution of colours, portrait painting, and several other branches, he is most excellent, so much so that many artists prefer him to Daswant." In the reign of Akbar, liberal pay and abundant honour drew crowds of artists, both foreigners and Indians, Muslims and Hindus, to his magnificent court, where the more distinguished were enrolled as Mansabdars or members of the official nobility."

Jahangir

Jahangir was a lover of beauty and painting. The art of painting flourished in his reign. He was himself a connoisseur of art as his father. The most famous painter of his court was Abul Hasan who was honoured with the title of 'Nadir-uz-Zama'. Abul Hasan's father, Aga Riza of Hirat too was an accomplished painter of his age, but his work was not to the standard of his son. Painting which initiated and nurtured by Akbar, reached the glorious heights under Jahangir and Shahjahan. Ustad Mansur was unique in his generation and became such a master in painting that he has the title of Nadira-ul-Asr.

"The artistic intuition and personality of Jahangir, his keen interest in painting, his enthusiastic royal patronage and the peaceful and settled condition of the country contributed to the development of the Mughal painting to its fullest extent. Jahangir reign is called the golden age of the Mughal painting." Jahangir himself had considerable skill with the brush. He writes in his autobiography, "My liking of painting and my practice in judging it have arrived at such a point that when any work is brought before me, either of deceased artists or of those of the present day, without the names being told to me, I say on the spur of the moment that it is the work of such and such a man. And if there be a picture containing many portraits and each face be the work of a different master, I can discover which face is the work of each of them. If any other person has put in the eye and eyebrows of a face. I can perceive whose work the original face is, and who has painted the eye and eyebrows." He had established a picture gallery consisting of many valuable paintings in one of his gardens. No doubt Mughal painting did much progress in the reign of Jahangir.

Farruk Bet, Mohammad Nadir, Mohammed Murad, Aga Riza and Ustad Mansur were the prominent painters of Jahangir's time. Though he did not favour Hindu painters, yet Bishan Das, Keshava Manohar, Madhav and Tulsi also flourished during his time.

Under Jahangir, portrait painting acquired unusual fineness, and scenes of hunting became very popular. "Since the Mughal artist was one of the retinue of the court, keen to please his patron, who was either the Emperor or a nobleman, he was more familiar with the important dignitaries of the court, the turesqueness and pomp of camp life, with armies on the march, hunting, battle and Darbar scenes. A keen appreciation of nature led him to draw curious birds, animals and unusual trees and flowers. Jahangir commissioned artists to depict for him any rare bird or beast, and in this way an interesting album was made." The Mughals loved blossoms and plants in bloom, and the artist's, brush was requisitioned to portray the likeness of anything beautiful and novel. Thus, under Jahangir, Indian painting reached its high watermark.

Shahjahan

The painting continued to flourish in his time. But he was more fond of architecture than of painting. Though Shahjahan was more interested in architecture but even then he continued the tradition of his father in the sphere of painting. Percy Brown has remarked. "With his (Jahangir's passing away) the soul of Mughal painting also departed."

The paintings of the time of Shahjahan are characterised by graphic colouring and ornamental borders. Proper attention was not paid to perspective, light and shade. Dr. Tara Chand says that the reign of Shahjahan saw the culmination of the art, the rules of perspective and forshortening, of modelling and shading were used. By constant practice the draughts-manship in Shahjahan's school of painting becomes very sensitive. The lines are not allowed to flow freely, but are studied and above all priority is given to the expression of grace and delicacy. The lines at times are so fine that it would require sometimes a magnifying glass to distinguish the delicate strokes. Among the artists mention should be made of Hindus who were more numerous. Among Hindus, Kalyan Das alias Chatarman, Anupchatar, Rai Anup and Manohar, and among the Musalmans, Muhammad Nadir Samarqandi, Mir Hashim and Muhammad Faqir Ulah Khan have been mentioned by Smith. The school of painting was now supervised by Muhammad Faqirullah Khan. Mir Hashim was an excellent portrait painter. Asaf Khan and Dara Shukoh were also patrons of the art of painting.

Aurangzeb

He was an orthodox Muslim. Unlike his predecessors, he was neither a lover of art nor extended his support to it. He got white washed the paintings on the tomb of Akbar and destroyed the paintings of the palace of Bijapur. The painters of Delhi and Agra fled away to different parts of the country. The reign of Aurangzeb marks the decline of the art of painting. The nobles who partonised artists, now paid them wages. In consequence the character and quality of work deteriorated. In the reign of Farrukhsiyar (1713-1719), however, painting received a fresh impetus, but the artists produced work, large in volume but much inferior to that done in the time of Akbar, Jahangir and Shahjahan. The colours lacked refinement, "and to hide defects increased use of stippling was made." Muhammad Shah also partonised the art of painting, but no artist of his time could capture its previous brilliance.

The Portrait Painting and Technique of Mughal Painting

The Mughal artist achieved great fame in the realm of portrait painting. In the reign of Akbar, the art of portrait painting made much progress, but in the time of Jahangir it was at its best. Akbar, Jahangir and Shahjahan had their portraits painted and they inspired the nobles of their court to follow them. The pictorial art was also used for illustrating books, either original or translations. "Babur's autobiography was illustrated with painting, by the best artist of Akbar's reign. Akbar got illustrated many works such as, Razm-Nama (Mahabharat) Ramayan, Waquat-i-Babri, Akbar nama, Hamzah-Nama, Timur Nama, Tarikh-i-Rashidi, Khamsa Nizami, Bahristan Zami and Anwar-i-Subaili. Other works such as Shahnama, Lilawati, Majnu Laila, Babarnama and many others were similarly illustrated with beautiful paintings.

The method, perspective shading and landscape in Mughal art has been described in the book "Technique of Mughal painting" by Dr. Motichand. The painters at Agra and Fatehpur Sikri used Indian and foreign paper as also parchment. Art paper of a very high quality was manufactured in this country from santal, linen, and grass. It was also imported from Persia and was known as Irani and Asfahani. Painting on canvas was also known and practised though not on such a large scale as that on paper. The colours used by the Mughal painters were natural as well as artificial and were made in the country. During the reign of Jahangir and Shahjahan, blending of colours became the common practice. "Smartly dressed nobles holding flowers in their hands and standing in formal rows were admired. Darbar scenes, depicting even minute details of carpet and architectural designs were much favoured. Harem scenes and those depiciting ladies at toilet were special favourites of the Mughal aristocracy. Beautiful ladies drinking or serving wine or listening to music were popular themes.

Music

The Mughal Emperor Babur is said to have been skilled in the art and to have written a treatise upon it and although no definite evidence of Humayun's attitude towards music survives, it is probable that he shared the family taste for song and dance. Akbar like his great ancestor Babur, devoted to music. Abul Fazal writes 'His Majesty' pays much attention to music and is the patron of all who practise this enchanting art. He himself was a skilled musician and no mean performer on the naqqara. Tansen was the most celebrated singer of the age. Another famous musician at Akbar's court was Baba Ram Dar who ranked next only to Tansen. There were other musicians of note at Akbar's court and according to Ain-i-Akbari there were thirty six musicians who were considered by Abul Fazal as first-rate singers. Akbar's interest and patronage of the art, led to great progress in both instrumental and vocal music.

Jahangir and Shahjahan, being much interested in music, extended generous patronage to competent musicians. The most remarkable musicians of Jahangir's court were Jahangir Dad, Parvez Dad, Khorram Dad, Makhu, Hamjan and Chaturkhan. Jahangir used to reward the musicians according to their merit. He used to invite musicians from all over the country and enjoyed their performance on the occasion of court festivals, such as, Nauroz, and his son's birthday etc.

Shahjahan himself was a skilled musician and sometimes participated in music in the company of notable musicians. There were at his court many distinguished musicians, such as Ram Das, Sursen, Jagannath, Mahapatra, Sukhsen, Lal Khan and Mirza Zulqarnen.

After ascending the throne Aurangzeb dismissed all court musicians. The dismissed musicians took out a mock-funeral procession symbolising the death of music to draw the emperor's attention to the wretched plight. But it had no effect on emperor and he ordered the coffin to be buried deep and well, lest music should escape from its grave. However, music did not disappear altogether. Apart from the active encouragement given to it by the earlier Mughal Emperors, music had always been popular with all classes as Rev. Edward Terry noticed during his brief visit to India. Female musicians continued to entertain the ladies of the royal harem. And some ladies of the royal families took keen interest in music and were themselves good singers. The nobles other men of rank, as well as the semi-independent chieftains, in the country continued to practice the art. The later Mughal emperors from the time of Jahander Shah to that of Bahadur Shah II were all lovers of music and they encouraged this art. But in the 18th century this noble art fell of its high standards and became debased. It became associated with courtesans and professional women.

Gardens

Even before the advent of the Mughals, Gardens had existed; but they were not geometrical in design. Agriculture and gardening were encouraged all over the vast Muslim Empire. The Iranians and Spanish Muslims were noted for their love of gardening. So were the Timurids in India whose gardening proved a great contribution to Indian artist. Firoz Tughluq had planned 1200 gardens around Delhi. Gardens were generally made on sloping grounds with platforms and water flowing in artificial channels coming into successive falls.

Babur's ancestor Timur laid out two gardens Bagh-i-Bulandi and Bagh-i-Dilkusha. Ulugh Baigh built Bagh-i-Maidan. Babur first Mughal emperor had a great passion for gardens. He brought to our country the new style in garden which had been developed in Persia and Turkistan and whose chief characteristics were artificial irrigation in the form of channels and tanks. The gardens were generally made in the squares divided into a number squares. In the main square fruit and flower trees were planted, each squares containing one kind of fruit or variety of flowers. Sometimes several flower trees were mixed up in one square.

The first Mughal garden in India was laid out by Babur at Agra and was named Hasht-bihisht or Nur-i-Afshan or popularly known as Ram bagh. Humayun also, gifted as he was with great aesthetic sense, must have beautified his residences with flower and fruit gardens. At Sarhind there was Dilkusha garden. It was one of the oldest gardens where Akbar had feasted on his way to the north-west. Akbar made many improvements in gardening by combining the Indian with the Iranian style of which the best specimen is the Shalimar garden in Kashmir. He laid out beautiful gardens in Agra Fort, Fatehpur Sikri and other places. The most remarkable and the largest garden associated with his name is that at Sikandra, where he lies buried. In the centre of this Garden stands his beautiful mausoleum. The Mughal garden was brought to perfection during the reign of Jahangir who laid out most elegant garden. The gardens were kept in order by Khwaja Waysi, well acquainted with horticulture. The garden was planted with many varieties of fruit trees and flower shrub. It also produced many kinds of vegetables. It was rented yearly for Rs. 50,000. One of his best charming garden is the Shalimar at Srinagar in Kashmir with its back ground of snow-clad mountains. The other remarkable gardens constructed during his reign were the tomb gardens of Itmad-ud-Daulah at Agra and his own at Shahdara near Lahore. Nurbagh, a Garden constructed in the reign of Jahangir at a cost of two lakhs near Agra is fully described in the Tuzik-i-Janangiri. Some of the gardens of the same type were situated in Lahore such as Bagh-i-Dilkusha, Bagh-i-Mirza Kamran, Bath-i-Nawlakh and Bath-i-Izzabad, near Delhi which was also known as Shalimar.

Some of the ladies as Bika Begum, the grand mother of Akbar and Mariam Makani, the grand mother of Jahangir were also interested in laying out gardens. Nurjahan's garden called Shahdara was built near Lahore. Jahanara Begum owned many gardens. One of them was situated at Ambala and another was at Surat. She also seems to have received some gardens as gifts. After the death of Mumtazmahal she received Begh-'i-Shahanara, whereas Begh-i-Shaherara was given to her by her father. Koshannara Begum also built a garden near the city of Delhi which is known after her name.

Shahjahan was equally interested in gardens and his Anguri Bagh in the Agra fort, the garden around the mausoleum of Mumtaz Mahal in the Taj, and the Shalimar garden near Lahore, are the most important. In Shalimar garden of Lahore Ali Mardan Khan had brought canal from river Ravi. The garden was planted with fruit and flower trees, including the much praised cypress and chanar trees. The Mughals built many delightful gardens in Srinagar (Kashmir) but none of them was lovelier than Shalimar of all the Imperial gardens in Srinagar. According to the author of Badshah Namah Qazwini, the Begh-i-Fayd Bakhsh was the best in 'area' beauty and charm. Shahjahan had laid it out in his princehood. The nobles followed the emperors and laid out large number of gardens in their own jagirs. Dara Shukoh laid down Talkatoorah garden at Delhi and the Vazir Bagh.

Aurangzeb had no taste for gardens. Nevertheless, the art of gardening did not disappear from the country, thought it fell from the high sandard of excellence that it had attained during the reign of the early Mughal Emperors. The garden system of the Mughal emperors was imitated by Hindu Rajas and in a modified form by the British. The nobles of Lucknow followed the example of the Mughal Emperors and beautified their capital with a number of well-laid out gardens.

(iv) Literature. Akbar the greatest Mughal ruler showed much greater interest in learning and developing literature.

Akbar's reign saw wonderful progress in the development of Persian Literature. Persian, already the language of polite conversation, became the official medium of record, and all people and public officials were required to learn Persian.

The most well known historical works of the time are Tarikh-i-Alfi of Mulla Daud, and Akbarnama of Abul Fazal. Ain-i-Akbari gives the names of 59 Persian poets of Akbar's court. Abul Faizi, the poet laureate of Akbar was the greatest poet of Persian in India. Nizamuddin Ahmad's Tabqat-i-Akbari; Jauhar's Tazkiratul-waqayat were works of a notable historical value. An early work of his reign was Tarikh-i-Akbarshahi of Muhammad Azif Quandhari, Abbas Sarwani produced Tuhfa-i-Akbarshahi (Tarikh-i-Shershahi). Some of the other historial works written during the period were Abdul Qadir Badayuni's Muntakhab-ut-Tawarikh Ahmad Yadgar's Tarikh-i-Salatin Agaghana, Bayazid Sultan's Tarikh-i-Humayun, Nurul Haq's Zabbat-ul-Tawarikh, Asad Beg's Waqayat and the Akbarnama of Shaikh Allahabad Faizi Sarhindi.

Shaikh Asbul Hak wrote Tarikh-i-Hakki which describes the history of Muslim India from the time of slave kings of Delhi to that of Akbar. The Muntakhabul Tawarikh was written by Hasan Bin Muhammad-al-Khaki-al-Shirazi. The Maasir-i-Abul Baki is a valuable and eleborate history of the Emperors. During Akbar's reign many notable works of Sanskrit, Arabic, Turki and Greek were translated into Persian.

The Tajak, a well known work of astronomy and the Tuzuk-i-Babari were rendered into Persian. Abul Fazal translated into Persian many outstanding Sanskrit works, such as, Kishan Joshan Gangadhar, Mahesh Mahananda and others. The Majmul Buldan, an excellent work of towns and countries, was translated from Arabic by Mulla Ahmad Qasim Beg.

Naqib Khan Abdul Qadir Badayuni and Shaikh Sultan of Thaneshwar translated Mahabharat and was named Razmnama, the book of wars. These writers also translated the Ramayana, and Haji Ibrahim Sarhindi translated the Atharva Veda. Lilawati, a Sanskrit treatise on Mathematics was rendered into Persian by Faizi and the Rajatrangini, a Sanskrit history of Kashmir, was translated by Maulana Sheri. Abul Fazal, himself translated the Panch Tantra (Anwar-i-Sahili) and Faizi the story of Nala Damayanti into Persian.

Jahangir had also a liking for literature. He also gave patronage to literary men. He wrote his autobiography "Tuzuk-i-Jahangiri. According to Elliot and Dowson, this work is very interesting; as a whole and assuming that Jahangir was mainly responsible for its authorship." The famous works written during his reign are Iqbalnamah-i-Jahangiri, Masir-i-Jahangiri and Zubb-ut-Tawarih.

Among the notable learned men, and poets were, Nasiri of Nishour, Ghiyas Beg, Naqib Khan, Mutamid Khan, Niyamatullah and Abdul Hag Dehlvi.

Shahjahan also gave partonage to learned men, writers and poets. Shahjahan appointed Abu Zalih (Kalim) as Court poet. A good deal of historical literature was produced in his time. Abdul Hamid Lahori, the Court historian, wrote Padshah-nama. Aminai Qazvini produced another Padshah-nama. Inyat Khan wrote Shahjahan-nama and Muhamad Salih produced Amal-i-Salih. The emperor's eldest son Dara Shukoh was also a scholar of outstanding merit. He was well-versed in Arabic, Persian and Sanskrit. He translated some of the Upanishads, the Bhagwad Gita and the Yog Vashistha. Sanskrit works were translated under the partonage of Dara Shukoh. Prabodh Chandra Uday was translated into Persian by Banwali Dass. The Ramayan was translated by Ibnhar Karan.

During the reign of Shahjahan poets from Persia came to this land in large numbers. Dr. B.P. Saxena writes, "The Persian language had come to stay in India, and it could not for long keep itself aloof from its new environments. It absorbed Indian ideas and Indian thoughts and it was used for Indian subjects.

Aurangzeb was a critic of Muslim theology and Jurisprudence and had no taste for poetry. But it was during Aurangzeb's reign that Persian was at its full bloom. The Emperor himself composed verses with great facility. Zeb Unnisha who herself was a poet of merit partonised those who took to learning. Her Divani-i-Makhji speaks of her poetic genius. Khafikhan wrote Muntakhabul-Lubab, Mirza Muhammad Qazim wrote the Nuskha-i-Dilkusha, a history of Alamgir reign, and Sujan Raj wrote Khulasa-ut-Tawarikh. Fatwa-i-Alamgiri, a digest of Muslim law, was also produced in his reign.

Aurangzeb's successors continued to partonise Persian literature until the time of Muhammad Shah (1713-1748) after which Urdu began gradually to take the place of Persian. Yet even in the 18th Century many books, specially on Sufism and History were written in Persian by Hindus and Muslims alike, but their literary value was small. Books on History continued to be written in Persian, first under the patronage of the rulers of the local dynasties established on the ruins of the Mughal Empire, and subsequently on account of encouragement from the English East India Company's governors and officers. "Some of the important chronicles are : Sair-ul-Murakherin by Ghulam Husain, Tarikh-i-Muzaffari by Muhammad Ali Ansari, Tawarik-i-Chahhari-i-Gulrar-i-Shujai by Hari Charan Das, Imad-ud-Saadat by Ghulam Ali Naqvi, Maadan-us-Saadat by Sultan Ali Safawi, Ibrat-nama by Khair-ud-din and Hadiqat-al-Aqalim by Murtaza Husain Bilgrani." Histories of the Court of Delhi continued to be written upto the end of Shah Alam II.

Urdu Literature

Babur used many Urdu words in the text of his Tuzuk-i-Babri. Akbar's intimate relations with the Rajputs indirectly helped the development of Urdu. During his reign, translations were made from Sanskrit work into Persian, and Hindus and Muslims came very close to each other and their social and political contacts deepened as never before. Abdur Rahim Khan Khanna excelled in Hindi poetry to which he gave a new metre, shorter and more delicate than the 'doha'.

Thus, during Akbar's reign the popularity of Rekhta (Urdu) increased. In the time of Shahjahan and Aurangzeb, Urdu (Rekhta) acquired a complete form and a greater content and power than before.

The famous poets of this period who wrote in Urdu are Chandar Bhan Brahman, Muizuddin Musavi Khan, J' afar Zaralli, Mirza Abdul Ghani Kashmiri and Mirza Bedil. They prepared the way for the greatest lyricist of the time, Wali who is regarded as the founder of modern Urdu poetry. He is most appropriately called the Father of Rekhta. He was born at Aurangabad and he went to Ahmadabad for his studies at the Madrasa of Maulana Wajihuddin Alvi, which drew students from far and near. After his return to Aurangabad he started writing poetry. He visited Delhi in 1700 when he came in contact with Shah Adullah Gulshan, a famous poet and Sufi of his time, who initiated him in Sufism. He also advised him to introduce the Persian style and Persian subjects into Rekhta and to substitute the idiom for the Deccan which he had followed.

'Wali's poetry is steeped in love. It is sweet and subtle with a strong emotional appeal, written in a style that is chaste and simple and haunting. He has successfully introduced the poetic motifs and imagery of Persian into Urdu'.

Wali's example was followed by a number of Muslim scholars who wrote Urdu poetry full of Persian and Arabic words and imagery. Abru, Hatim, Naji, Mazmun and Mazhar were the earliest Urdu poets of Delhi who flourished in the second and third quarters of 18th century.

Thus, from the middle of 18th century Urdu began to follow the Persian poetic form and convention. Urdu poets, like Mir Taqi Mir, Khwaja Mir Dard, Sauda, Soz, Masahafi and Insha gave new turn to Urdu poetry. These poets refined and polished the Urdu language and greatly enriched its vocabulary. Dr. Sarkar observes Urdu as it came to be introduced in the North in the 16th Century was not a very refined language and it was only in the 18th Century it became a literary one. Urdu became important when it was made a court language by the English East India Company in the second quarter of the 19th Century. Thus, the Urdu language is one of the finest achievements of the Indo-Muslim Civilization.

Other Languages

The Mughal rulers, particularly Akbar and after, also patronised Sanskrit learning. During his rule Banuchandra and Siddha Chandra wrote a commentary on Bana's Kadambary! During his reign Ramayana and Mahabharata are also translated into Persian. The famous story of Nala and Damayanthi was also rendered into Persian by Faizi. Panchatantra was also translated into Persian.

During the time of Jahangir and Shahjahan a large number of Sanskrit works were translated into Persian. Aurangzeb was orthodox and had no soft cheer for Sanskrit learning. He stopped extending patronage to Sanskrit scholars.

Hindi literature received new encouragement under, Akbar. Akbar's courtiers included some of the prominent literary figures such as Raja Birbal, Raja Man Singh, Raja Bhagwan Das, Prithiviraj Rathor, Tulsi Das, the most outstanding poet lived during this period. His 'Ram Charit Manas' (Ramayana) was the most outstanding work. Sur Das also lived in his court.

Under the Mughals, Gujarati literature was greatly enriched. Besides Tamil, Telugu and Bengali literature also flourished during this period.

(v) Social and Cultural History of the Marathas. The Peshwas were not only the secular but the ecclesiastical heads also. They united to a certain extent the rights and prerogatives of the Pope and the Emperor. This position of them is naturally affected all the institutions. Murder to them was not only a crime but a sin also. And as the crime had its legal punishments, the sin had its religious penance as prescribed by the Sastras. During the reign of Sahu, one Shidoji Rao murdered his concubine and cousin. At the intercession of his brother he obtained a free pardon, but he was ordered to perform Prayashchitta for cousin's murder.

The Peshwas also regulated the social affairs of the state. They did not exercise the authority of regulating the social affairs because they were Brahmanas. But it formed a part of their duties as the chief magistrates of the state.

Jurisdiction over Non-Hindus

As the non-Hindu ruler of the country was required to enquire about the social customs of the Hindus and decide disputed social and religious questions, so the Peshwas were also called upon to decide about the religious rights and customs of their non-Hindu subjects. Thus the year 1754-1755, a dispute about the priesthood of the Parsis was decided by an officer of the Peshwa.

Spirit of Toleration

The extensive jurisdiction exercised by Peshwas over their non-Hindu subjects did not cause any discontent for these Brahmana rulers were uncommonly tolerant and generous to the people of other faiths. Not only were the old grants continued even new Inams were given for the maintenance of mosques and shrines. They liberally contributed to the construction of mosques and churches. Cannons were fired thrice at the request of a Portuguese clergyman to celebrate a Roman Catholic festival. Baji Rao II permitted the Portuguese clergymen at Bassein to exercise all their old rites with the single exception of cow slaughter. The other Maratha chiefs did not lag behind. Daulat Rao Scindhia and his officers always joined the Muharram procession dressed in green as Muhammadans should do.

Superstition

The Peshwas were not free from superstitions. In 1721-22, one rupee was given as a present to an Agnihotri to counteract the evil effects of the fall of a lizard in the hall of audience. In 1751-52, there was an earthquake in the province of Kalyan Bhivandi and good Brahmans were ordered for a Shanti ceremony.

Influence of Orthodox Views

Sometimes the Peshwas were influenced by orthodox ideas. In 1744-45, the Peshwa was informed by a person from Bassein that during the Portuguese regime some Brahmans of Yajurvedic class introduced by the new unorthodox practice of giving their daughters in marriage to nephews (by sisters). But now as the righteous government was established and as the new practice was quite contrary to the Dharmasastras, a fine of Rs. 50 together with the punishment of excommunication should be inflicted on those who adhered to this practice. The suggestion was accepted and instructions were accordingly issued to the officers in charge of Bassein. In 1789-90 Madhav Rao II strictly ordered the Prabhus not to obstruct the remarriage of a willing widow in their community. Baji Rao II ordered that no Brahman should sell his daughter or keep her unmarried after she was nine years old. It was also ordered that failure to observe this will not be excused.

Widow Remarriage

Though orthodox and superstitious, the Peshwas were not opposed to the remarriage of a willing widow. Among the non-Brahmans, however, not only widow remarriage but marriage of a woman to a second husband in case of prolonged and continued absence of the first, depriving her of any means of livlihood was also permitted. An instance of such marriage is found in the papers of Chhattrapati Sahu.

Victims of Violence

The Hindus of Maharashtra were always considerate to the women and the Government always extended its support to the women in difficulties, whenever necessary. A document is available, which narrated the incident that the wife of a Hindu person while going to her mother's house was raped by a Muslim on her way. She reported the matter to the authorities. The Mohammadan was arrested and beheaded and the woman after Prayaschita was admitted to her caste. It is a pity that after two centuries of Western education we are still unprepared to show that sympathy for such unfortunate victims, which the Peshwas readily extended to them in similar circumstances. The Peshwas compelled a reluctant husband to take back his deserted wife, through a sense of social duty, for restitution of conjugal rights could not be claimed by a Hindu wife.

Informal Marriage

An informal marriage, though not complete for legal purposes, was declared valid if children were born to the pair. But such laxity of laws was allowed only among the lower castes, Examples are not lacking when the parent's fault was not allowed to add a lasting stigma to the social position of the son even among higher castes.

Involuntary Social Offence

There were certain persons who could not avoid dining with their captors, while prisoners in a Muslim camp. In those days of constant warfare, everybody ran the risk of being taken a prisoner by their Mohammadan enemies. Such people could be readmitted subject to governmental sanction into their rank. They also could not do without such order exclude anybody from bid caste.

Not only an innocent man be protected from the unreasonable oppression of his caste-men, but a man who had willingly or unwillingly committed a social offence could, if repentant, and willing to perform the necessary penance, be forced into his caste.

Exaction of Dowry Prohibited

The Peshwas as the head of society exercised control over everything social and religious. The Peshwas as the head of society exercised control over everything social and religious. The Peshwas prohibited marriage exactions. Baji Rao II strictly forbade any exaction by the bride's father from the bridegroom, and threatened to punish all parties concerned in such transaction.

The following penalties were prescribed :

1. The relatives of the bride receiving any such sum to return it to the relatives of the bridegroom and to pay an equal amount as fine to the government.
2. If the relatives of the bridegroom or any person settling the marriage failed to give information to government of the amount paid to the relatives of the bride, the relatives of the bridegroom should forfeit to governments double the amount paid by them to the relatives of the bride, and the person settling the marriage double the amount received by him.

Forcible Marriage

The Peshwa declared a forcible marriage as null and viod. A marriage was nullified in 1778-79, although Kanyadan and other ceremonies were over and only Hom alone remained to be preformed. Strangely enough they sometimes went out of way to order the wedding of marriageable girls without being approached by their parents.

Prisons and Department of Police

Some rooms in the fort were used as regular prisons. According to Elphinstone "the prisoners unless they were people of consideration were always neglected and sometimes allowed to starve". Hard labour in building fortifications were not unknown. Elphinstone's remarks were undoubtedly based upon the worst days of Maratha administration. But the prisoners were treated according to the standard of time.

The Maratha prisoners sometimes got leave for going home to perform some religious ceremonies like the Shradha of dead parents, marriage of grown-up daughters, and the sacred thread ceremony of grown up sons, which the Peshwa as the ecclesiastical head could not permit to the neglected. The prisoners were however, to come to the prison after the ceremony was over.

At times some consideration was made for the health of the prisoners. The prisoners were transfered from one place to another if the climate did not suit them. The wives and relations of prisoners were sometimes permitted to live with them in their prison rooms to look after them whenever their health demanded it. The servants and the relatives in such cases were fed by the government during their residence in the prison.

Treatment of Political Prisoners

The political prisoners were well treated. Good arrangements were made for their boarding and lodging and their comforts, although they were strictly watched, and their communication with the outside world and sometimes with their own people, was strictly prohibited.

We do not know much about the internal management of prisons under the Peshwas. Efforts were no doubt made to reform an offender. The greatest defect in the Maratha system was that the prisoner had hardly any right. He might be very leniently treated and he might suffer all sorts of hardships. Everything depended upon the nature of his offence, his rank and wealth.

The Police

The village police was under a Patil, and the chief police officer in the rural republics was the Mahar. The district police was under the Mamlatdar. In big cities the police was placed under an officer called Kotwal. His duties included regulation of prices and taking of census. His duties were as follows :

1. He disposed of the disputes of importance.
2. He used to fix the prices of goods and list of the prices fixed was daily submitted to the government.
3. The Kotwal should arrange to supply labourers as required by Government from among the artisans and the members of the several castes in the city.
4. Sales and purchases of land sites should be made with the permission of the Kotwal who should prepare the necessary documents and receive the fees due to government.

5. The Kotwal should take the census. He should keep a record of all persons coming into and leaving the city.
6. All disputes relating to roads, lanes and houses should be disposed of by the Kotwal.
7. The Kotwal should furnish a monthly amount to the government.
8. The Kotwal should issue orders for any proclamation being made by the beat of the drum.
9. Professional gamblers should not gamble without the permission of the Kotwal, who should levy on them the usual fees. Other persons were not allowed to gamble.

The powers of the Kotwal were immense, so sometimes they were abused also.

The Metropolitan Police

The Metropolitan Police at Poona became a model body during the administration of the last of the Peshwas. The efficiency and honesty of this body had extorted the applause of critics like Elphinstone and Jone. Jone says, "It is little remarkable for anything but its excellent police which alone employs thousand men. After the firing of the gun, which takes place at ten at night, no person can appear in the streets without being taken by Kotwal. So strict is the discipline observed that the Peshwas himself had been kept prisoner a whole night for being out at improper times". Lt. Edward Moor and his brother officers visited Poona in 1792 and they heard that the Police of Poona was "Uncommonly well regulated".

The Maratha institutions, compared branch by branch with those of contemporary Europe, cannot fail to extort our admiration, by the superiority and excellence in many cases.

2

European Penetration

(i) Rediscovery of India's Past

The coming of the Europeans in India was a significant event in the history of our country. The Portuguese were the first in the line. It was due to the great demand of the Indian commodities in European markets throughout the Middle ages. These things used to reach Europe either by land or by sea. The land route was practically closed by the Turks. There arose the necessity of finding a new route to India. Prince Henry of Portugal who is commonly known as the "Navigator" did a lot in this field. Diaz and Gama started their expeditions one after another, Gama reached Calicut in 1498. After that they were able to establish trading centres in India, (*i.e.*, Calicut, Cochin and Cannanore).

De Almeida (1505-1509) was the first Viceroy of the Portuguese in India. He followed "Blue Water Policy" during his period. Both Almeida and his son were defeated and killed in 1509 by the Egyptians.

Albuquerque (1508-1515) was the second Viceroy of the Portuguese in India. He was a great conqueror. He conquered and annexed Goa in 1510. He built a fort at Cochin. He appointed a large number of Portuguese officers for the work of administration. Albuquerque was a great man. He was really be called the founder of the Portuguese Empire in India. After Albuquerque the Portuguese power began to decline.

After the Portuguese, the Dutch and the English established their trading centres. Later on the French also thought of trying their luck in India. Accordingly they established their trading centres in India. The French and the English companies fought the three Carnatic wars in the Decan and these wars sealed the fate of the French in the Deccan.

First Carnatic War (1746-1748)

The first Carnatic War was merely an echo of the War of Austrian succession which broke out in Europe in connection with the succession of Maria Theresa to the throne of Austria.

The then Governor of Pondicherry was Dupleix. He wanted to strengthen his position as against the English. Dupleix gave a suggestion for maintaining neutrality to the Madras Governor. The Governor was not willing to have such neutral relations. So Dupleix sought the help of Anwar-ud-Din, the Nawab of Carnatic. The Nawab told both the English and the French Companies not to quarrel and thereby not to break the peace of the country. The English did not like the idea of Nawab and proceeded with troops. On behalf of Dupleix, La Bourdonnais, Governor of Mauritius hastened to India with troops. In July 1746 the French and British squadrons faced each other for sometime. Then the French besieged Madras.

In the meantime the English sought the help of Anwar-ud-Din to direct the French to leave Madras and maintain peace. But in the end the French under La Bourdonnais captured Madras. Difference arose between Dupleix and La Bourdonnais. La Bourdonnais accepted a bribe of one lakh Pagodas and restored the same to the English for 40,000 pounds. Dupleix repudiated his action and recapture Madras. The Nawab asked for the restoration of Madras to him. Dupleix refused to do so. So a battle took place between the forces of Nawab and the French. It was called the battle of St. Thomas or the battle of Adyar. In this battle, the French army defeated the Nawab's forces. The battle of Adyar is regarded to be one of the decisive battles of India.

Further Dupleix tried to capture Fort St. David also but failed The English in turn tried to capture Pondicherry but the French defended the same successfully.

The war came to an end by the Treaty of Aila-Chappelle in 1748 According to this treaty :

1. The English got back Madras.
2. The French got back Louisburg in North America.
3. Temporary negotiations were made between them to maintain their respective territories.

The Second Carnatic War (1748-1754)

The Hyderabad State was created by Nizam-ul-Mulk. In 1713, he was appointed the Viceroy of the six Subahs of the Deccan. After a long period of administration he died in May 1748. There was a struggle between his second son Nasir Jung and grandson Muzzafar Jung. Both of them desired to get the leadership of Deccan. So Muzzafar Jung joined hands with Chanda Sahib who wanted to be Nawab of Arcot. Chanda Sahib also opened negotiations with Duplex. Accordingly he helped them. With the help of the French they defeated Anwar-ud-Din in August 1749 in the battle of Ambur. Anwar-ud-Din was killed in the battle; his son Mohammed Ali took refuge in the fort of Trichirapalli.

In the meantime the English helped Nasir Jung. He took the field in 1750. Muzzafar Jung was defeated, captured and imprisoned. Unfortunately a change took place. Nasir Jung was deserted by his troops and was captured and put to death. Chanda Sahib was recognised as the Nawab of Arcot. After the death of Muzzafar Jung in 1751, Salabat Jung was put on the throne by Bussy.

At this juncture Clive appeared on the scene and occupied Arcot. The French efforts failed to relieve Arcot; Chanda Sahib also failed to relieve Arcot. He had to give up the siege of Trichirapali Chanda Sahib was himself defeated and killed. The whole of the Carnatic fell into the hands of the English.

Dupleix met defeat after defeat at the hands of the English. So he was recalled in 1754 and he died in 1764.

Dupleix was successed by Godeheu. He arranged terms of peace with the English. Accordings to the new treaty :

1. Both the nations agreed not to interfere in the internal affairs of the Indian states,
2. Both the French and the English retained their old positions.
3. The English got a town in Northern Circar.

Bussy remained in the Deccan and continued to exercise his influence. But the new treaty made the English stronger.

Third Carnatic War (1756-1763)

The treaty made by the French and the English Companies in India was a short lived one in 1756 the Seven Years' War started in Europe. It echoed in India also.

The French Government sent Count Lally as the Governor and Commander-in-Chief. He reached India with great difficulty. He had some success at the start. He brought St. David under the French control. But he recalled Bussy from the Deccan. It was a great blunder on his part. As soon as Bussy left, the French influence ended.

In the meantime Salabat Jung went over to the English and gave them Northern Circars. Lally tried to get Madras but failed. He was compelled to retire to Pondicherry. He was defeated by Sir Eyre Coote in the battle of Wandiwash in January 1760.

The battle of Wandiwash was a decisive battle. It sealed the fate of the French. Bussy was imprisoned.

In April 1760, Karaikal was captured by the English. Lally surrendered at Pondicherry in January 1761.

In Europe the Peace of Paris was concluded between the two powers in 1763. So also in India there was an exchange of prisoners of war.

Lally returned to France. But he was condemned and executed. According to the Peace of Paris the French territories were restored to them. But the French were not allowed to fortify them. It cannot be decided that the three Carnatic Wars completely destroyed their chances of founding French empire in India.

Dupleix

Dupleix wanted to establish a French empire in India. He critically analysed the political condition in India and came to the conclusion that by helping one state against the other, the French could add to their resources and ultimately set up an empire of their own in the country.

Dupleix did well in the very beginning of his career. He was able to put Chanda Sahib on the Carnatic throne. Similarly he was sufficiently efficient to put Muzzafar Jung on the Deccan throne. After the death of Muzzafar Jung he was able to put Salabat Jung in his place.

Dupleix was responsible for getting Northern Circars from Salabat Jung. It was due to him that the French influence was in its height in South India. When Clive appeared, things changed. He captured Arcot and thereby posed a danger to the French. Chanda Sahib failed to carry out the instructions of Dupleix. So he was defeated and the plans of Dupleix miscarried.

Dupleix was a good diplomat as that of Clive. But Clive was also a good soldier which Dupleix was not. It is true that Dupleix was no match for Clive. No wonder while Dupleix failed, Clive succeeded.

Dupleix did not get sufficient soldiers and enough fiinds at times of crisis. It was a great handicap on the part of Dupleix. Hence, he failed miserably as against the English soldier.

Moreover, the masters of Dupleix did not give him proper guidance to achieve glory as against the English. They ignored his sentiments.

Nobody encourage him, nobody appreciated him. So Dupleix will always remain a tragic figure in history. He was let down both by his fortune and by his countrymen. He rightly pointed that "he had sacrificed his youth, his fortune and his life. He had spent money out of his own pocket to finance the wars".

According to Henri Martin, the failure of Dupleix was due to the French Government and the Company.

Elphinstone says that, "Dupleix was the first who made an extensive use of disciplined Sepoys in India."

Major Lawrence says that, "Dupleix is a striking and brilliant figure in Indian history. His political conceptions were daring and imaginative and he aroused a dread in his English contemporaries which is at once a tribute to his personal power and testimony in their sagacity."

According to Roberts, "Dupleix is a striking and brilliant figure in Indian history. For even if we give up the old uncritical estimate we need not deny his real claims to greatness..."

Malleson says that, "Dupleix was a great administrator and diplomat with a wonderful capacity for organisation and great persistence and tenacity of purpose."

Sir Alfred Lyall admitted that, "Dupleix was a man of genius and political vision who strove gallantly against all those obstacles".

Robert Clive came to India as a clerk in the East India Company. He showed such remarkable military genius that he became commander-in '-chief. It cannot be denied that his services to the British Empire in India were great.

Robert Clive was responsible for the capture and defence of Arcot in 1751. In collaboration with Lawrence he was able to frustrate all the designs of Dupleix.

During the Second Carnatic War, Clive appeared on the political scene of India and occupied Arcot. All efforts to dislodge him from Arcot failed. Even when Chanda Sahib sent half of his army under his own son to relieve Arcot there was no better success than before. Clive's capture of Arcot proved to be the turning point in the contest between the French and the English. Clive has therefore been called as the "hero of Arcot" in the history of India.

Robert Clive from his early days was very interested in knowing things in the administration. He learnt his soldiering from General Lawrence and his diplomacy from Governor Sounders In 1756, he co-operated with the Marathas to put down the pirate stronghold of Ghariah.

In 1757, Clive defeated Siraj-ud-Daulah supported by the French in the battle of Plassey. It was a glorious victory for the English. He laid the foundations of the British power in Bengal and provided the basis for further expansion into the interior of the country.

The period of second Governorship of Bengal of Lord Clive is remarkable for the successful handling of the political and administrative problems which confronted the Company in 1765. His masterly handling of the situation silenced all opposition and created an atmosphere of calm and quiet at least for sometime. During this time he established Oudh as a buffer State. He was not only a great warrior but also a great administrator and statesman.

Lord Chatham compared Lord Clive with Frederick, the Great of Prussia.

According to Burke, Lord Clive settled great foundations. When he, "forded a deep water with an un-known bottom, he left a bridge for his successors over which the lame might hobble and the blind might grope their way."

According to P.E. Roberts, inspite of his faults, there was the stamp of grandeur on all the words and actions of Lord Clive.

The system of dual Government of Bengal which was set up by Clive is not easy to explain. In the administration of Bengal he did a lot for the improvement of the Company.

It goes without saying that Lord Clive was the founder of the British empire in India. At the same time it cannot be denied that he was the architect of the ruin of the people of Bengal. "The corruption, the oppression and the mal-administration under which they groaned for bears were in no small measure due to him."

According to one writer, "Lord Clive's career in India may be briefly summed up as follows : first a merchant, then a soldier, and then a statesman."

According to Dodwell, "Clive was a man of insight rather than of foresight."

Lord Macaulay says that, "our island has seldom produced a man more truly great than Robert Clive, either in arms or in council."

After Clive

During the next seven or eight decades British continued their fight for supremacy and consolidation in India. Warren Hastings, the first Governor General of India (1774-85) waged a number of wars against

Marathas, Haidar Ali, Tipu Sultan and the Rohillas to make greater acquisitions for the supremacy and to consolidate its hold. He also introduced a number of administrative reforms with the same object. Cornwallis, the successor of Warran Hastings, tried to consolidate the gains of his predecessor. He purified administration and tried to bring order out of chaos through his famous Permanent Settlement of Bengal. He crushed the power of the Mysore and reduced the Marathas to the position of subordinate allies. He brought a number of Indian rulers under the suzerainty of the British through the system of subsidiary alliances. But it was only under Marquis of Hastings (1813-1818) that the power of the Marathas was crushed and the Rajput states were brought under the British control. He also deposed the Peshwas and annexed their territories in the Deccan to the British Empire. A large number of Indian states were brought under the control of the British company either through the policy of anneaxation or the Doctrine of Lapse during the period 1845 and 1856. Some of the areas which were thus brought under the British control included Punjab, Sindh, Oudh, Satara, Jhansi, Nagpur etc. Thus, by 1856 the British enjoyed an unquestioned supremacy over the territory from the Indus to Brahmaputra and from the Himalayas to the Cape Comarin.

The year 1857 was a turning point in the history of modern India. During that year a great national uprising — the Mutiny took place, which has been described by the historians as the last effort of the old order to regain national independence and honour. It was the result of a combination of a number of political, administrative, economic, religious and military causes. It may be noted that the British ultimately succeeded in finally controlling the rebellion, it led to the wounding up of the company, which was responsible for the building of the British Empire in India.

The change was of great significance because the policies which the British Crown followed after 1858 fundamentally differed from the policies followed by the company. From 1858 to 1922 the Government of India confined its activities mainly to the collection of revenue, maintenance of peace and the defence of Indian frontiers. It made no efforts to reorganise the Indian society or raise the moral or material standards of the people. It made no effort to increase the national wealth of the country either. In short "they provided the appertenances of the civilisation but it did not undertake the work of civilisation themselves."

Towards the close of the nineteenth century a national movement was launched with the objective of securing greater participation of the people of India in the administration of their own country. This movement gained greater momentum during the twentieth century particularly after Mahatma Gandhi assumed its leadership. The initial demand of self-government was subsequently changed into 'Purn Swaraj'. As a result of this struggle the British grip over India began to loosen slowly but surely. Ultimately the British were forced to grant Independence and two independent states of India and Pakistan were created in August 1947.

Growth of Indology

The contact of Indian scholars with English literature facilitated the synthesis of the East and West. Various foreign writers Like Sir William Jones, H.T. Colebrooke, H.H. Wilson, H.T. Princep, Fergusson Alexander, Cunningham, Max Muller and E.B. Havel paid glowing tributes to Indian culture. Besides a host of scholars have done wonderful service for the growth of indology.

Robert Orme was treated as the official historiographer to the English in India from 1767 to 1801. His theme was the Military transactions of the British Nation in Hindustan from the year 1745.

Meckenzie Colin, the Surveyor General of India in Calcutta collected Indian manuscripts and antiquities with the help of Indian scholars. H.H. Wilson, the orientalist made a catalogue of his manuscripts.

Sir Alexander Cunningham must be considered the father of Indian Archaeology. It was on the foundation laid by him that later Indian archaeological research and studies grew to their present dimensions.

James Burgess who succeeded Cunningham as Director of Archaeology promoted epigraphic studies in South India. George Bwhler, a German by birth like most Indological scholars spent his working time mostly in London. In 1880 he was Professor of Sanskrit and Indology in Vienna. He started and partly completed the monumental work 'Encyclopaedia of Indo-Aryan Research.'

Alexander Rea and Bruce Foote did a lot for the same, James Ferguson came to India and joined the Royal Asiatic Society in 1840. His contribution to South Indian art is famous. Kielborn started his Indian career as Superintendent of Sanskrit Studies in the Deccan College, Poona.

Hultzseh was a master of Sanskrit and Pali and he knew the chief Dravidian language sufficiently to help him in his professional work.

Bishop R. Caldwell, J.H. Nelson and J.F. Fleet did a wonderful job in this field. Robert Sewell, Sir Walter Elliot and V.A. Smith have contributed much for Indology. Col. Henry Davidson Love who was principal of the old Engineering college, Madras was the author of the stupendous masterpiece 'Vestiges of old Madras'.

It gives the stories of the history of Madras from the very beginning to 1809.

H.H. Dadwell was a professional historian and he is known for his valuable work on 'Dupleix and Clive.' Father Heras have done a lot for Tamilian historiography.

Sir Robert Eric Martimer Wheeler became a junior investingator of the staff of the Royal Commission on historical monuments on the strength of the study of Romans-Rhenish, pottery. His findings at Arikkamedu near Pondicherry give a beautiful clue for Roman trade in India.

The eminent historian C.H. Phillips who headed the S.O.A.S. for quite sometime and who is reputed for his work on the East India Company has been keeping up British interest in Indological studies.

A.L. Basham was perhaps the most famous scholar who treated, in his 'The Wonder that was India', Indian culture with a kindly eye.

J.D.M. Derrett and Hardgrave have made wonderful contributions for Indological studies.

E.F. Irschick, C.J. Baker and D.A. Washbrook and similar western scholars have been studying the contemporary political scene in Tamilnadu and writing on the themes which relate to the emergence of Justice Party and the several Kazhagams and their increasing roles in regional life and politics.

The French Institute of Indology, Pondicherry has made very substantial contribution to Indological studies. It is part of the vast French Academic establishment which has been looking after oriental research relating to India and Indo-China. G. Jouveau Dubreil, an eminent French Indologist laid the foundation for the great tradition of Indological research in the institute. J. Filliozet was the distinguished Director of the Institute.

The Saraswati Library and the Madras Library Society have done a lot for Indological studies.

Thus, the growth of Indology is an interesting and important study in the social and cultural history of India.

Social and Cultural policy of the East India Company

The East India Company was founded in India by the English in 1600 A.D. The then ruler of England was Elizabeth I and she gave all sorts of help for the same. They established their factories at Surat, Agra. Ahmadabad and Broach.

During the initial years the company followed the policy of peaceful trade advented by Sir Thomas Roe. It avoided all attempts for gaining territorial possessions, because it felt that it could prove ruinous to the English interests in India. Later they followed a policy of territorial acquisition.

During this period the company took steps for spreading Christianity. At the same time there was religious toleration and freedom of worship to each individual. The Hindus, the Muslims and the Christians lived amicably during the period. Gradually conversion by the English gaining ground. The political power of the British granted social supremacy. There were landed aristocratic people. Different classes depend on them. Especially the moral society depended upon them. The wealthy man was his counterpart in the urban society.

The position of women gradually began to improve. Under company rule untouchability existed in the society. Missionaries began to convert the people of lower rank so as to uplift them on par with other castes.

The company took the cause of developing primary education among Indians as suitable means of gaining their opportunities. The Missionaries under the direction of the company established many educational institutions in different places. East India Company not only established institutions for imparting instructions in English but also established Sanskrit colleges at Madras and Banaras. The institutions imparted European education as well as Indian education.

It was for the first time on June 3, 1814, that East India Company came out with an announcement to send about a lac of rupees for Indian system of education, especially Hindu system of education. It appointed a committee in 1823 to make arrangements for education in Bengal. The company took steps to spread education in Bombay and Madras.

The Company built many factories on the European model. Many residential buildings were constructed during the period. In 1659 it secured the site of the present city of Madras from the Raja of Chandragiri and built the fortified factory called Fort St. George.

Policy of Non-interference

Cornwallis left India in 1793. He was succeeded by Sir John Shore (1793-98). During the term of his office Sir John Shore followed the policy of neutrality (Policy of non-interference) as laid down in the Pitt's India Act. This policy which was carried to such an extreme point that it lowered the prestige of the English company of India. The most important event of Sir John Shore's time was the attack of the Marathas on the Nizam and the defeat of Nizam in the battle of Kharda in March 1795. The Nizam begged for British help but the same was refused by Sir John Shore on the ground that such help was likely to entangle the English company into the internal affairs of the Indian states. Such a treatment made the Nizam bitter and he had to submit to humiliating terms of the Marathas. However, the Nizam was able to recover his position on account of dissensions among the Marathas and on the whole the Nizam did not loose much. Anyhow the Nizam was not in a mood to forget the British betrayal of his cause. His policy of non-interference was discontinued by his successor Lord Wellesley in 1798.

(ii) Activities of Christian Missionaries

After inflicting a naval defeat on the 'Spanish Armeda' in 1588 the British acquired naval supremacy. This encouraged certain merchant adventurers of London to form a company for trade in the East Accordingly they formed the East India Company in 1600 A.D. After that many Christian missionaries came to India.

Prior to this the Portuguese, the Dutch, the French and the Danes had started visiting India in connection with their trade. Their Missionaries did a wonderful job for humanity and for their progress. Their cultural activities particularly in the field of education cannot be minimised or underestimated.

Portuguese were the first among Europeans who came to India and they of course were the people who started modem system of education here. St. Francis Xavier, the followers of Jesuit religious seat came to India in 1542 A.D. He preached Christianity in the villages. He distributed small books related to Christianity in the villages. He started a university named Kochin.

Their main centre of activities were Bombay, Goa, Damon, Diu, Ceylon, Chittagong and Hubli and they started primary schools in those places. Those who followed Christianity and their children were given free education. The children of the poor people were also given food, books etc. But they were to be the followers of Christianity.

The Dutch, the French and the Danes also started many educational institutions. For the promotion of Tamil language and literature the two German Bishops named Zieganbalgu and Plastchom did wonderful services.

Under East India Company the Missionaries made good deal for the propagation of Christianity and education. They also encouraged Hindu system of education. They made local languages, the medium of instruction and prepared course books, grammar and dictionaries etc.

'London Missionary Society' and 'Church Missionary Society' also worked much for the expansion of education. In Bombay and Madras they had started many schools and colleges.

For the growth of Humanitarianism they did a lot. They rendered remarkable service to the human beings. In the medical field they built many mission hospitals. They provided medical aid for the poor and the needy. They started many orphanages for poor and the downtrodden people. In the social field they did excellent service for the growth of humanitarianism.

3

Changes After 1858

After 1858 Indian social life had two distinct divisions : (1) Urban life and (2) Rural life. To understand this life we have to know the political conditions prevailing in the 18th century. The Mughal empire began to decline in the life time of Aurangzeb. Marathas were the most successful in ousting the Mughals. At this juncture Europeans interfered in the political affairs of India. Indian society has been a rural society. The rural society lived in the villages. The 1921 census enumerated 4,98,527 villages containing 87 per cent of the Indian population. Muslims live both in the existing villages and founded their new settlements.

In the 18th century it was the kshatriyas who had undergone a transformation in its social status.

Divide and Rule

The communal franchise introduced by the British in the early years of 20th century was advocated on the grounds of religious disharmony.

From the beginning of the Carnatic Wars the British began to follow divide and rule policy in India. To achieve political objects they did a wonderwork by following the policy of divide and rule. Unfortunately the Maratha chieftains are divided and their internal dissensions created inroads into their unity and the British succeeded in playing one Maratha chief against another. By 1818 the British grabbed the entire Maratha territory. In the same manner they acquired many states. Through Subsidiary Alliance and the Doctrine of Lapse the British annexed Hyderabad, Oudh, Mysore, Sindh and Punjab. With the fall of the Marathas, almost all the princely states of Rajputs entered into a subsidiary alliance with the British.

The British every now and then followed the policy of divide and rule and achieved its objects. During the time of Lord Curzon the Partition of Bengal took place in 1905, The new province named as "Eastern Bengal and Assam" was set up. Its total area was 106,540 square miles and its population was 31 million of which 18 million were Muslims and about 12 million Hindus. It was termed by the public as an attempt at breaking the political unity of the province, an attempt at playing the Hindus against the Muslims and at disrupting the "new and surging spirit of nationalism." It was an act of divide and rule by the British. There was a great upsurge in India by boycotting English goods. Finally, in the years 1911 Partition of Bengal was annulled. In this way the British sowed the seeds of dissensions and divisions in the minds of both the Hindus and the Muslims. Day by day the dissensions and differences grew more and more. But by the close of the century the British had started putting one religion against the other. It was also the social division in our social structure which helps them to 'divide and rule.'

The British were also responsible for dividing the country on the religious grounds. Though there existed two distinct societies in the pre-British era, there was much reconciliation among the general population. The seeds of two nation theory was first sown by the British in 1909 when they granted separate electorate to the Muslims. This approach was further strengthened when they granted separate electorate to the Sikhs in 1919. It was only the strength of other factors which kept the country one, but the British were directly responsible for inculcating this two-nation theory in the minds of the people of India.

During the time of freedom movement a wide gap began to emerge in the society between the Hindus and the Muslims. As a result of the British policy of divide and rule they were forced to grant Independence by dividing or partitioning India as two independent states of India and Pakistan in August 1947.

Hindu-Muslim Relations

There is a great controversy amongst the scholars whether the Muslims were absorbed in the Indian society or not. While Pandit Nehru in his 'Discovery of India' expressed the view that the Muslim invaders were absorbed in India. Their royal dynasties were completely Indianised and they considered India as their motherland.

The Muslims tried to retain their exclusive identity in India which ultimately resulted in the demand of a separate state of Pakistan and the partition of India into two parts.

During the Muslim rule the Hindus dominated the economic life of the country and Muslims sought their cooperation. Except Aurangzeb, the other Mughal rulers tolerated Hindu religion. Akbar the great Mughal maintained cordial relations with the Hindus. In short, it can be said that with the lapse of time a spirit of harmony, toleration, and co-operation appeared between the Hindus and Muslims.

Similar relationship in other words the same relationship continued during the British rule prior to Freedom Struggle. The British who came to India as traders turned as rulers began to follow the 'divide and rule' policy. It was their tactical policy by which they obtained many fruits during their regime. During the Revolt of 1857 the Indian soldiers both Hindus and Muslims worked together and maintained brotherly relationship. Moreover, the rulers of both religions extended their co-operation and co-ordination for the same.

Even after this both Hindus and Muslims had maintained good relations and they fought for common cause. Both Hindu Saints and Muslim Maulvies preached love and brotherhood among them. During the Freedom Struggle the Muslims started Khilafat Movement. The leaders of Hindu fold under the leadership of Mahatma Gandhi supported the Muslim cause and opposed the British tooth and nail.

The leaders of both sides fought for their freedom against the British. To eradicate social evils like sati, infanticide and purdah they did wonderful service. They worked hand in hand for the welfare of the Muslims and Hindus. Muslims leaders like Sir Syed Ahmad Khan, Beck, Ali Brothers, M.A. Jinnah, Agha Khan and Maulana Abul Kalam Azad rendered remarkable service for the Muslim community. So also the Hindu leaders like Gandhiji and Nehru did a lot for Hindu-Muslim unity.

In spite of this a wide gap developed between the Hindus and the Muslims during the freedom movement. It was due to the British attitude and their policy of divide and rule. Hence, the Muslim League objected to mass contact Movement of the Congress under the leadership of Jawaharlal Nehru. The middle classes among the Muslims were not satisfied with their future of India. They felt that the Hindus were more than a match for them in practically every sphere of life. So they raised the cry of Pakistan where some very big jobs were sure to fall to their share. Finally the Cripps' proposals of March 1942 recognised the claim of the Muslim League for Pakistan. No wonder it was a severe blow to the conception of Indian unity. Thus, strained relations began between the two communities. It led to colossal devastation and death and massacre in the country.

Racial antagonism of the rulers

Though initially the British were very cautious in not interfering in the affairs of the native people but slowly they initiated this process. It was more extensive in the case of Hindus and Muslims. After 1858 the policy of the British government towards India created a sense of bitterness in the minds of the people. In 1859 and 1860 there took place disputes between the European Indigo planters and the Bengal peasants. The situation became very serious and disturbances took place. The racial antagonism of the rulers greatly affected the peasants.

Sir John Lawrence (1864-69) followed the so called policy of masterly inactivity with regard to Afghanistan. He had to fight the Bhutan war. The British officials forced the Bhutanese to sign a treaty.

During the time of Lord Noth Brook (1872-76) the Gaekwad of Baroda was ill-treated and his relatives were tortured. This antagonism was vehemently criticised by the people.

During the time of Lansdowne (1888-98) the troops were sent to Manipur to tackle the situation. The antagonism of the officers created a sense of uneasy calm.

In the case of Chitral (lies north east of Kashmir) also, their attitude was vehemently criticised by the people.

Impoverishment of the peasants

During this period the peasants lived in small villages, mud houses and thatched sheds in the country. They were opt to rest content with the production of sufficient to eat and drink and wherewithal to clothe themselves. With the apathy to better life or (Ignorance of the value of wealth) there could be no agricultural progress and large scale farming was impossible. However it is difficult to accept the view that the people of India were not rich and they produced the barest needed by them. In fact it was the wealth of India, which brought about the influx of the people, including the British, from outside India.

The "Permanent Settlement" was no measure for the relief of the country. The peasants continued to suffer for more than six decades when the indigo labour revolts attracted the government to the impoverished ryot and the Bengal Land Act was passed in 1859. Its abusive character is substantiated with the fact that "Permanent Settlement" was confined to Bengal and in other (provinces the land reforms were effected with a view to raise the revenue.

The increasing demand or revenue had made cultivation uneconomical. As a result the desertion from agriculture was not only improving the rural economy but also intensifying the political danger. The anti-industrial policy had increased the pressure on land and the people were left with no other alternative but to live on agricultural yields. As a result of this pressure, the land-plots were divided into smaller holding. It led to stagnation and deterioration of agriculture. There was low yields and the labour was going waste. The increasing rent made the peasants miserable. The landed aristocracy too made the peasants more miserable by their cruel attitudes. The small holdings and landlordism was the direct cause of increasing indebtedness of the rural population. The agricultural debt increased by leaps and bounds. This indebtedness was the crux of the agrarian economy and presents the true picture of the impoverishing rural population. The indebtedness made the money lender all the more powerful. The peasants suffered a lot by indebtedness. Morever, they had to sell their products at the cheapest rates and later on to purchase at exorbitantly high rates.

This impoverished condition of the peasants made the government to think about improvement of the peasants.

Ruin of Artisans and Craftsmen

The conditions of artisans and craftsmen were miserable during this period. Initially the British had come to India to buy goods from India but after the industrial revolution in England, the position changed. England produced goods on a massive scale on machines and exported them to India. Due to the development of means of transport and communication, these machine made goods reached every part of India. As a result of this, indigenious Indian industries suffered a severe set back as they could not face the challenge of the English factory made goods. The rural and urban handicrafts were formerly patronised by the Mughal emperors and native things began to disappear. The Indian artisans and craftsmen suffered a lot. They led a pathetic life. They had no help from any quarter. The English gradually gained momentum to establish their industries. The artisans and craftsmen were unable to meet the challenge posed from the British industry. The Indian artisan had to give up his vocation and had no option except to work as a labourer in a factory or on a farm.

However, one outcome of the introduction of capitalist economy was the rise of Indian capitalist class. The British carried on their business through Indian wholesalers, retailers, agents and contractors. Thus, big business gave impetus to the Indian bourgeois class, while the Indian artisans and craftsmen were rendered jobless.

Poverty and Famines

India has suffered from famines since time immemorial. The frequency of famines increased during the 19th century. The recurrence of famines was a great danger both to social harmony and political stability. Rocked by the continuous famines, the British government appointed a famine commission in 1880.

Famine of 1860-61

There was a famine in North Western provinces in 1860-61. It was due to the disturbances of 1857. Cultivation suffered and villagers fined heavily. During the two years preceding the famine rainfall was deficient. The people had to face the drought of 1860. So the poor people deserted their villages to find work in the neighbourhood. There was "a minimum of two lakh deaths" Colonel Baird Smith was deputed to tackle the situation. No fruitful result came from him.

Famine of 1865-66

The famine of 1865-66 covered a vast area. The districts of Bihar bordering on either bank of the Ganges, North Bengal, Orissa and the districts in Madras Presidency lying along the Bay of Bengal were suffered. There was a terrible loss of 1.3 million lives in Orissa. The relief given by the government was extremely belated, inadequate and ill organised.

The Campbell Famine Committee

Sir Gerrage Campbell laid the foundations for a definite famine policy. The committee made recommendations which in certain respects anticipated those of the Royal Commission of 1880. Sir John Lawrence, the then Governor General of India declared that his object was "to save every life" and that district officers would be held responsible if preventible deaths occurred.

Famine of 1868-70

A famine of great severity overtook Northern India in 1868-70. It covered the parts of the Punjab, North Western Provinces, Central India and Central Provinces. Local officers were instructed to save every life in those areas.

Famine of 1873-74

The famine 1873-74 in Bengal and Bihar occupies a unique position in the history of famines in India. The famine was actually very severe. The government took timely measures and provided foodgrains for all. For normal work normal wage was assured. However later on the wages were reduced and the work was increased.

Famine of 1876-78

The greet famine of 1876-78 revaged the country for 3 years and was a great calamity of its kind in respect of the area and the population affected, the duration and intensity of distress. In all, a total of 2,05,600 sq. miles covering a population of 36.4 million was affected. Under Sir Richard Temple relief measures were taken in Bombay and Madras. Efficient assistance was given to the suffering people.

Strachey Commission

The Government of India appointed a strong commission under General Richard Strachey in 1880. Relief should elsewhere be administered on the following basic principles :

1. Employment on works must be offered before the physical efficiency of applicants had been impaired by privation. The work should be of permanent utility.
2. The Government recognised that the grant of relief was the duty of the state and not of the general public.
3. The Government should trust private trade to supply and distribute food, giving it every possible facility.
4. Easy terms of land revenue and rents should be made by the landlords.
5. The cost of relief must be so localised as to bring home to its administrators a sense of personal responsibility for expenditure.
6. In times of excessive drought, facilities should be given for the migration of cattle to grassy forest areas where abundant pasturage was procurable.

   The recommendations of the commission were greatly accepted and steps were taken to create new resources by which in normal times a surplus of revenue could be secured to meet the extraordinary changes thrown on the state by famine. It was finally decided that Rs. 15 million should always be entered in the budget under the head "Famine Relief and Insurance." In 1883 Provisional Famine Code was promulgated.

There was poverty in some provinces. The same was eradicated by series of measures in 1884-85. The great famine of 1888-89 and another great famine of 1897-97 were controlled by extensive measures.

Lyall Commission

Under Sir James Lyall a commission was appointed to look after the conditions of famine. It largely adhered to the views expressed by the Strachey Commission.

Famine of 1900

India was visited in 1900 by a drought the greatest in extent and intensity which had been experienced for 200 years. More than 400,000 sq. miles of area was affected. Moreover, 60 million people were affected. It affected Bombay, the Central Provinces, Punjab, Rajasthan and Central Indian Principalities.

Mac Donald Commission

The Government appointed a commission under the Presidency of Sir Anthony Mac Donald. Their report was published in 1901. It summarised the accepted principles of relief and emphasised the benefits of 'moral strategy'. A Famine Commissioner was appointed. In many ways, it helped the affected people.

In 1905-06 there was a famine in Deccan districts of Bombay Presidency. Relief measures were taken considerably.

There was a famine in Bengal in 1943. It was due to this that food situation went from bad to worse. However, the government took relief measures to ease the situation.

4

Development of Education

I. Progress of Education under East India Company upto 1835

During the eighteenth century, the process of decay of Hindu and Muslim seats of learning was accelerated due to whirlwind of political confusion which gripped the country after the downfall of the Mughal empire. The Britishers fished into the troubled waters of Indian politics and gained political ascendancy in Bengal and Madras by the end of the eighteenth century. By the midnineteenth century, the British established their control over entire India. The Court of Directors in London was mainly interested in amassing the wealth of India and not in educating the people of India.

Hence, prior to Macaulay's Minute 1835, the management of education was left to private institutions. However, some piecemeal efforts were made by individuals like Warren Hastings and Jonathan Duncan and certain Christian missionaries, in the field of education. Warren Hastings established the Calcutta Madrasa in 1781 for the study of Persian and Arabic. In 1791, Jonathan Duncan the British Resident at Benaras, made a significant contribution to the establishment of Sanskrit College at Benaras for the study of laws and literature of the Hindus. In 1705, Sir William Jones established the Bengal Asiatic Society of individuals in their individual capacity but the British East India Company was rather averse to the issue of promotion of education of the people till the passage of the Charter Act of 1813. However, certain Christian missionaries motivated by proselytizing zeal evinced some interest in introducing education through the English medium. The Serampore Mission was greatly responsible for the introduction of Western education though the mission was also interested in the study of Indian languages.

(a) The Charter Act of 1813

Lord Minto, the Governor-General, made a significant observation in 1811 that science and literature were fast deteriorating in India. In England, the public opinion was in tune with the view of Lord Minto. The new awakening resulted in the provision for education when the Company's Charter was renewed in 1813. The Charter Act of 1813 provided for a sum of not less than one lakh of rupees every year for the revival and improvement of literature and encouragement of learned Indians and for the introduction of knowledge of the sciences.

This Act was the first legislative recognition of the right for education. However, the East India Company allotted one lakh of rupees not for mass education but for the learning of Sanskrit, Arabic and Persian because in the judicial department. Indians conversant with Sanskrit, Arabic or Persian were required to work as assessors with British judges. These assessors were required to expound Hindu or Muslim law from Sanskrit or Arabic or Persian books.

In the political department, the knowledge of Persian and vernaculars was essential for handling correspondence with the native princes of India. Thus, the administrative needs of the East India Company required the services of those Indians who were well-conversant with the classical and vernacular languages.

(b) Growing popularity of Western education and contribution of Raja Ram Mohan Roy

On 3rd June, 1814, the Court of Directors wrote a letter praising the excellence of Sanskrit. It said that the literature and science of India contained knowledge in law, ethics, medicine, a mathematics, astronomy and other subjects and so it would be advisable to encourage education in Sanskrit. This explains why the Sanskrit college of Calcutta was established in 1823 by the Governor-General, Lord Amherst. But Raja Ram Mohan Roy wrote a letter of protest to Lord Amherst declaring "that the Sanskrit education could only be expected to load the minds of the youth with grammatical niceties and metaphysical distinctions of life which are of little or no practical use to their possessors or to society. The pupils there will acquire what was known two thousand years ago with the addition of vain and empty subtleties since then produced by speculative men." The protests of Raja Ram Mohan Roy produced the desired effect. The government responded adequately and accepted the education of English in principle. A grant was sanctioned for the Calcutta Hindu College which was set up in 1817 by Raja Ram Mohan Roy with

David Hare and other enlightened Bengalis. The aim of this college was to teach English and Indian languages as well as Western humanities and sciences.

(c) The Anglicist and Orientalist Controversy (1823-1835)

In 1823, John Adams, who succeeded Lord Hastings temporarily as the Governor-General, appointed a General Committee of public instruction to decide how best the annual grant of one lakh of rupees which had been accumulated so far under the Charter Act of 1813 could be spent for the spread of education in India. But there arose a controversy among the members of the committee on the issue of the type of education to be imparted to the Indians and the medium of instruction necessitated for the purpose. Two schools of thought emerged; the one led by H.H. Wilson which supported oriental learning and the other led by Travelyan and later on strengthened by Lord Macaulay who stood for English education. The orientalists argued that the original intention of the Charter Act of 1813 in granting one lakh rupees per annum was for the development of oriental learning and, therefore, money should not be spent for any purpose other than this. On the other hand, the oriental learning was the best for the orientals and suited to their inclinations and aptitudes. Moreover, any effort to develop English learning would seriously injure the existing efforts of the private agencies in Pathshalas and Madrasas. The orientalists believed that Sanskrit and Arabic literature were not interior to English literature. There were great treasures in the ancient Hindu thought which India could not afford to neglect.

On the other hand, the arguments of the English school of thought too were not less strong and weighty.

1. The Anglicists argued forcefully that the intentions of the authors of the Charter Act of 1813 was to devote the granted funds only for the English education.
2. The exponents of the English school, specially Lord Macaulay argued that Arabic and Sanskrit were not suitable for judicial administration.
3. Moreover, the spread of English education would train the Indians to understand the English system and it would provide cheap India clerks.
4. The spread of the English culture would develop a demand for English goods in this country and give a great impetus to the English industries.

Lord Macaulay was appointed by the Governor-General Lord William Bentinck, as the chairman of the Committee of Public Instruction. Macaulay believed that instructed in European knowledge, if in some future age, the Indians demanded European institutions "that will be the proudest day in English History". Such was his **fervour** for the cause of English education that he submitted his Minute which was entirely in favour of English education without securing the consent of the members of the Committee of Public Instruction.

(d) Macaulay's Minute (1835)

Macaulay's Minute was a masterpiece characterised by its eloquence, brilliance, wit and incomparable style. In his Minute, Macaulay championed the cause of English by arguing in the following manner :

1. He disputed the view that by literature British Parliament could have only meant Arabic and Sanskrit literature. In fact, the Charter Act of 1813 was completely silent about the particular languages or sciences which were to be studied by the Indians.
2. Macaulay argued that the government ought to employ its public funds in teaching what is worth knowing. He asserted that nobody could ever deny that 'a single shelf of a Good European library was worth the whole native literature of India'. However, this assertion was an exaggeration but apparent merits of Western could not be denied.
3. Lord Macalay refuted the contention of the orientalists that after getting English education, the Indians would not remain submissive. He declared : "Are we to keep the people of India ignorant in order that we may keep them submissive?" He believed that if educated Indians demanded democratic institutions at any future age, that would be the proudest day in English history. That day did come much earlier than Macaulay predicted.
4. Lord Macautay laid emphasis on English as it was suited for running the administration. Thus, English education would serve the interests of the British Empire. Macaulay concluded the minute by writing thus : "I conceive that we have at present no right to the respectable name of a Board of Public Instruction. We are Board for wasting the public money for printing books which are of less value than the paper on which they are printed while it was blank."

However, it can be contended that Lord Macaulay's Minute was designed to create a class of person who should be "Indians in blood and colour but English in taste, in opinions, in morals and in intellect."

1. All the funds at the disposal of the Government would hence forward be spent in imparting to the Indians a knowledge of English literature and science.
2. While "the colleges of oriental learning were not established, the practice of supporting their students during their period of education was to be discontinued."
3. The government funds were not to be on the printing of oriental works.

The merits and demerits of English education are too well-known to be discussed in detail. In its favour, we say that it threw open the floodgates of the treasures of English knowledge and revolutionised the whole gamut of thought in India. The common language and common thought gave Indians a political unity. Under the impact of English learning in India. Indian behaviour and mode of life changed.

II. Development of education between 1836 and 1853

The years between 1836 and 1853 witnessed a considerable progress in the field of education. Many schools and colleges were established in various parts of the country. The Anglicists founded twelve new schools in the Bengal Presidency alone. Lord William Bentinck founded a Medical College at Calcutta. An engineering College was established at Roorkee by Lord Dalhousie.

(i) Educational reforms by Lord Auckland

In the field of education. Lord Macaulay, as President of the Committee of Public Instruction, did a good job under Lord Auckland, the Governor-General. One of the most important measures of Lord Auckland in the field of education was the institution of number of scholarships in the principal government schools for the encouragement of Indian scholars.

Another important measure was the adoption of vernacular as the medium of instruction to the masses. The Court of Directors had been repeatedly expressing their opinion in its favour and the Macaulay Committee, feeling the need, forwarded a manifesto to the Governor-General as to how it could help.

Auckland accepted the vernaculars for the primary schools and put the policy into practice as far as the funds could permit.

In order to spread medical science in India yet further, Lord Auckland established such colleges in Madras and Bombay. As a result of Lord Bentinck's resolution of March 7, 1835, as already stated certain money grant had been withdrawn from the Indian colleges which taught the classical languages. Despite the opposition of Christian missionaries in India, in his Minute of November, 1839, Lord Aucklamd declared that government scholarships would hence forward be available to these institutions as well.

(ii) Other educational developments and the role of missionaries

(a) Vernacular education though going to the background was also offered a consideration by Lord Auckland who granted Rs. 500 a month to the Asiatic Society of Bengal.

(b) Lord Hardinge, the Governor-General of India, laid down condition that all appointments in government departments would be given to those persons who were well-versed with English.

(c) Before 1854 certain important steps for the development of English education and openly for propagating Christianity were also taken by the Christian missionaries.

The Bible class in their schools was compulsory. The first important institution was opened in 1716 by the Danish Missionaries for training teachers in Madras. English schools were opened and the missionaries like David Hare, Thomas, Carey, Marshman and Ward did a lot of work. The Wilson College of Bombay and the Christian College of Madras were important missionary achievements. The St. John's College of Agra was started in 1853 and institutions were founded at Nagpur, Masulipatam and other places, which soon flourished.

III. Charles Wood's Despatch (1854)

The turning point in the history of education in India, however, came in the time of Dalhousie in 1854. A Parliamentary Committee appointed for the purpose of reorganising educational system in India made its recommendations on the basis of which Sir Charles Wood, the president of the Board of Control, drafted his despatch of 1854 which for many years remained a guiding star in the field. Sir Charles Wood declared that in India the British had to deal with "a rare of people slow to change, bound up by religious prejudices and antiquated customs". Therefore, the British approach to the subject required a change for which he made the following recommendations in his despatch which is popularly known as the "Wood's Despatch of 1854".

1. **Diffusion of the arts, science and philosophy of Europe**

   The aim of the educational system and policy should be the diffusion of the arts, science and philosophy of Europe so that trustworthy men may be produced capable of holding responsible offices under the British East India Company.

2. **Medium of Instruction**

   The Wood's Despatch declared that English was the most perfect medium of instruction but it should not be insisted upon at all stages. It should be used only when a sufficient knowledge of it has been gained. The Despatch gave importance to the existing vernacular languages because it was through the medium of vernacular languages that European knowledge could filter down to the masses.

3. **Macaulay's Filtration Theory Discredited**

   Macaulay's filtration theory which meant imparting of education only to the upper classes with the belief that therefrom it would filter down to the masses would be abandoned and in its place the indigenous schools should be made a foundation of the system.

4. **Official support to private enterprise**

   The system of grants-in-aid should be started with definite release to encourage private enterprise to open educational institutions.

5. **Award of scholarship and professional education**

   A comprehensive system of scholarship should be instituted to help the deserving students and professional institutions should be established for training students in law, medicine, agriculture methods of teaching in schools etc.

6. **Impetus to elementary education and female education**

   The Wood's Despatch insisted that greater attention should be paid to elementary schools. Special facilities and encouragement should be provided for female education.

7. **Establishment of Department of Public Instruction**

   Wood's Despatch recommended that a separate Department of public Instruction should be established in every province under a Director of Education assisted by inspectors of schools who should make periodical reports of educational work in the respective provinces.

8. Establishment of Universities on the model of London University

For the encouragement of higher education by conferring degrees, the government should establish universities which could be both affiliating and also examining bodies. Each university should have a Chancellor and Vice-Chancellor and should organised on the pattern of the London University with a senate to frame rules for conducting examinations, and controlling funds, and professorships of the different branches of education.

A beginning should be made with Universities at Bombay, Calcutta and Madras where a sufficient number of educational institutions to supply properly qualified candidates for receiving degrees was available. Under the University control would be colleges affiliated to the university which would impart education from Intermediate to the Degree level. Below the college level would be a network of schools such as Primary, Middle, High and Anglo-Vernacular Schools which could impart education in lower classes through the vernacular medium. The Wood's Despatch is said to be the "Magna Carta" of education in India. It outlines in definite terms the educational machinery that India was going to have. The provision for grant-in-aid was a great step taken which encouraged the private enterprise to come forth and exert their might in the field of education. The provision to encourage indigenous schools was a laudable step and female education and professional education all received due attention.

IV. Educational progress between 1855 and 1882

In 1858, the rule of British East India Company ended and the Indian administration was taken over by the Grown. During the reign of sixty-four years of Queen Victoria (1837-1901), many strides were taken in the field of education in India.

1. Despatch of Stanely (1859)

In 1859 Lord Stanley, the first Secretary of State for India, declared through his "Despatch" that though the Indian administration was taken over by the British Crown, yet the British Government would continue to implement the recommendations. Of Wood's Despatch and there would be no reversal of the principles of Wood's Despatch. Stanley Despatch made provision for the promotion of primary education. It also provided for a more liberal and flexible grant-in-aid system.

A further impetus was given to the programme of establishing a department of education in every province, with a Director, teaching staff and inspecting officers.

2. **Progress of University Education**

   In 1857, the Calcutta, Bombay and Madras Universities were established. In 1878, the Punjab University was founded. Several reputed educational institutions were established during 1855 and 1882. Among the most distinguished institutions were St. Xavier's College, Calcutta (1860), Forman College, Lahore (1864), St. Xavier's College, Bombay (1869), Reid College, Lucknow (1877) and St. Stephen's College, Delhi (1882). The number of colleges rose from 23 in 1854 to 72 in 1882.

3. **Impetus to Professional Education**

   By 1854, medical colleges were established in Calcutta, Bombay and Madras. In 1860, a medical coiiege was founded in Lahore. From 1854 onwards law colleges were establishes in various parts of India. During the four years (1858-62), the Survey School of Madras was turned into the Madras Engineering College. On the other hand, a school of art and industry at Madras, the J.J. School of Art at Bombay, an agricultural college at Saidapet near Madras, the Mayo School of Art (1875) at Lahore, and Forestry School (1878) at Dehradun were founded.

V. The Hunter Commission (1882)

A landmark in the history of education in India is, however, the report of the Hunter Commission submitted in 1882. There were complaints that the Wood's Despatch of 1854 had not been properly followed. In the circumstances Lord Ripon, the Governor General, appointed a Commission composed of 22 members with Sir William Hunter as its Chairman to report on the manner in which effect had been given to the principles of the Despatch of 1854. The Hunter Commission was also required to report on "the present state of elementary education and the means by which this can be extended and improved". The progress of the college work and some other aspects of education were also be reported upon; though the general operation of universities was out of the Commission's terms of reference.

(1) The Recommendation of the Hunter Commission

The Hunter Commission submitted its report after a thorough investigation into the matter. It made the following important recommendations :

(a) Encouragement to primary education

Primary education was seriously lagging behind and it should be strongly encouraged by reserving a part of provincial revenues for the purpose of financing the programmes of development of primary education. The commission recommended that elementary schools should be handed over to the management of municipal councils and district boards and other bodies subject to the inspection and supervision by the government.

(b) Secondary education

Regarding secondary education, the Commission expressed its appreciation that it was making commendable progress, particularly in Bengal, where the system of grant-in-aid worked well and where after every one government-maintained school, there were too maintained by private agencies. The Commission recommended that all the secondary schools should be progressively handed over to the private enterprises which should be encouraged by grant-in-aid and that in future the secondary education should be ordinarily provided by the government only where private co-operation was not available. At the same time, the standard of education was not to be permitted to decline.

(c) Grant-in-aid for indigenous schools

The Hunter Commission made recommendations for the encouragement of indigenous schools by grant-in-aid on the basis of "Payment by Results." The aided schools and colleges were to be allowed lower rates of fees than those charged by similiar government-owned institutions and these colleges should be encouraged to employ more Indian graduates trained in European universities.

(d) Emphasis on secular education and physical education

The Commission emphasised that though any sort of religious education was to be always excluded, yet some arrangement should be made to satisfy the popular demand regarding the development of the sense of right and wrong among the students. For this purpose, moral text books could be prepared. On the other hand, in the government-owned or an aided college, the principal or a Professor could deliver a series of lectures in each class on the duties of man and a citizen. Besides moral education, due emphasis was to be laid on physical education.

(e) Encouragement of education among Muslims

The Commission recommended that special attention should be paid towards development of education among the Muslims.

(2) Significance of Hunter Commission and its impact on education

The Hunter Commission constitutes an important stage in the history of education in India. Majority of its recommendations were adopted by the government with the result that with the devolution of control to the local bodies, the British element in the teaching and the inspecting departments was considerably reduced. Another significant improvement after 1882 was the development of the Punjab University which was founded in that year, this, lessening the burden of the Calcutta University. The progress in primary schools from 1882 to 1901 was displayed by the number of students in them, rising from 22 lakhs in 1882 to 32 lakhs in 1901. In the secondary schools, this number increased from 42,993 in 1886 to 6,33,728 in 1901, while in the colleges, the number of students increased from 11,501, in 1886 to 23,009 in 1901.

VI. Educational reforms of Lord Curzon

One of the greatest achievements of Lord Curzon, writes Frazer, lay in the field of education. One may, however, differ as to how much of this achievement was positive and how much negative. The existing system of education had been built on Macaulay's Minute of 1835 and Wood's Despatch of 1854. Among the defects from which education suffered was that the masses of India were not touched by it. Moreover, it was "too slavish an imitation of English models and was fitted to turn out an army of clerks rather than leaders of public opinion and thought." On the other hand, there was a lack of the Central control.

In order to put his views into practice, in September 1901, Lord Curzon called a conference of the highest government officials and the official representatives at Simla. No Indian was invited and among the non-officials, only Dr. Miller, the Principal of the Madras Christian an College, received an invitation to attend. There was great secrecy in the conference and its deliberations were not published. After discussions in this conference, a Universities Commission, under the Chairmanship of the Law Member, Sir Thomas Raleigh, was appointed in 1902. The only Indian member appointed to the Commission was Syed Hussain Belgrami, the Director of Public Instructions in the Nizam's Dominions. However, the Hindus lodged their protest for lack of their representation on the Commission. So later on, Justice Guru Das Bannerji of the Calcutta High Court, was included. After five months of discussions and deliberations, the Commission submitted its report in June 1902 in which Guru Das gave a note of Dissent. The report submitted by the Commission was published on October 1902 and on its basis the Universities Act of 1904 was passed.

(1) The provisions of the Universities Act of 1904

(i) The governing bodies of the Universities were to be reconstituted and the size of the senates was reduced to a minimum of 50 and a maximum of 100.

(ii) The number of elected fellows was to be fixed at 20 for Bombay, Calcutta and Madras Universities and for the remaining Universities, the number of elected fellows was fixed at 15.

(iii) Powers of the universities were enlarged and they were also to resume teaching functions for the post-graduate classes, appoint professors and lecturers for the purpose and promote study and research.

(iv) The Syndicate of Universities were given statutory recognition and University teachers were to get an adequate representation on them.

(v) The Senates were to be responsible, for maintaining a proper standard of examinations, courses of study, text books and working facilities for the students.

(vi) Undergraduate teaching was left to the colleges and strict conditions and terms were laid down for affiliation of new colleges which were to be subject to inspection by the university authorities.

(vii) All the policies of university and affiliation and disaffiliation of colleges were to be subject to the approval of the government.

(viii) The Vice-Chancellors were to be appointed by the government

(ix) The Governor-General was empowered to define the territorial jurisdiction of different universities.

Commenting on the University Act, C. Chirol wrote thus : "As was to be expected, under a Viceroy who was a great autocrat with an overwhelming faith in the efficiency of government machinery, the chief purpose of the Act of 1904 was to tighten the hold of the government on the universities. Practically nothing was henceforth to be done without the approval of government".

The Indian leaders, specially Sir Phirozeshah Mehta, Sir S.N. Banerji and G.K. Gokhale, vehemently criticised the Act. Lord Curzon was blamed for having ulterior motives rather that educational aims. It was asserted that his aim was to prevent the universities from becoming nurseries of nationalism and to keep the masses in the state of illiteracy and backwardness so as to enable England to continue her imperialist rule in this country.

VII. Important landmarks in the fields of education during 1910 and 1947

1. Government resolution of 1913

After Lord Curzon, India for years witnessed a continuous agitation. A better system of education was demanded and there was persistent demand for more funds for higher education and technical and vocational training. Under these circumstances education was transferred in 1910 from the Home Department to a separate department of its own. Sir Harcourt Butler, the first education member of Lord Hardings' Executive Council, issued a resolution in 1913. The resolution declared that areas of the university control would be limited within every province. In other words, a university would be established in every major province. New affiliating universities for Patna, Nagpur and Rangoon and teaching universities for Aligarh, Dacca and Benaras were promised.

Within the next five years of this resolution, universities were established at Benaras, Mysore, Aligarh and Patna. The expenditure on schools and colleges from private sources such as missionaries and others also increased and in 1916-17 it reached the figure of Rs. 1,128.83 lakhs.

(2) The Saddler Commission (1917)

Lord Chelmsford, the Governor-General, appointed the Saddler Commission in 1917 to report on secondary and university education under the Calcutta University alone. But the Commission made a vast study not only of the Calcutta University but of other Indian Universities as well. The Commission submitted a comprehensive report dealing with almost every aspect of secondary and higher education. Its recommendations are as follows :

- (i) The university intermediate classes should be transferred to secondary schools and admission into the university should be at the existing intermediate examination stage.
- (ii) The degree course duration after the intermediate examination should be three years.
- (iii) The Board of secondary education should replace university in its control of secondary and intermediate education.
- (iv) The government should transfer the control of the University of Calcutta from the Centre to the provincial government.

(v) Efforts should be made to establish a University at Dacca within a short time.

(vi) The organisation of university teaching service should be on a different basis from that of the government services.

(vii) A special board should be founded in order to encourage the education of women.

(viii) The medium of instruction up to high schools should be the vernaculars of the province while English should be used as the medium of instruction beyond the high schools stage.

(ix) There should be a complete overhaul of the university examination system.

(x) The development of professional and vocational training should be seriously taken up by the university.

The Government of India accepted these recommendations. Though retaining still the general policy on higher education in the hands of the central government, the Act of 1919 transferred the charge of education department into the hands of Indian ministers responsible to the provincial legislatures. A university at Lucknow and another at Dacca were established in 1920. Allahabad got its university in 1921 while the University of Delhi was established in 1922.

(3) The Hartog Committee

In 1928 the Hartog Committee reviewed the progress of education made since the transfer of education to the control of Indian ministers. It drew the attention of authorities to the problems of stagnation, leakage and wastage, the disparity in literacy between men and women, the high percentage of failures at the matriculation leave, lack of professional and vocational training and the mad rush of admissions at the university stage.

(4) Formation of General Advisory Board

In 1935, the Government of India Act was passed. The Bureau of Education which was created after the Montagy-Chelmsford Reforms in 1921 was converted into the Central Advisory Board. The C.A.B. (Central Advisory Board) defined the various stages in the educational ladder, *viz.*, (i) primary stage for minimum general education and training, (ii) lower secondary stage as a self-contained course of general education or a foundation for higher secondary education, (iii) higher secondary stage for preparing students for admission to the university and technical courses.

(5) Report of Wood and Abott

In 1937, Wood and Abott submitted their report on vocational education and administration. They laid emphasis on the establishment of full-time junior and senior technical schools. It was at the recommendation of Wood and Abbot Report that the Government High School, Delhi was converted into a Polytechnic.

(6) Wardha Scheme of Education

In 1937, Mahatma Gandhi initiated discussions on a independent scheme on national education. He convened an All-India National Education Conference at Wardha and the conference drew up a scheme of Basic Education known as to Wardha Scheme. It provided seven years free and Compulsory education with the mother tongue as the medium of instruction. Craft was to be the centre of teaching and correlation as the technique of instruction. The basis education emphasised the activity principles, the imbibing of Indian culture and Indian philosophy. The curriculum was suited to the rural and urban masses. This system of education was given a trial in a number of provinces where the Congress formed ministries. The basic education received greater impetus so much so that the Sargent Committee (1944) recommended it as a national scheme and the Congress Government after Independence declared it as a national system of elementary education. However, during the post-independence period, the craft-oriented basic education became popular for some time but the present system of elementary education gained ground and the craft-centered basic education could not attract many students, because their parents insisted on the study of English which was not to be taught in basic schools.

(7) The Sargent Commission

The next landmark in the history of Indian education was the Report of Sargent Commission on Post-war Education Development in India. The Commission dealt at length with the stages of education, various aspects of education, examination reforms, teacher's training, health education, recreational and social activities. It was as a result of the Sargent Commission that (i) The Ministry of Education was constituted at the Centre, (ii) The University Grants Commission was constituted, (iii) the All India

Council of Technical Education and (iv) the Central Bureau of Education were set up.

VII. Development of education during post-Independence period

The first milestone in the development of education in independent India was the enactment of the Indian Constitution which defined a number of matters concerning education. The provision for free and compulsory education for all children until they complete the age of fourteen has been made. Again the state shall promote with special care the education and economic interests of the weaker sections of the people and in particular, of the scheduled tribes and scheduled casted. In Part xvii of the Indian Constitution, Hindi has been declared as the official language of the Union. Hence, the progressive use of Hindi language for official purposes of the Central Government and the regional languages for the internal administration in each state has been recommended. The place of English as the language of High Court, Supreme Court and of administration till it is replaced by Hindi has been defined.

A. Radhakrishnan Commission

In 1948-49 the Union Government appointed the University Education Commission with Sir Radhakrishnan as its Chairman. The Commission made detailed recommendations regarding the teaching staff and their service conditions, regarding the standard of teaching, research, professional education and examinations. The Commission recommended higher salary scales and better service conditions. It recommended opening of occupational institutions, organising refreshed courses, increase in working hours, prescribing of good text books, improving of library facilities and setting up of laboratories.

Regarding curriculum, it laid emphasis on acquaintance with ones physical environment, introduction of basic ideas of science effective use of languages, appreciation of higher values, and social cooperation. The Commission laid stress on increased facilities for post-graduate research and teaching. The commission laid stress on increased facilities for postgraduate research and teaching. It advocated increased facilities for the study of professional courses like agriculture and commerce, etc. It suggested improvements in the method of appointment of examiners, in paper setting, in the system of scoring and in the organisation of examiners.

B. Secondary Education Commission (S.E.C.)

In 1952, the Union Government appointed the Secondary Education Commission under the chairmanship of Dr. A. Lakshmanaswami Mudaliar, Vice-Chancellor, Madras University. The terms of reference before this Commission were to examine the existing system of secondary education in this country and to suggest measures for its reorganisation and improvement. The Commission submitted its report in August 1953 and presented recommendations on almost all aspects of secondary education. The major recommendations were the installation of higher secondary system with diversified pirses the three-language formula, the emphasis on educational and vocational guidance, improvement in the system of examination, improvement in the teaching staff and improvement in methods of teaching. These recommendations of the Secondary Education Commission were discussed by the Central Advisory Board of Education in January 1953 and accepted with certain modifications. A scheme of higher secondary education was launched all over India. An All-India Council of same has been widened. The National Council of educational Research and Training, having with it over a dozen wings, was established at the Centre for guiding education at its various levels developing special aspects of education and providing educational guidance and facilities to the States. The Secondary Education Commission laid emphasis on the following aspects :

(1) Development of democratic citizenship

The Commission states that the education system must make its contribution to the development of habits, attitude and qualities of character which will enable its citizens to bear the responsibilities of democratic citizenship and to counteract all those fissiparous tendencies which hinder the emergence of a broad national and secular outlook. Secondary education must develop the capacity for clear thinking, the intellectual integrity to sift truth from propaganda and falsehood and scientific attitude of mind to think objectively and dispassionately. The democratic type of education should take into account all the psychological, emotional, social and the practical needs of the child. It must cultivate the qualities of discipline, co-operation, social sensitiveness and tolerance it must foster the development of a sense of true patriotism leading to sound internationalism.

(2) Vocational efficiency

One of the urgent problems of the country is to improve productive efficiency and to increase national wealth and thereby to raise the standard of living. In this respect, the Secondary Education Commission recommends appreciation of dignity of manual labour and promotion of technical skill for the advancement of industry and econology, Education should emphasise agricultural, technical, commercial and other practical courses besides the academic one.

(3) Development of personality

The next aim of the secondary education is to release the sources of creative energy among the students so that they may be able to appreciate their cultural heritage, and to cultivate rich interests which they can pursue in their liesure time. The scope of secondary education must be widened so as to make it broad based enough to include a wide variety of subjects and interests for the complete development of various aspects of personality physical, moral, mental, social and practical. Secondary education should thus fulfil the needs of the growing individual and, at the same time, achieve the goals of the nation.

(4) The three-language formula

Reviewing the whole situation of the complexity of the language problem in India and taking into consideration both the historical background and future needs of the country, the Secondary Education Commission made the following recommendations :

1. The mother tongue or the regional language should be the medium of instruction throughout the secondary school stage, subject to the provision that for linguistic minorities, special facilities should be make available.
2. At the higher secondary stage, at least two languages should be studied, one of which being the mother tongue or the regional language. The language to be studied at the secondary stage should be :
   (i) Mother tongue or regional language or a composite course of the mother tongue and a classical language.
   (ii) One other language should be chosen from among the following :
      (a) Hindi (for those whose mother-tongue is not Hindi).
      (b) Elementary English (for those who have not studied English at an earlier stage).
      (c) Advanced English (for those who have studied English at an earlier stage).
      (d) A modern Indian language other than Hindi.
      (e) A modern foreign language other than English.
      (f) A classical language.

The Secondary Education Commission states : "It will be noticed that in this curriculum, a pupil will ordinarily be required to take one other language besides his mother tongue. It may be Hindi or English or any other language according to his needs and choice. This arrangement will meet the ordinary requirements of most pupils".

The Central Advisory Board or Education did approve of the above system suggested by the S.E.C. and it prepared a new programme, popularly known as the three-language formula. The Union Government accepted this three-language formula in 1957. According to this formula, every student in the secondary schools will be required to study as a part of the core curriculum the three languages, namely :

I. (a) Mother tongue or

(b) regional language or

(c) a composite course of mother tongue and a regional language or

(d) a composite course of mother tongue and a classical language or

(e) a composite course of a regional language and classical language

II. English or a modern European language

III. Hind (for non-Hindi speaking areas) or another modern Indian language (for Hindi speaking areas)

Later, this three-language formula was modified by the Indian Education Commission (1965). This modified three-languages formula as recommended by the Indian Education Commission runs thus :

(a) The mother tongue or regional language

(b) The official language or the Union or an associate language (*i.e.*, English or Hindi) and

(c) A modern Indian or European language not covered under (a) and (b) and other than that used as the medium of instruction.

The obvious corollary of this formula when implemented is thus : In Hindi-speaking states, the students will study Hindi under (a) English under (b) and other modern Indian language under (c) In non-Hindi-speaking states, the students will study the mother tongue or the regional language under (a) English under (b) and Hindi or any other Indian language or any European language under (c) The Indian Education Commission feels that non-Hindi speaking students should not be compelled to study Hindi if they are unwilling.

(5) Organisational pattern of secondary education

The traditional structure of education has been 4 or 5 years primary education followed by three years middle standard education followed by 2 years high school education, leading to the matriculation examination.

The Secondary Education Commission modified the 2 years high school education and substituted it by 4 years higher secondary education. Later on the Central Advisory Board approved 3 years higher secondary education instead of 4 years, thus making it eleven years school in all.

(6) Vocational bias to secondary education

The S.E.C. has suggested vocational bias to the secondary education. But, unfortunately, we find that only 12 per cent of the students who go to secondary schools take up vocational courses. In other countries, the percentage is 60 to 70. Hence, there is need for a vocational bias to secondary education. Every student should learn some craft or skill. Every student should imbibe the dignity of labour.

(7) Social and moral values

The S.E.C. has laid due emphasis on social and moral values so that the students may develop an integrated personality. In this connection, Shri K.G. Saiyidin has aptly remarked thus : "If I was asked to define broadly the main objectives of out educational reconstruction, I would say that we are trying to build a bridge between education and life and make out educational ideology responsive both to the new urges and aspirations of the people and the age as well as the older basic values of our culture. The latest trend is, therefore, to bring about a synthesis between the various aspects of individual, *viz.*, the social, cultural and utilitarian, liberal and vocational, theoretical and practical old and new, personal and national and thus to balance the objectives of secondary education so that it may lead to the happiness of the individuals and welfare of the nation.

C. Indian Education Commission (1965)

The Central Government appointed in 1965 the Indian Education Commission (I.E.C.) under the chairmanship of Dr. S. Kothari, Chairman, University Grants Commission, with 16 other members who are educationists of repute (ten from India and six from foreign countries). The Government of India defined the purpose of the Commission thus : "The Commission will advise the government on the national pattern of education and on the general principles and policies for the development of education at all stages and in all its aspects." The Indian Education Commission submitted its report on 30th June, 1966. Its recommendations are summarized as follows :

(1) Elementary education

(i) Tuition fee at the primary stage should be abolished in all government, local authority and private schools as early as possible preferably before the end of the Fourth Plan.

(ii) Free text books and writing material should be provided at the primary stage. The students should be presented with a complete set of books for the next year as soon as the results of the annual examinations are declared.

(iii) Steps should be taken to ensure at the end of the lower primary that no promising child is prevented from continuing his studies further and to this end, a scholarship of an adequate amount should be provided to every child who may need it. It has been presumed that the target should be to provide scholarship for 2.5 per cent of enrolment at the higher primary stage by 1975-76 and 5 per cent of the same enrolment by 1985-86.

(iv) Special attention should be paid to the education of women, handicapped children, backward classes, backward tribes, tribal people and scheduled castes.

(v) In view of the present unsatisfactory position regarding school buildings, it is necessary to take steps to clear the backlog of unconstructed school buildings as well as to provide additional buildings for new enrolment.

(vi) Allocations for construction of school buildings should be increased in the central and state budgets and community resources mobilised. Loans and grants-in aid should be given on a liberal basis to private schools for the construction of buildings.

(vii) The norms and guidance already available for specing and planning of school buildings should be put into practice. To avoid delays in the construction of government buildings, a separate unit of the P.W.D. should be set up for the execution of education building programmes. At a later stage, an Education Building Consortia may be set up.

(2) Aims of education

The Indian Education Commission emphasised the need for an urgent reform in education to endeavour to relate it to the life, needs and aspirations of the people and thereby make it a powerful instrument of social, economic and cultural transformation, necessary for the realisation of the national goals. For this purpose, education should be developed so as to increase productivity, achieve social and national integration, accelerate the process of modernisation and cultivate social, moral and spiritual values.

(a) Education and productivity

For the promotion of productivity, I.E.C. emphasised the (i) science education should become an integral part of schools course; (ii) work experience should be introduced leading to technology and industrialisation and (iii) secondary education should be increasingly and largely vocationalised.

(b) Social and national integration

To achieve this objective, I.E.C. recommends that (i) common school system of public education should be adopted as a national goal; (ii) social service for a total of 30 days at the lower secondary stage and 20 days at a higher stage should be obligatory for all students; (iii) suitable arrangements should be made for teaching mother tongue, Hindi and other modern Indian languages; (iv) teaching of languages, literatures, philosophy and history of India together with Indian architecture, sculpture, painting, music, dance and drama should be well-organised for the promotion of national consciousness.

(c) Education and modernisation

The I.E.C. emphasises that education should be concerned with the awakening of curiosity, the development of proper interests, attitudes and values and building up of such essential skill as independent study and capacity to think and judge for oneself.

(d) Education and moral values

I.E.C. endorses the recommendations of the Committee on Religious and Moral Instruction and urges that such values should be made an integral part of the school programme. The I.E.C. observes, "A syllabus giving well-chosen information about each of the major religions should be included as a part of the course in citizenship or as a part of general education to be introduced in schools and colleges upto the first degree". Thus, the four priorities mentioned by I.E.C. *viz.*, productivity, national integration, modernisation and moral values, faithfully represent the pulse of the nation at the present moment.

(3) Guidance and counselling

Guidance and counselling should be regarded as an integral part of education, meant for all students and aimed at assisting the individual to make decisions and adjustments from time to time. Guidance should begin from the lowest class in the primary school and in view of the large number of schools involved, the programme may be introduced through simple measures such as (i) familiarising teacher under training with diagnostic testing and the problems of individual differences; (ii) organising in-service courses for primary teachers; (iii) production of occupational literature and (iv) helping pupils and their parents in the choice of further education.

Guidance at the secondary stage should, among other things, help in the identification and development of the interest and abilities of the pupils. The ultimate objective should be to introduce adequate guidance services in all secondary schools with a trained counsellor in charge of the programme. On the other hand, all the secondary school teachers should be introduced to guidance concepts through pre or in-service training. The training colleges should be suitably staffed for the purpose.

The Indian Education Commission further recommended that the teachers should be oriented to the special techniques of dealing with talented children, specially for providing an atmosphere for free expression and creative work. The neglect of backward children leads to the wastage of educational facilities and human resources and it is necessary for a developing country to refuse this wastage to the minimum. Steps should be taken to diagnose the causes of under-achievement of the backward pupils are the secondary stage and to formulate and implement the remedial achievement within the school system with the help of interested teachers and child guidance clinics where available and parent teacher associations.

(4) Suggestions regarding university education

The Indian Education Commission also made certain recommendations regarding university education :

(i) Some orientation to professional education is necessary for junior lecturers in higher education, (ii) Newly-appointed lecturers should be given some time to acclimatise themselves to the institution, (iii) Regular orientation courses for new staff should be organised in every university and where possible in some colleges, (iv) In bigger universities or groups of universities, these courses may be placed on a permanent basis by establishing a staff college.

(5) Education of the handicapped

The Indian Education Commission made the following recommendations regarding the education of the handicapped :

(i) By 1986 education for 15 per cent of the physically handicapped, 5 per cent of the mentally handicapped and 10 per cent of totally handicapped should be provided.

(ii) In each district there should be at least one good centre for these children.

(iii) For the above purpose, special programme should be developed and special schools established.

(iv) Many handicapped children should be educated in the normal schools.

(v) The Ministry of Health, Ministry of Education and Social Welfare Board must have a co-ordinated plan for action in the field of the handicapped.

(vi) NCERT should undertake research work in this field.

The government accepted most of the recommendations of the IEC and this has resulted in a better organisation of the educational system in the country.

(6) General appraisal of education in India

Educational activity during the post-Independence period has followed a clear pattern of development, the logic of which became unambiguously explicit. Till about the midfifties, everything remained more or less the same as before 1947. There was only a certain amount of qualitative expansion at every level of education. In the midfifties came the Second Fiver Year Plan, which laid due emphasis on professional and technical education. The decisions to establish I.I.T.s., Regional Engineering Colleges and to assist university education through the U.G.C. were all taken up from the midfifties onwards. Expenditure on universities in 1950-51 was 5.4 per cent of the total allocation for education. In 1955-56 it rose to 5.5 per cent and remained exactly at the same level till 1960-61 after which it began to rise somewhat steeply. Similarly, expenditure on elementary and secondary education increased.

Though many strides have been made in the field of education, yet there have been certain imbalances. The Education Commissions usually play safe. Even when they make an honest appraisal of a difficult situation, they generally present their findings in bland and soothing terms. The neglect of elementary education was not the only casulty of the strategy of educational planning. We have yet to attain the target of free and compulsory education.

Yet another equally important casualty was adult education, In India adult education is generally taken as equivalent to eradication of illiteracy, in out country, more than 60 per cent people are illiterate. Adult education, however, has a connotation even beyond the eradication of illiteracy. It is an attitude of mind as well as strategy of growth. It assumes that knowledge and skill have to be imparted to everyone whether he went to a school or not. Even if a person has undergone high professional training in a particular field, after a few years he requires some further training. At least this is the theory underlying the concept of adult education; and theory is followed in actual practice in most advanced countries of the world. In out country, the situation is different. There is no strong emphasis on improvement of skills. We are content with functioning at a moderate level of performance. Yet another defect of out educational system is the neglect of teachers education. In order to maintain satisfactory standards of educational attainment, perhaps no other input is more essential than the quality of those employed to instruct now-a-days, a first class graduate prefers to be a clerk in the LIC or a bank rather than to take up a teaching profession in a school. If teacher's quality is poor or indifferent, the damage that they can do would extend to their whole life span. It is aptly said by a writer : "If an advocate makes a mistake, it lies in the file, if an engineer makes a mistake it is plastered but if a teacher makes a mistake it is reflected throughout the nation." There are two aspects of this issue which need to be examined. One is the salary and the other is status given to teachers as a class. While there has been a certain amount of improvement in salary scales at the higher levels of education, teachers at the lower levels continue to be grossly under-paid. This means that the profession of teaching fails to attract the better kind of people and only those who are unable to find jobs elsewhere come to teaching.

Though it cannot be denied that much has to be done in spreading elementary and adult education and improving the teacher's status, yet great strides have been made in the spread of women education, secondary education and higher education. There has been a commendable increase in the medical colleges. According to the Census Report of 1981, the literacy figure is slightly below 40 per cent. Indian scientists, doctors and technicians have made a mark even in the foreign countries. Due to the unemployment of the educated class, there has been a brain drain. Our most accomplished and competent doctors and engineers are prone to serve in foreign countries due to lack of attractive jobs in our country.

A developing country like India should arrest this trend and utilise the services of the talented young men in the best interest of the people.

Indian education would certainly be revolutionised if elementary education is made free and compulsory, craft-centred education at secondary level becomes a reality, brain drain is checked, pace of adult education is accelerated, strong library movement is launched throughout the country and above all, the status of teachers is raised by providing the teaching community with all the benefits that help them in maintaining a higher standard of living.

5

Renascent India

The emergence of reform movements in the 19th century marks the beginning of new era in Indian society.

Western education and Industrial Revolution brought about a new awakening in the minds of the Indian intelligentsia. The enlightened and educated Indians developed consciousness about the pristine glory of Indian culture and realised that the existing social evils such as the sati system, purdah system, untouchability, ban on widow remarriage, and host of other evil practices were leading to human degradation. On the other hand, the proselytizing zeal of the Christian missionaries, the political unification and economic exploitation of the people at the hands of the British made Indian society still more vulnerable. In such circumstances, various social and religious reformers rose to the occasion to meet the challenge of the times. The first objective of these reformists was to purge society of its long-standing social evils. A brief description of the movements launched by a galaxy of social and religious reformers in India is given below :

I. The Brahmo Samaj

In 1815, Raja Ram Mohan Roy (1772-1833) who is regarded as the Father of Indian Renaissance, established the Atmiya Sabha for holding theosophical discussions and meditation. The prayer meetings of this organisation finally led to the formation of Brahmo Samaj, which commenced functioning on 20 August, 1828. Tarachand Chakravarti was its secretary. In January 1830, the Brahmo Samaj began to work in the new building in the Jorasanko area of Calcutta.

(1) Brahmo Congregation

The Brahmo Samaj meetings, which were held on Saturday evenings, were very instructive. Here, the Bengali translations from the Upanishads were read. There were preachings of sermons. Persons who held liberal views became the members of the Brahmo Samaj. The orthodox Hindus were critical of the Brahmo Samaj on account of the liberal and progressive views of its members.

(2) Raja Ram Mohan Roy's modern and progressive ideas

(a) Raja Ram Mohan Roy shines significantly in the galaxy of those reformers who inspired by Western culture, science and technology, entertained modern and progressive ideas. He was so imbued with Western thoughts that in the controversy between the Anglicists and Orientalists regarding the medium of instruction in India, he supported the Anglicists. When there was a move to establish a Sanskrit College in 1823, Raja Ram Mohan Roy wrote to the Governor-General Lord Amherst : "The Sanskrit system of education would be best calculated to keep this country in darkness". Ram Mohan was indeed not against Sanskrit. He himself had founded the Vedanta College where Sanskrit literature was taught. But what he wanted was that the Indians should keep pace with the strides in science and technology of the West so that the country might become modernised.

(b) Raja Ram Mohan Roy undertook a profound study of the Bible and studied Hebrew and Greek languages. His famous treatise: "The precepts of Jesus, the guide to peace and happiness", displayed his orientation with the teachings of the Jesus and the Christian ethics. This publication evoked an angry reaction of the orthodox Hindus. On the other hand, Christian missionaries were also critical of this book for different reasons. Marshall branded him as the "Father of Lies". Ram Mohan Roy replied that abuse has no place in a solemn religious controversy.

(c) Ram Mohan Roy firmly believed that there was only one theism and that "a Hindu theism, an Islamic theism and Christian theism" were only historical varieties. According to him, there is one Supreme Reality in the world.

(d) Raja Ram Mohan Roy was deeply concerned with the eradication of social evils like sati, child marriage, polygamy etc. In 1811, his brother died and his brother's widow Alokmanjari decided to commit sati though Ram Mohan Roy made an unsuccessful attempt to prevent her from doing so. Alokmanjari's self-immolation gave a rude shock to the mind of Ram Mohan Roy. He rightly believed that very few widows gave consent to commit sati. Mostly the bodies of widows were consigned to flames by overcoming their reluctance. This was a heinous crime perpetrated on the innocent womenfolk. Ram Mohan whole heartedly supported the Government General Lord William Bentinck when the latter enacted legislation abolishing sati in 1829.

(e) In the field of politics, Ram Mohan Roy made his mark as a liberal democrat. He was a staunch advocate of the freedom of press. Though a landlord by birth, his sympathies were with the underprivileged section of the society. He vehemently condemned the drain of wealth, the salt monopoly and certain aspects of the permanent settlement which were prejudicial to the interests of the poor. He was in touch with the latest political developments in the international field such as the French Revolution of 1830, and the Reform Act of 1832. In 1830, he defied the prejudice against crossing the ocean and went to England to request the British Government to increase the allowances of the nominal Mughal Emperor Akbar II who deputed him as his emissary and conferred on him the title of "Raja". He also personally witnessed the proceedings of the House of Commons when the Charter Act of 1833 was due to be passed. But, unfortunately, his frail body could not survive the strains and stresses and on 17th September, 1833 he passed away in England.

(3) Execution of Trust Deed to run the Brahmo Samaj

Land was bought and a house of prayer was constructed in 1830. A trust deed was executed to create a trust to run the Brahmo Samaj and its Church. Ram Mohan Roy included the following ideas in the trust deed :

1. The "Church" was for the worship of one God.
2. No images were kept and rituals were not allowed.
3. Anyone belonging to any religion could participate in the worship of God.
4. All religions were to be respected.
5. World brotherhood was given due emphasis.

Indeed Brahmo Samaj absorbed good principles of Christianity and made Hinduism broad based but the orthodox Hindus manifested their displeasure with the liberal ideals of this organisation. Suppression of sati, foreign travel, ban on images and rituals, no belief in gods and goddesses and other liberal ideals were alien to the thinking of the tradition-bound orthodox Hindu community.

(4) The Brahmo Samaj not a mass movement

The members of Brahmo Samaj belonged to the upper classes and castes. As the Samaj failed to attract the people from the lower section of society, it could not become a mass movement. While it struck roots in Bengal and strongly influenced the cultural life there, its impact on the other parts of the country was very limited. In Raja Ram Mohan Roy's death the Samaj lost an ardent leader. However, the Brahmo Samaj was lifted from its moribund condition and revitalised by Maharishi Debendranath Tagore, the eldest son of Dwarkanath Tagore and the father of Rabindranath Tagore.

(5) Debendranath Tagore (1817-90)

Debendranath Tagore was the most important leader among the second generation of the Brahmos. He became a Brahmo in 1838. After the death of Ram Mohan Roy, Debandranath managed the affairs of Brahmo Samaj.

(a) Brahmo Covenant

Debendranath Tagore prepared a covenant for the Brahmo Church. Every devotee had to accept it and promise to follow a religious life as prescribed by the Vedanta and worship of God daily reciting the Gayatri Mantra. The Vedas became the basis of the Brahmo Samaj and the concept of infallibility of Vedas was given up. Debendranath signed the covenant and formally became a member of Brahmo Samaj in 1843. He did not believe in external forms of worship such as idol worship, pilgrimages and costly rituals.

(b) Role of Tattvabodhini

The Church of Brahmo Samaj under Debendranath Tagore became an active institution with the Tattvabodhini Sabha acting as its missionary wing. Tattvabodhini Patrika, a monthly journal with Shri A.K. Datta as its editor, was published. On the other hand, the books of Ram Mohan Roy were re-printed and a school was established in order to impart religious education to the young students. In 1857 Keshab Chandra Sen joined the Brahmo Samaj and Debendranath and Keshab joined their hands to revitalise the Samaj and succeeded in their mission to a considerable extent.

(6) Keshab Chandra Sen (1838-84)

Keshab Chandra Sen became a missionary of the Brahmo Samaj in 1857. In 1862 he was elevated to the status of an Acharya. It was his endeavour to broaden the basis of the Samaj by launching a programme of extensive reforms such as female education, removal of the purdah system, abolition of polygamy, and introduction of temperance. The initiative emanated from Keshab and his young followers in Brahmo Samaj. Keshab demonstrated the indefatigable enthusiasm and indomitable will to convert the Brahmo Samaj into a dynamic all India organisation. He undertook the journey to various parts of India and being at erudite scholar and brilliant orator, he succeeded in his mission of spreading the teaching of the Brahmo Samaj. It was due to his tireless efforts that the Prarthana Samaj could be established in Bombay and Veda Samaj in Madras.

(i) Split in Brahmo Samaj

In 1866 a split occurred in the ranks of Brahmo Samaj. Debandranath supported by the old Brahmos developed difference of opinion and could not agree with Keshab and his young associates who stood for the above mentioned progressive reforms. Thus, Brahmo Samaj was split into two organisations : (1) Brahmo Samaj of India led by Keshab and (2) the Adi-Brahmo Samaj led by Debendranath. After this split Debendranath retired as the active member of Adi-Brahmo Samaj and Raj Narayan Bose assumed the status of presidentship of this organisation.

(ii) Keshab Chandra's efforts for reforms

Keshab was an ardent supporter of women's emancipation. He worked for the end of the exploitation of the workers. He desired to introduce prohibition because the use of liquor was adversely affecting the health as well as the budget of the poor workers. It was his intense desire to spread literacy. He started a weekly newspaper known as the Sulabh Samachar and also founded an association for publishing books and journals. After returning from England in 1870. He founded the Indian Reforms Association consisting of five departments such as (1) Female improvement department, (2) Education of working classes, (3) Procurement of cheap literature, (4) Prohibition and (5) Charity. Each department was headed by a Secretary. Under the auspices of this association, the above reforms were introduced at a rapid pace.

On the other hand, the credit of the passage of the Native Marriages Act of 1872 goes to Keshab to certain extent. In 1870 he visited England and co-operated with the British Government for passing the Native Marriages Act in 1872. This Act made monogamy more or less obligatory. It overlooked the caste considerations in marriage. The Act freed the parties concerned from observing age-old Hindu customs and conventions, the minimum ages for the bride and the bridegroom were fixed at 14 and 18 years respectively and monogamy was not to be violated. This Act was indeed a great landmark in the movement of social reforms in India.

(iii) Cooch-Behar case and the expulsion of Keshab Chandra from the Brahmo Samaj

Unfortunately, Keshab Chandra violated some of the basic principles of Brahmo Samaj, which he himself had been preaching enthusiastically and this eventually led to his expulsion from the Samaj. The reason for this drastic action against him was the Cooch-Behar Marriage Case in March. 1878. He gave his eldest daughter who was not even 14 years old in marriage to the Maharaja of Cooch-Behar who was below 16 years. The members of Brahmo Samaj were shocked at this breach of principle and the appalling divergence between practice and precept. All the time Keshab had been advocating the principle of raising the age of marriage but to the discomfiture of his followers, the same principle was flagrantly violated by Keshab in the case of marriage of his own daughter. The marriage was solemnised not in Brahmo style but in traditional Hindus style by Brahmanical priests in the presence of Hindu images.

The expulsion of Keshab Chandra participated yet another split in the ranks of the Brahmo Samaj. Those who differed with Keshab Chandra seceded and on May 15, 1878, they organised a new Samaj, popularly known as Universal Brahmo Samaj. Its membership was open ably to those persons who would strictly adhere to the principles of Brahmo Samaj and reject idol worship and the caste system. Keshab Chandra passed away in 1884 at the age of 46 years and after his death, the Brahmo Samaj began to decline because of the lack of cohesion in its ranks and introduction of rituals and practices which were originally condemned by its celebrated supporters. However, it is no exaggeration to say that for about half century, Brahmo Samaj played a significant role in the renaissance movement in Bengal in particular and Maharashtra in general.

(iv) The Prarthana Samaj

The Brahmo Samaj and its impact in Maharashtra greatly contributed to the renaissance there. The Pararthana Samaj had been established in 1867 in Bombay by Dr. Atmaram Pandurang under the influence of Keshab Chandra Sen who had visited Bombay in 1864. In 1868 Keshab Chandra again visited Bombay and further strengthened the Prarthana Samaj. Its most celebrated members were R.G. Bhandarker and M.G. Ranade. The avowed objective of these leaders was to establish a reform movement within the fold of Hinduism. They had great veneration for great saints and reformers of Maharashtra such as Jnaneshwar, Namdeo, Tukaram and Ramdas and they professed to follow the path shown by these great saints.

The members of the Prarthana Samaj avoided the religious controversies and concentrated their attention on the eradication of social evils.

(1) Performance of the Prarthana Samaj

The guiding principle that motivated the followers of the Prarthana Samaj was love of God through service to man. This organisation engaged itself manifold constructive activities :

(a) It aimed at spreading education and ran night schools to cater to the needs of the working class.

(b) It established a Foundling Asylum and Orphanage at Pandharupur. It also established a social service league.

(c) It started a Depressed Classes Mission for improving the lot of the depressed people.

(d) It worked for improving the lot of women, and tried to introduce reforms such as inter-caste marriages, widow marriages, encouragement of women's education and the eradication of evils like the purdah system and child marriage.

(2) Role of M.G. Ranade in Prarthana Samaj

M.G. Ranade was one of the illustrated luminaries of the Prarthana Samaj. He had attained the stature of being a great reformer, educationist, nationalist, economist and historian. He became a professor in the Elphinstone College in Bombay and later on worked as the Oriental Translator to the Bombay Government. He was also elevated to the position of a High Court Judge in Bombay. He worked for the emancipation of women. In 1861, he founded the Widow Marriage Association. In 1870 Ranade rendered help in the establishment of the Sarvajanik Sabha at

Poona. The aim of this organisation was to apprise the Government of the hopes and aspirations of the people and to ventilate public grievances. When a Parliamentary Committee was appointed in 1871 to enquire into the economic position of India, the Sarvajanik Sabha prepared a useful report on the economic situation in Maharashtra with the help of Ranade. The Sarvajanik Sabha started the publication of a Quarterly Journal, to which Ranade contributed articles.

Ranade's calibre as a historian is evident from his famous treatise entitled "Rise of the Maratha Power." In his public, life, he had to encounter public criticism from orthodox Hindu circles. When he helped Swami Dayanand, the founder of the Arya Samaj, to deliver a lecture in Poona, he had to face severe criticism from orthodox Hindus because Dayanand denounced idolatry, caste system and child marriage. Ranade tried his best to enlist Government's support for the eradication of the social evils in the teeth of the opposition of the orthodox Hindus.

(3) Role of Gopal Krishna Gokhale and Pandita Ramabai

Besides being a political leader, Gopal Krishna Gokhale was a great social reformer. He was one of the founders of the distinguished organisation known as "The Servants of India Society". He was also a member of the Deccan Education Society. These voluntary organisations upheld the principles for which Prarthana Samaj stood. On the other hand, Pandita Ramabai worked incessantly for women's emancipation. In this exalted sphere of action, she enlisted the support of Prarthana Samajists like Ranade, Bhandarkar and Chandavarkar. With her help the supporters of Prarthana Samaj were able to establish Arya Mahila Samaj.

Thus, a great galaxy of reformers of Prarthana Samaj such as Agarkar, Gopal Hari Deshmukh, B.M. Malabari, V.R. Shinde, S.V. Kamble and Vishnu Shastri Pandit worked for the eradication of social evils and thereby ushered in an era of reformation and renaissance in the tradition-bound Indian society.

(V) The Arya Samaj

Dayanand, the founder of the Arya Samaj, was born in 1824 in the prosperous town of Morvi in Kathiawar. His father, a Brahmin of the highest order, held a respectable post in the government of the State and was a rigid, austere Brahmin thoroughly orthodox and uncompromising in his religious beliefs and practices. His mother, on the other hand, was the personification of sweetness, gentleness and goodness.

The education of Dayanand, whose original name was Mulshanker, commenced when he was five years of age and he was invested with the sacred thread in his eighth year.

(1) The turning points in Dayanand's early life

It was his father's piously-intended insistence upon his son's observing the fast of Shivratri which turned the son into the most virulent and successful opponent of image worship of his time at the age of fourteen. On the other hand, the death of his beloved sister had turned Dayanand's attention to investigations into the mysteries of birth and death. He was told that Yogabhyas was the method by which he could understand the mystery of death and birth. But the Yoga could not be mastered till he left home. His father already having reason to suspect such workings in his son's mind decided to weave a web of affection round him but Dayanand resisted his parent's plan with determination and declined to be married. The marriage was postponed for a year. A week before the day fixed for marriage, Dayanand fled from home and became an ascetic. He was soon traced out and imprisoned under a strong guard. The same night the boy succeeded once again in escaping and this time for good, never seeing his father again.

(2) Dayanand's Pursuit of Knowledge and Truth

From 1845 to 1860, young Dayanand wandered almost all over India in pursuit of knowledge and truth. In search of teachers of fame and Yogis of merit, he penetrated into the inner-most recesses of the Himalayas. He crossed and recrossed the valleys of Indian rivers, the Ganges, the Jamuna and the Narbada and mounted the highest accessible tops of the hills near the vicinity of those rivers. It was here that he delved deep into the mysteries of nature. After studying for over thirty years, he gave finishing touches to his education when he waited for two years and half on Virjanada, a master spirit.

(3) Dayanand's Entry into Public Life

After acquiring education, Dayanand entered public life, visiting some of the most important towns of U.P. where he preached his teachings. It was on 10th April, 1875, that he founded the Arya Samaj in Bombay. In 1877, the Arya Samaj was also established at Lahore and it was this place which became its centre and where its principles received their final shape. From 1877 to 1883, Swami Dayanand spent his time in preaching and teaching and writing books as well as establishing and organising Arya Samaj's throughout India. Dayanand's speeches were delivered in

Hindi. Swami finished the compilation of his treatise entitled "Satyartha Prakash" in 1874. He died on 30th October, 1883 at Ajmer as a result of the slow effect of a subtle poison administered to him mixed in food by a concubine of Maharana Sajjan Singh of Jodhpur. Swami Dayanand had gone there on the invitation of the Maharana and had taken a strong exception to his living with the concubine.

(4) Teachings of Swami Dayanand

(a) Swami Dayanand believed that some persons might have more of the divine in them in proportion to what others have. But this should in no way mean that they are the same as God. In fact he held, no man is infallible, however exalted he may be.

(b) The only approved forms of worship according to him, are "Studi" Contemplation, "Prarthana" prayer and "Upasana" communion.

(c) Swami Dayanand believed in Karma and also in the transmigration of soul. He believed in fate only as much as it conformed with the doctrine of Karma and not beyond that.

(d) The man has the power, and he has the will to make or unmake his destiny.

(e) Although due respect should be paid to the living parents, there is no need of ancestor-worship.

(f) Vedas are an infallible and inexhaustible source of all knowledge.

(g) Swami Dayanand did not believe polytheism nor did he have belief in pantheism.

(h) He had no belief in the mythology of the Puranas and condemned the caste system which, according to him, had been a source of many evils in the Hindu society. Nobody is a born Brahman or born Sudra. Sudra is he who does evil and Brahman is he who does good.

(i) God and soul, according to him, are two distinct entities, each having certain attributes of its own. Yet they are inseparable and are related to each other as Pervader and the Pervaded. Three things are external : God, Soul and Prakriti.

(j) The transmigration or earthly bondage of soul has a cause. Cause is ignorance which is a source of all sin. The freedom of soul from ignorance is its salvation. But salvation lasts only for a period, on the expiry of which the soul assumes the body again.

(k) All truth must satisfy five tests :

(1) It must not militate against the nature and attributes of God.

(2) It must not be opposed to the teachings of the Vedas.

(3) It must stand the test of the well-known eight kinds of proof based on natural laws.

(4) It must have the sanction of true, holy and learned men.

(5) It must be in consonance with the dictates of one's own conscience.

Every doctrine must be subjected to these five tests.

The watchword of the Arya was "Back to the Vedas" which are prefect and source of all science and knowledge.

(5) Qualifications of a member of Arya Samaj

A person must subscribe to the following principles before he could become a member of Arya Samaj :

(1) God is the primary source of all knowledge.

(2) God is all truth, all knowledge infinite and the cause of all universe. To God alone worship is due.

(3) Vedas are the books of true knowledge. Every Arya must read them.

(4) All actions must conform to virtue and be performed after a thorough study of the right and wrong.

(5) An Arya should always be prepared to accept truth and renounce untruth.

(6) The primary task of the Arya Samaj is to benefit the whole world by improving the physical, spiritual and social conditions of the people.

(7) All should be treated with love and due regard to their merit.

(8) Ignorance should be dispelled and knowledge diffused.

(9) Everyone is to consider his own good to be included in that of the others.

(10) In personal affairs all are to have freedom but no person is to stand in the say of the general good.

(6) Main programmes and activities of the Arya Samaj

The basic principles on which the social ideas of the Samaj were based were : (1) Fatherhood of God and brotherhood of man, (2) Equality of sexes, (3) Absolute justice and fair play between man and man, nation and nation, (4) Equal opportunity to all according to their nature, Karma and merit and (5) Love and charity to all.

Commenting on the social activities of the Arya Samaj, Valentine Chirol has aptly remarked thus : "The influence has been constantly exerted to check the marriages between mere boys and almost infant girls which have done so much physical as well as moral mischief to Hindu society and also to improve the wretched lot of Hindu widows whose widowhood with all that it entails of menial degradation often begins before they have ever really been wives".

(i) Establishment of Orphanages

In order of alleviate the pathetic conditions of the destitutes, various orphanages had been established under the auspices of the Arya Samaj. The first Hindu orphanage was established by the Arya Samaj in Punjab at Jullunder during the lifetime of Swami Dayanand, with a splendid and commodious building. Later on, a number of other orphanages on similar lines were established at different places in northern India.

(ii) Relief Operations of Arya Samaj during Famines

In 1897-98 there were severe famines in the country. A very commendable service was rendered by Arya Samaj in organising relief operations for the famine-stricken people. Thousands of children were rescued and for them several new orphanages were founded in Punjab. In 1908, the Arya Samaj provided relief to the people of the famine-affected areas in the U.P.

(iii) Educational enterprises of the Arya Samaj

(a) Under the auspices of the Arya Samaj, the Dayanand Anglo-Vedic College was founded in Lahore in June 1889. This institution constituted a monument of tribute to the departed Swami. After the death of Swami Dayanand, the session of Lahore Arya Samaj opened. Commenting on the deliberations of this session, of Lahore Arya Samaj opened. Commenting on the deliberations of this session, the Arya Patrika wrote thus : "there was one united purpose that the glorious life of the departed Swami should be immortalised and the proposal to found an Anglo-Vedic College in honour of his memory was unanimously adopted. The sight that followed was worth observing. Though the meeting was composed mostly of middle class men, from 7,000 to 8,000 rupees were subscribed on the spot. Women and children and even poor menials zealously came forward with their mite". The avowed objectives of the college was to (i) encourage, improve and enforce the study of Hindu literature, (ii) to encourage the study of classical Sanskrit and of the Vedas and (iii) to encourage and enforce the study of English literature and science.

The progress of this college was so fast that the total number of students was 903 in December 1913. Soon a DAV College at Jullunder, another at Hoshiapur and the third at Kanpur were added the total amount of funds at the disposal of the management of these institutions on 31st March, 1929 was Rs. 26,51,206.

(b) In 1928 the Arya Samaj was divided into two groups which differed on the policies and principles on which the DAV College of Lahore was to be run. The difference of opinion was whether English and science or the Vedas should be given the first place in the institution. Those who held the opinion that the Vedas should be given the first place were termed as the religious fanatics and were debarred from the management of the college. But they started a new institution three miles away from Hardwar and named it Gurukula. The Gurukula was founded in 1902 as a result of the efforts of Munshiram, an advocate of Jullunder.

(iv) Development of the Arya Samaj

In 1928, the Arya Samaj had the following two all-India Organisations: (1) The Sarva Deshik Arya Pratinidhi Sabha and (2) The Paropkarani Sabha founded by Swami Dauanand himself. The Arya Samaj had nine provincial assemblies. According to the Census Report of 1901, the number of the Samajis was 500 in Punjab, 413 in UP, 200 in Delhi, 52 in CP and Berar, 100 in Ajmer, 30 in Bombay, 20 in Bihar and Bengal and 10 in Burma. Besides, there were members of the Arya Samaj outside India.

(v) General appraisal of Arya Samaj

(1) Swami Dayanand's Arya Samaj was rendering a great service to the country but the Punjab Census Report of 1901 remarked that its leader were unfortunately too much pre-occupied with keeping their reforms within the Hindu society. The principles of fatherhood of God and of absolute fairplay between man and man and nation and nation applied only within the Hindu

community outside of which they interaction. The Imperial Paper of Lahore wrote on 3 October, 1888 that the leaders of Arya Samaj were inciting its members against the Muslims advising them to avenge themselves upon that community because they believed that all the evils such as child-marriage and purdah system were products of the Muslim rely in India. However, there is no element of truth in this Imperial Paper as the British Government was bent on erecting a wedge between the Hindus and the Muslims in order to prevent the growth of national movement in India.

(2) Swami Dayanand who launched the cow protection movement said that the Vedas held the cow sacred. He established a society for cow protection and raised funds for the purpose.

(3) Swami Dayanand launched the Shuddi movement. He had the courage to fight against Hindu orthodoxy and stubborn obscurantism. His Shuddhi movement was designed to reconvert those Hindus who embraced other religions to Hinduism. This was a momentous step because till then it was impossible for Hindus who has once left the Hindu fold to be reconverted to Hinduism.

(4) The Arya Samaj also made efforts to afford protection to the untouchables. In this respect, Valentine Chirol has remarked thus : "Again in the treatment of the untouchable low castes, the Arya Samaj may claim to have been the first native body to break new ground and to attempt something akin to the work of social reclamation of which Christianity in a lesser degree, Islam had hitherto the monopoly."

(5) Swami Dayanand, who was great nationalist inspired the people to have faith in themselves. He made the Indians conscious of their country's pristine glory and greatness. He was a staunch supporter of Swadeshi and gave the slogan "India for Indians."

However, among the Hindus, the movement was getting popular as the time passed. In 1911, thus, its membership stood at 243,000 in Punjab and this was six times what it was in 1891.

VI. Theosophical Society

The Theosophical Society was established in 1875 by Madam H.P. Blavatsky and Col. A.S. Olcott in New York in the USA. These founders came to India and established in 1882 the main centre of the Theosophical Society at Adyar, a suburb of Madras.

(1) Role of Annie Besant in Theosophical Society

Born in 1847, Miss Wood, whose name was Mrs. Annie Besant lost her father when she was only five. Her early childhood and maidenhood were beset with all sorts of difficulties. When she married a clergyman in 1867, her fortune did not improve. Being frustrated in married life, she decided to leave her husband and devote the rest of her life to the welfare of humanity. Her fight for the rights of English girls working in the match factories revealed a great organiser and preacher in her. Soon she joined the Theosophical Society and came under the intimate influence of Madam H.F. Blavatsky who trained her into a mystic. As such she came to India in 1893 and for twenty long years kept herself intensely devoted to the religious and social upliftment of this country. Mrs. Annie Besant undertook a deep study of India's past glory and her glorious literature. She discovered how great India was and how great she yet would be. Commenting on her personal qualities, C.Y. Chintamani says : "In her greater intellect and learning, were united an indomitable will, concentrated purposefulness, undaunted courage, indefatigable zeal and a determination never to rest until her work was done. And added to these was her matchless oratory."

(a) She preached about in India telling the people of their marvellous forefathers and of the great part they have yet to play.

(b) She translated the Bhagwat Gita into English and started the Central Hindu School and College at Benaras which later on grew into the Hindu University.

(c) India was losing herself into the glare of materialism of the West. Mrs. Annie Besant preached that India had her own personality and individuality from which the West could yet learn much. She killed Indian diffidence, breathed courage and will power wherever she went and prepared the country for the great part it had to play in world politics.

(d) Later on, she became president of the Theosophical Society and in this capacity, she went several times to England between 1908 and 1913. She studied the Irish Home Rule Movement of Redmond and was highly impressed by it. When she returned to India, she decided to start a similar movement in this country. She started a Home Rule League and under its auspices established organisations throughout the country and distributed vast quantities of propagandist literature.

(e) In 1916 Mrs. Annie Besant effected a compromise between the Moderates and the Extremists in the Congress. Prior to that, she had started a weekly journal named Common weal and later on brought a daily paper which she named New India. Through them she spread her liberal principles in India. All these activities landed her in jail in 1917, together with Wadia and Arundale. When she was released after three months, she was honoured by Indians by electing her the President of the Indian National Congress in 1917.

(f) Mrs. Annie Besant worked for women's emancipation. She tried to improve the lot of the women, fought for their rights and tried to free them from their disabilities. She believed that female education would go a long way to emancipate the womenfolk.

VII. The Rama Krishna Mission

Swami Vivekananda established the Rama Krishna Mission in 1897. in memory of his spiritual mentor and preceptor Rama Krishna Paramahamsa who is regarded as one of the greatest saints of India. The Rama Krishna Mission became an international institution serving the cause of humanity and propagating the laudable principles of Hinduism. The avowed aim of the Mission was to facilitate a synthesis of traditional Hinduism and Western knowledge. Since Swami Vivekananda was highly indebted to Rama Krishna Paramahamsa, it is desirable to throw light on the life and principles of the latter.

(i) Rama Krishna Paramahamsa

(1) Rama Krishna Parmahamsa's early life

The onginal name of Rama Krishna Paramahamsa was Gadadhar. He was different from other boys of his age. He was thoughtful and relished the company of saints and occasionally fell into trances. In 1855 he became the chief priest in the Kali temple at Dakshineshwar on the river Ganga about five miles north of Calcutta. Here in this temple revolutionary changes took place in the life of Gadadhar. To him the image of Kali was the real Goddess herself. He had intense spiritual intoxication and he was completely absorbed in the worship of Kali whom he regarded as his mother and as the mother of the entire universe. However, the devotion Goddess Kali became a consuming passion in him. In his devotion, he was unconscious hunger, thirst and other physical desires. He developed complete detachment and exceptional priest, giving up all the usual ceremonies of worship.

(2) Rama Krishna's orientation with precepts of a great ascetic named Totapuri

After contact with Totapuri, a great ascetic, Rama Krishna was able to formally become an ascetic. He learnt from Totapuri the monistic philosophy of Shankara. According to this philosophy the world is maya and that the human spirit is the same as God. Under Totapuri's spiritual guidance, Rama Krishna attained the Stature of an ascetic and came to be called Paramahamsa.

(3) Rama Krishna's inquisitions about teachings of Islam and Christianity

Rama Krishna learnt the doctrines of Islam. He also lived like a Muslim following the food habits, mode of dress and religious practices of the Muslims, and in that capacity, he was able to have the vision of God. He also vigorously followed the principles of Christianity.

(4) Worship of Sharadamani

Rama Krishna was married to a five-year old girl who was known as Sharadamani Devi. When she was 18 years old, she came to Dakshineshwar to live with Rama Krishna. Their relationship was purely spiritual. Sexual gratification had no place in their mutual relationship. Rama Krishna developed a great sense of veneration for his wife and he began to look upon her as the visible representation of the Divine Mother, the name by which he called God.

(5) General Appraisal

Rama Krishna attracted many people. Keshab Chandra Sen was one of his staunch admirers. Rama Krishna's discourses were enchanting and of a high order. He agreed that ritualistic worship of God is useful but he rightly insisted that abandonment of desire, lust and avarice was more important. Rama Krishna asserted that in the eyes of God, there is no difference between a Brahmin and an untouchable. He insisted that the spiritual ecstasies should be accompanied by the love of poor. In 1886 Rama Krishna passed away. Sharadamani, his wife, was 33 years old at that time. Rich tributes were paid to him by the contemporary ascetics and his disciple described him as a "Wonderful mixture of God and man."

(ii) Swami Vivekananda (1863-1902)

Narendranath Datta, the most prominent and the most favourite disciple of Rama Krishna, became famous all over the world as Swami Vivekananda. At the age of 20, he came under the spiritual spell of Rama

Krishna Paramahamsa. In 1886 Rama Krishna passed away. Swami Vivekananda became a sanyasi and decided to dedicate his whole life to work for the ideals and principles of his great teacher.

(1) Swami's role as a staunch exponent of Hinduism in India and the USA

Swami Vivekananda believed that the best way of paying tribute to his great spiritual guide Rama Krishna Paramahamsa was to spread his message all over the country. He established network of monasteries all over India. In these monasteries, the monks lived a disciplined life. The Swami was a man with a mission. He came to know that a "Parliament of Religions" was to be held in 1893 at Chicago in the U.S.A. and he decided to attend it. He would expound Hinduism which was treated with much contempt and was much misrepresented to the people of the West. In the proposed "Parliament of Religions", Swami saw an opportunity to place before the Americans the excruciating difficulties of the poor in India and to plead for material support. His idea was liked by the Maharaja of Khetri who promised him financial support for the proposed voyage.

In 1893 Swami Vivekananda sailed from Bombay for the West coast of the USA. At Chicago he was faced with difficulties. He was a stranger and his funds were fast dwindling. However, several generous Americans came to his aid. One of them was Prof. J.H. Wright of the Harvard University. Prof. Wright insisted that Swami should represent Hinduism at the Parliament of Religions. As a representative of Hinduism., Swami Vivekananda possessed no credentials and this problem was discussed with prof. Wright who said, "To ask Swami for credentials is like asking the sun to state its right to shine". The Swami had an exhilarating experience in the meeting of the Parliament of Religions where he addressed the audience with the words : "Sisters and brothers of America". These words evoked a thunderous applause and the Swami during the course of his speech referred to Hinduism as the "Mother of Religions". Later on, he read a paper giving a lucid account of the principles and practices of Hinduism. In another speech, he said : "I came here to seek aid for my impoverished people." In 1896 he established the Vedanta Society of New York. On the other hand, his books on Yoga aroused deep interest among the Americans and Europeans. He won recognition as a true spokesman of Hinduism. Even the eminent historian Valentine Chirol called him "the first Hindu whose personality won demonstrative recognition abroad for India's ancient civilisation and for her newborn claim to nationhood."

(2) Establishment of the Rama Krishna Mission

When Swami Vivekananda was in America, his disciples in India wanted to establish a permanent organisation which would give a concrete shape to the principles of service to the downtrodden people. When the Swami came back to India, he was apprised of this proposal. So in 1897 Swamiji called a meeting of his trustworthy disciples and it was decided to establish the Rama Krishna Mission. On 5th May. 1897 Vivekananda established the Rama Krishna Mission, which was to be both a humanitarian as well as a religious organisation. Its main objective was to build up a feeling of fellowship, among the members of all religions, and to alleviate the poor financial conditions of the under-privileged sections of society. The Mission launched massive relief measures for the famine-stricken people in Murshidabad and other places. In April 1898, a bubonic plague broke out in Calcutta and panic seized the people who began to migrate to other places. On this occasion, the Rama Krishna Mission organised various preventive measures to combat the plague and provided relief to the poor affected by the disease. Under the auspices of Rama Krishna Mission, various schools, dispensaries, and hostels had been established in various parts of the country and about 100 Missions were operating in India doing useful humanitarian work for the benefit of the poor.

The Rama Krishna Mission undertook the publication of books and newspapers. *The Prabuddha Bharata*, an English newspaper, and the *Udbodhana*, a Bengali paper, were started. Many spiritual books, including those on Rama Krishna and Vivekananda, were also published.

On 4th July, 1902, Swami Vivekananda passed away leaving Hinduism in a far better condition than he had found it. He at least succeeded in making the Hindus conscious of their strength and weakness. The nucleus of his message was religious toleration and emulation of the dynamic spirit of the West for the amelioration of the poor and a happy synthesis of materialism of the West and the spiritual values of India.

6

Indian Islam

(i) The Muslim Reformist Movements

Much to their discomfiture, the Muslims had been displaced by the British from the mastery of the country. They were suspected by the British for their part in the Mutiny. They were in consequence inclined to sulk and to go into a kind of retreat. They clung to their Persian culture while the Hindus took advantage of British education. Proud of their own culture and literature, the Muslims refused to avail themselves of the educational facilities provided by the British. But since they had no sufficient resources of their own, their literacy growth was stopped. They thus lapsed into ignorance and backwardness. Their association with the ruling race remained undeveloped and they remained unlooked and uncared for. In general professions, too, the Muslim position was hardly enviable as, for instance between 1852 and 1862 out of total number of 240 Indian pleaders for the High Court, only one Muslim was admitted. Between 1858 and 1878, as many as 3,000 degrees were conferred on the Hindus while 57 degrees were conferred on the Muslims.

Gradually the Muslims grew disgruntled and dissatisfied. The British were the cause of their unenviable position and therefore, a slow simmering against their rule began to be vocal.

1. Reform Movements among the Muslims

Muslim community was free from caste system and untouchability. But it had its own social evils such as the purdah system, polygamy, child marriage, superstitions etc. The religious reform movements like the Brahmo Samaj, Prarthana Samaj and Arya Samaj were bound to have an impact on the Muslim educated class, which desired the Muslim society to be purged of these social evils. It is desirable here to refer to certain movements among the Muslims, which aimed at reforms in the Muslim society in India.

2. Wahabi Movement

The Wahabi Movement which, though religious in its aims, talked of the Muslim backwardness, and opinions were roused against the British discrimination towards them. This movement had started in Arabia towards the close of the 18th century and was brought to India by Sayyad Ahmed Brelvi. The movement preached hatred towards foreign rule. But the Muslims were not materially benefited by the Wahabi Movement which failed to break the British disfavour to this community. On the contrary, the British aggrandized to a considerable extent. Out of 2,141 in the services of the Government of Bengal in 1871, 711 were Hindus while 92 were Muslims, the rest being all Europeans. Here was an economic discredit which the Muslims had gathered from their antagonism towards the British. The best solutions of the problem lay in seeking British favour by peaceful approaches.

3. Role of Sir Syed Ahmed Khan for upliftment of Muslim Community

The Muslim leaders realised that a continued hostile stance towards the British was futile. The prominent among these new Muslim leaders who favoured Anglo-Muslim accord was Sir Syed Ahmed Khan. A nationalist and a lover of Hindu-Muslim unity in the beginning calling the two communities the "two eyes of the beautiful bride that was India", Sir Syed grew loyal to the British.

(a) Efforts to woo the British

During the Mutiny, Sir Syed Ahmed Khan had helped the British and received as a reward a pension of Rs. 200 per month and several other honours. In 1864, Sir Syed organised the "Translation Society" renamed later as "The Aligarh Scientific Society" and through this, step by step, he built up the Muslim loyalty towards the British. He established a Muslim school at Delhi which was soon raised to the status of a college and the declared aim of this institution was to make the Muslims useful subjects of the British Crown.

(b) Establishment of Aligarh Muslim College

Sir Syed Ahmed Khan established contacts with the Hindus who gave liberal help in the foundation and development of Muslim Anglo Oriental College at Aligarh. Unfortunately, later on Sir Syed Ahmed Khan was weaned away by Mr. Beck, the English Principal of Aligarh

Muslim College. A new phase of his anti-national and rather anti-Hindu activities continued and this helped in a considerable measure the Muslim communalism to develop.

(c) Influence of Maulvi Chirag Ali

Influence of Maulvi Chirag Ali was helpful to Syed Ahmed Khan in improving the lot of the Muslims. Chirag Ali stood for the abolition of polygamy and other social evils in Muslim society. Like Syed Ahmed Khan, he strongly believed that Muslims should co-operate with the British and enter the administrative services.

But, unfortunately, the activities of the communal elements among the Muslims continued and these activities culminated in the demand for Pakistan. The British government adroitly exploited Hindu-Muslim discord to its advantage.

(ii) Aligarh Movement

The main features of Aligarh Movement. Sir Syed Ahmed Khan was the founder of the Aligarh Movement. This Movement was the liberal interpretation after Quran. Through education he wanted to uplift the Muslims from backwardness and conservatism. In 1873 he started an English medium school for Muslims at Aligarh. It was later developed into the Muhammadan Anglo Oriental College in 1877. The college became the centre of Muslim activities in political and social fields.

Role of Sir Syed Ahmed Khan (1817-1898)

Sir Syed Ahmed Khan was vehemently opposed to the activities of the Indian National Congress. He dissuaded the Muslims from joining Congress.

Sir Syed Ahmed Khan pleaded for free inter course between the Europeans and the Muslims and tried to get the Muslim society rid of social evils and superstitions. He was particularly opposed to purdah and alavery and stood for the emancipation of women. To popularise these ideas amongst the Indian Muslims Sir Syed Ahmed Khan started a monthly periodical entitled Tahzib-ul-Akhlaq (Reform of Morals). He was helped by the poet Khwaja Altaf Hussain Hati, Maulvi Nasir Ahmed and Maulvi Shible Nurrani.

Objectives and Programmes :

1. To spread western education among Muslims without breaking their inclination towards Islam.
2. To enforce the secular education through the religious education and to impart it through educational institutions.

3. To introduce social reforms in the Muslim social organisations.
4. To evolve a distinct social and cultural community among the Indian Muslims on modern lines.
5. To propagate against polygamy and see that it is ended.
6. To fight against the ban on window-remarriage.
7. To bring a life of harmony between Islam and the adopted western liberal customs.

Because of its forceful propagation and wide intelligentsia following, the Aligarh Movement spread like wild fire in Bombay, Punjab, liberal customs.

In 1887 when the third Congress session was taking place at Madras, he convened Muslim conference at Lucknow on the same day and exhorted them to keep away from the Congress. He said that the Hindus and the Muslims constitute two different nations and they could not sail together.

He opposed the introduction of the system of election to the legislative councils on the plea that by virtue of their numerical majority, the Hindus would capture all the seats and the Muslims would have to suffer under the Hindu rule. He appealed to the Muslims to join hands with the British Government to safeguard their interests.

Role of European Principals

The European principals of the M.A.O. College, Aligarh played significant role in promoting Muslim separatism in Indian politics. Theodore Beck, who became the principal in 1883, was regarded as an "Empire builder in far off lands". He supported the opinion of Sir Syed Ahmed that the Anglo-Muslim alliance would promote the Muslim interest whereas alliance with Congress would throw them into troubles.

Pro-Muslim Policy

From 1888 onwards, the British Government developed antagonism against the Congress and initiated a Pro-Muslim attitude. In that year A.O. Hume opted for agitational approach to achieve the Congress demands. Lord Dufferin criticised Congress as representing only a microscopic minority of the people and decided to follow a policy of creating cleavage between the Hindus and Muslims.

Lord Curzon implemented his policy by creating the Muslim majority province of East Bengal in 1904. The division of Bengal on communal lines gave support to Muslim separatism and resulted in acts of violence.

Role of Lord Minto

Lord Minto deliberately wanted to prevent the Muslims from going to the nationalist fold. He was eager to receive a Muslim delegation to press their communal demands. Colonel Dunlop Smith, the private secretary to the Viceroy, wrote to Principal Archbold of Aligarh College that Lord Minto would be happy to receive a Muslim delegation. The principal encouraged Nawab Mohsinul-Mulk, Secretary of the college to organise a deputation. Accordingly a delegation of 35 prominent Muslim leaders of different provinces led by H.H. Agahkhan met the Viceroy on 1st October 1906 at his Simla residence.

They demanded the introduction of separate electorates for Muslims if the principle of election was to be introduced in the forthcoming constitutional reforms. Lord Minto conceded their demand and promised communal electorates for Muslims if the system of election was introduced in a Municipality, District Board, or a Legislative Council. The Viceroy considered 1st October 1906 as a very eventful day in the History of India. Finally, this paved the way for the birth of All India Muslim League.

Certain other minor Muslim movements were also launched, which aimed at reforming the Muslim community. These included the Anjuman-i-Himayat-i-Islam set up at Lahore in 1885, which made valuable contribution to the educational, social, political and intellectual development of the Muslims. In 1894 Navaraat-ul-Ulema was established in Lucknow to get the Muslim community rid of social evils. In North Western Frontier Province of India, Khan Abdul Gaffar Khan started a movement known as Khudai Khimatgar, which fostered the feeling of brotherhood among the Muslims. Similarly, Inayatmulla Khan started Khaksar movement which emphasised the need of discipline and military training amongst the Muslims.

Deoband Movement

In 1866, the Deoband School of Islamic Theology was set up at Deoband by Rashid Ahmad Gangolai and Mohammed Qasim Namtari to promote studies in classical Islam and moral and religious regeneration of Muslims. The school did not support Western education and culture. Its religious teachings that encompassed a liberal interpretation of Islam earned a high reputation. The school's followers included notable personalities such as Maulana Abdul Kalam Azad, Mahammad-UI Hasan and Shibiti Namani, who founded the Nadwatal Ulum and Darul-UIum in Lucknow in 1894-96.

Jawaharlal Nehru felt, "I think that the Muslim rank and file has more potentiality in it. Perhaps because of certain freedom in social relations, than the Hindu masses, and is likely to go ahead faster in socialistic discretion, once it gets moving". This comment profoundly reflect the role and place of Muslims in the Indian society.

Besides the two striking movements (The Ahmadiya Movement and the Aligarh Movement), the Dar-ul-ulum Deoband also played a significant role for the uplift of Muslims. To eradicate the evils in the Muslim society it rendered remarkable services to the community.

Dar-ul-ulum Deoband opposed superstitious beliefs of the Muslims and stood for Western education. It exercised a tremendous influence upon the Muslims for their welfare in the society. It gave high regard to their religion as well as reformist leaders. The ideals and ideologies and their principles and philosophies were followed by its followers so as to promote the welfare of the Muslim society.

Ahmadiya Movement

The awakening among the Muslims was limited in degree, for they did not seek to take advantage of any of the political or educational system introduced by the alien English, who deprived them of their princely status. Gradually they understood their folly and tried to rectify it. Syed Ahmed started the Aligarh Movement and founded the Mohammedan Anglo-Oriental College which grew into the Aligarh Muslim University as mentioned earlier. In 1889 Mirza Gulam Ahmad founded the Ahmadiya Movement based on more or less on the liberal principles.

This movement designated itself as the standard bearer of Mohammadan Renaissance. Like the Brahmo Samaj (founded by Ram Mohan Roy) it based itself on the principles of universal religion of all humanity. He was very much influenced by the principles of western liberalism, theosophy as well as the religious reform movements of Hindus.

Jehad was strongly opposed by Ahmadiya Movement and as Hans Kohn puts it stood for the brotherly relations among the people belonging to different religious communities.

The main task of the Ahmadiya movement was to spread western liberal education among the Indian Muslims and inculcate the feeling of fraternity in them. In order to achieve its objectives it started many schools and colleges and published a large number of periodicals and books in vernacular and English languages.

Muslims worked on a career of national democratic progress in the forthcoming periods. As O' Malley puts it, "The tragedy of the great results in 1857-58 marks the death of the old order, and brought political, economic and cultural disaster to the Indian Muslims. It made their success, their aloofness, their suppressed hatred for the new order more naked than ever...... The key to the whole situation was adaptation to the new environment, use of the new forces that had come into play, acceptance of the new instrument of progress that had been created through English Education."

But very soon, the Muslims entered the field of education and successfully created an intelligentsia. Many Muslims appeared in the commercial as well as industrial field of the country. There lied the success of the Ahmadiya Movement.

The foremost aim of the Ahmadiya movement was the attainment of a social as well as political purpose. Socially the movement aimed at bringing about a resurgence among the Muslims and at countering the influences of Hindu and Christian Missions. Politically they wanted to promote an understanding with the British and to instill nationalism among the Mohammedans.

During the British rule Muslim society had also degenerated. There were certain evils in the society like child marriage, polygamy and purdah. Even certain superstitions had crept into their religion and society.

Towards the closing years of the nineteenth century this movement made its appearance. Mirza Gulam Ahmad of Qadian belonged to Gurudaspur district. He stubbornly opposed the missionary activities of Hindus and Christians. The Ahamadiya movement was opposed to the missionary activities of Arya Samaj and Christianity, as well as the efforts of Sir Syed Ahmed Khan to westernise the Muslim community.

Mirza Gulam Ahamad rendered remarkable service for the Muslim community. Evils of Muslim society were securely attacked by him. Superstitions of the people was vehemently criticised by him. His Ahamadiya Movement thus rendered yeoman service to the Muslim society.

(iii) Parsis and the Sikh Movements

The members of the other sects did not lack behind the Muslims or the Hindus and launched movements for their purification. In 1851 the enlightened leaders of the Parsi community founded the 'Raghnumai Mazdayasuan Sabha' (The Religious Reform Association) to reform their creed and society. They started a weekly journal Rast Gaftoor for the same purpose. To acquaint the people with the real teachings of Zoroaster, two institutions were set up where the priests got training. They also undertook the study of the Parsi scripture, 'Avesta' in a scientific manner. The Parsis also adopted the English education and manners. Some Parsi leaders devoted attention towards the improvement of the lot of the children and women. Seva Sadan set up by B.M. Malabari, which did commendable social welfare work. The other prominent Parsi leaders who made valuable contribution to the social, political and economic progress of the country included Dadabhai Naoroji, Sir Pherozshah Mehta, Sir Din Shaiduiji etc.

The above association worked for the "regeneration of the social conditions of the Parsis and the restoration of Zoroastrian religion to its pristine purity".

K.R. Cama did a lot for the spread of education among the Parsis. B.M. Malabari as mentioned earlier also rendered great service to the Parsi community. In 1910 was held a Zorostarian conference.

Dadabhai Naoroji engaged himself in a variety of social activities. He dedicated his whole life for public service. He was the first to found several organisations for the social, political and intellectual uplift of the Indian people. In 1867, he along with his friends founded the East India Association.

Pherozshah Mehta Worked for extension of educational opportunities for all. For the Parsi community he did a lot.

In the resplendent galaxy of illustrated religious teachers, Guru Nanak shines significantly. He was the founder of Sikhism and the people of this sect hold Guru Nanak with utmost reverence. It is fitting here to give a brief reference of his teachings.

1. According to Guru Nanak, there is only one God. He is a true Lord and creator whose true name, *viz.*, Sat Nam, should be worshipped.
2. True worship of God and a righteous life will enable an individual to realise God.
3. God is omnipresent, omniscient and omni-potent. His idol should not be made.
4. Every individual needs a guru for reaching God. It is with the grace of God that an individual finds a proper guru, who is like a ladder.
5. All are equal in the eyes of God and it is futile to speak of caste or creed.

6. The human beings should show fraternity, love, compassion and good will.

Guru Nanak's precepts evoked a remarkable response from his followers. He succeeded in bringing about a synthesis between the principles of Hinduism and Islam. Guru Nanak was succeeded by several distinguished Gurus.

Unfortunately, the Sikh community was subjected to great persecution under the Mughals, especially during the days of Aurangzeb. Guru Arjun Dev (1581-1606) complied the Adi Granth, the holy book of the Sikhs. During Aurangzeb's reign, untold atrocities were perpetrated on the Sikhs. Their Guru Tegh Bahadur was executed by Aurangzeb. Under the inspiring leadership of Guru Gobind Singh, the Sikhs were armed and they emerged as a martial community. Each Sikh was required to carry with him five KS or symbols of his faith, such as (i) Kesh (long hair); (ii) Kirpan (sword); (iii) Kachha (shorts); (iv) Kanga (comb) and (v) Kara (bangle).

With the passage of time, Sikh power gathered momentum and the Sikh Kingdom was at its zenith during the days of the distinguished Maharaja Ranjit Singh. But, unfortunately, after his death, the Sikh kingdom declined and it was annexed by the British by 1849. When the Mutiny occurred in 1857, the Sikhs remained loyal to the British. During British rule, a large number of Sikhs joined the armed forces and won laurels for their bravery. When the exponents of various Reform Movements preached for social reforms in various parts of India, the Sikhs could not remain aloof. An urge for reforms manifested itself in Punjab. A brief description of reform movements among the Sikhs is given below :

1. Nirankari Movement of Dayal Das

In Punjab, there were Hindus who gave up the worship of their deities. They began to follow the Granth Sahib. But they were not complete Sikhs. Among the Khatris, Aroras and Banias, there were persons who were half-Hindus and half-Sikhs. When such was the situation, the Nirankari Movement was launched by Dayal Das, a merchant of Peshawar. He was against image worship and the custom of doing obeisance to the holy men. He did not believe in Brahmanical ceremonies and pilgrimages. He regarded God as Nirankar, *i.e.*, formless. The followers of Dayal Das were known as Nirankaris. Unfortunately, the Nirankaris were criticised and ostracised by the Hindus as well as the Sikhs. The Nirankaris built a place of worship on the Layee, four miles away from Rawalpindi. The

Layee temple was known as Dayalsar where the sandals of Dayal Das were placed side by side with the Granth for the purpose of worship.

After the death of Dayal Das, his eldest son Darbara Singh constructed certain new centres of worship for the Nirankaris. After independence, the Nirankaris gave up Dayalsar and Amritsar became the centre of worship and later on, Chandigarh became the centre of worship. In essence, the Nirankari Movement was designed to bring about a happy synthesis between Hinduism and Sikhism.

2. Radha Swami Cult

The Radha Swami Cult is the product of the impact of Sikhism on Hinduism without the tradition of the militant Khalsa. This new sect was established by Shiv Dayal, a Hindu banker of Agra. The teachings of this sect are characterised by the happy blending of Sikhism and Hinduism. According to the founder of this sect, God is a synthesis between Radha (representing the soul) and Swami (the master). Shiv Dayal's principles were given in his famous treatise entitled Sar Bachan (Essential Utterances). He was regarded by his followers as the first guru.

After his death, there occurred a split in the Radha Swami cult. One group consisted of those who followed the original principles, with Agra as the centre of worship. The other group consisted of those followers who regarded Jaimal Singh as their guru and their centre of worship was situated near the river Beas. The number of Beas Radha Swamis rapidly increased during the days of Sawan Singh Grewal, the successor of Jaimal Singh. Many Hindus, Parsis and Christians have joined this sect.

3. Namdhari Movement

The Namdhari Movement popularly known as Kuka movement, was launched by Balak Singh who was the son of a goldsmith in the Hazro village of the north west frontier relation. Balak Singh did not like the lure of money and called upon his followers to lead a life of virtue and austerity. After Balak Singh's death, his loyal disciple Ramsingh became the leader of the sect. His followers sang hymns and while dancing, they used to give high-pitched whimpers (kuks). Hence they were called Kukas. But after some time the movement could not gain momentum and it fizzled out.

4. Educational Movement

The Sikhs were not isolated from the main current of the reforms and renaissance of the 19th century. They wanted to retain their distinct cultural identity. In Amritsar and Lahore associations known as Singh Sabhas were formed to protect Sikhism from the influence of Arya Samaj.

On 5th March 1892, the foundation stone of the Khalsa College was laid in Amritsar. The Singh Sabhas did much spade work in the national field. They encouraged the establishment of educational institutions and the publication of books, magazines and newspapers. Besides these constructive activities, the Singh Sabhas developed a consciousness among the Sikh community regarding their rights and cultural identity.

Thus, on the Indian national scene, the Sikhs represented a united community, noted for hard work and martial qualities. The State of Punjab has made great strides in the fields of education, science and technology during the post-Independence period and the sturdy Sikh community has made a significant contribution to progress and prosperity of the State.

7

Growth of New India

I. Social Reforms

(i) Phule

Jyotiba Phule, the harbinger of the liberation of the depressed classes of the Indian society was the first leader among the down trodden people. His services were remarkable, inspiring and daring in his period of life.

Early Career

Jyotiba Phule was born in Pune, the citadel of orthodox Hindus and the centre of exploitations by the Aryans on the Sudras. He was born in 1827 in Mazhi Community, a scheduled caste. His father was Govinda Rao who was engaged in flower trade. Phule started his education in 1841 but had to become a drop out due to the economic conditions of the family in 1847. He had to assist his father in his trade in order to win their bread. He was married while he was 13 years old. His bride was Savithri, a 8 years old girl. His neighbours were a Christian paster and a Muslim teacher. He studied the book "Human Rights" by Tomas Paine. He got inspiration about the rights of every human being irrespective of his caste, colour and creed. Hence, he developed an ambition to reform the society and restructure it based on Liberty, Equality and Fraternity. He became a daring youth because of his training in Gymnastics.

Turning point in life

The year 1848 became a turning point in the life career of Phule. It made him a revolutionary reformer. His zeal for reform became insatiable and made him a dauntless hero of the downtrodden. It was in that year Phule came to realise the untouchable agony of the depressed classes who had been exploited by the so called higher caste Hindus for centuries together. He happened to participate in the marriage procession of his Brahmin friend. But the members in the procession spoke abusive language and forbid him from participating in it. This incident became an eye opener for Phule and made him resolute to do away with this system in the society. The untouchability practised and perpetrated by the Brahmins had to be eradicated from this caste ridden society.

Phule began to formulate his policies for the elevation of the depressed classes. His avowed object was to establish Equality, Equal justice and Rationalism in the Indian society. He commenced his work by founding a separate school for girls in 1848. He appointed Savithri, his wife as the teacher in that school. His effort to start a separate school for the weaker sex alone aroused opposition from the caste Hindus. They created all problems and hurdles in running the school. Undaunted Phule surmounted all such obstacles.

Phule continued to open separate schools for the children of Mahar Mangu, and Samar castes. He founded two more schools for girls in 1851 and 1852. He started orphanages and centres for rehabilitation of the widows. He also advocated the social reform of widow remarriage. In 1873, he adopted the son of a Brahmin widow who had deserted him. He named him "Yaswantan." He made a deep analysis of the class structure of the Indian society and was able to find out the trickery of the Brahmin supremacy. He wanted to expose their malicious malignity and their intention to perpetuate their superiority in the society through their "Purohit Myths" in 1869. He published another book on the same theme called "Slavery through Brahmins in Indian Empire" in the year 1873. He decided to reform the Indian society by freeing it from exploitation, superstitions and dominations and thereby establishing an egalitarian society.

He considered that all people are children of God, the Almighty and hence no middlemen in the form of Brahmins are needed in between people and God. Their interception is not necessary. Purohits had to be dispensed with. Any social celebration can be conducted without the participation of the purohits. He himself conducted the first ever "Self honour Marriage" on 25th December 1873. He preached to the people not to invite the purohits for any of their social as well as religious functions. Thereby he wanted to liberate the Indian society from the thraldom from Brahmins.

Phule also condemned the people's belief in astrology, sorcery, witchcraft, and demons. He asked the people to cultivate rational

Share in India" and the Columbia University conferred on him Doctoral Degree. He returned to India on 17th October 1917 and undertook the job of the secretary of the army in Baroda as he had already promised to the King Sayaji. There he was ill-treated by the personnel of the King because of his birth in the low caste. He relinquished his job and returned to Bombay.

His early services to the Underdogs

He convened two conference for the depressed classes at Bombay in 1917 in which he highlighted the inhuman treatment met out to the downtrodden by the caste Hindus in the name of religion, customs and traditions. In 1918 he convened an all India conference of the depressed classes at Bombay in March 23 and 24. The King of Baroda, Sayaji Rao presided over the deliberations.

Ambedkar demanded separate electorate for the depressed classes to the South Borough Commission. The separate electorate should also be in proportion to the population of the depressed classes. He demanded that social equality should be established before granting Dominion Status to India. In 1920 he conducted another conference in which he arranged for all classes of people on equal status.

Preferred to become Professor

He entered into the career of a Professor of Politics and Economics in Ham College in Bombay. He wanted to study law in London through the earning of his teaching profession. His lectures ensnared students of other faculties also. He acquired the friendship of the King of Golhapur who had a deep urge for social reforms. Ambedkar published a magazine. "Mook Nayak" (Hero of the dumbs) in 31st January 1920 with the generous assistance of the ruler Golhapur.

Legal Studies in London

Ambedkar went to London to fulfil his desire of learning Law in London. He observed the canon economy and lived a life austerity in London. He submitted a thesis on "Provincial Decentralisation of Imperial Finance in British India" to the London University in 1921. He went to Bonn University in Germany and studied economics there. He submitted a thesis on "The Problem of the Rupee-its origin and its solution" for his D. Sc. degree. Thus, he returned to India with the Barrister degree to sene the people in the more appropriate way.

Services of Dr. Ambedkar

Ambedkar adopted Kabir, Jythiba Phule and Lord Buddha as his mentors and pioneers in his endeavours for the social reforms.

He formed a society for the people of depressed classes. A free hostel for the school children was opened under its auspices. Financial assistance was offered to such children for their dresses and books. He penetrated even into the remote villages and educated the depressed people to give up their inferiority complex. He made them to realise the necessity of education. He launched agitations against the laws prohibiting the depressed classes from being recruited in the army. He was offered the membership of upper house of the Bombay Legislature in recognition of his intelligence.

Resolution of S.R. Pole

S.R. Pole, a Brahmin member of the Upper Chamber of the Bombay Legislature, introduced a resolution in the house in 1923. According to it, risers, lakes and ponds are the public property and hence the depressed class people should also be given chance to utilise them like those of other people. It was legislated and implemented.

Based on this legislation, the Municipal Council of Makath also proclaimed that ponds are common to all people. But the class Hindus refused the entry of the depressed classes in the ponds. Ambedkar convened conferences annually. In 1927 that conference was held at Makath. On the second day of the conference Ambedkar went in procession to the disputed pond and took water in it. The class-Hindus unleashed violence on the depressed class people and held agitation against the proposed temple entry of the downtrodden. Ambedkar observed fast against this. He filed a case in the court. After four years of trial the judgement was given in favour of the depressed classes permitting to take water from common sources of water.

Ambedkar wanted to go to the temple of Thakkur Thuvar in Bombay. The priest of the temple too fixed the date for his visit. When Ambedkar went to the temple, the class Hindus rose up in arms and drove away Ambedkar from the temple.

Ambedkar started an "Educational Society for the Depressed Classes." He pleaded the Bombay Government for the opening hostels for the students of the downtrodden. The government also complied with the demands by opening five such hostels. The government appointed a commission to investigate the real conditions of the depressed classes in which Ambedkar also found a place. The commission visited many places in India and highlighted the appalling miserable conditions of the depressed people. Ambedkar also met the Simon Commission at Poona in October 1928 to appraise the pitiable plight of the depressed classes in India.

Communal Award and Poona Pact

Ramsay Mac Donald, the Prime Minister of Britain announced on August 10, 1932, the Communal Award. The award was based on the British theory that India was not a nation, but a congeries of racial, religious and cultural groups, castes and interests. A fixed number of seats were allocated to each minority and special separate electorates were assigned to each. This scheme encouraged every, minority group to consider it as a national unit with its particular interest separate from the interests of the general body of Indians. Nothing could be more efficacious method of fractionalising the country and preventing the growth of the consciousness of nationality. Gandhi, realising its mischievous character resolved to resist it with all his force. He considered that the separate electorate for the depressed classes was calculated to disrupt the Hindu community, without affording any advantage to the depressed classes. He started his historic fast unto death on September 20, 1932. Dr. Ambedkar and leaders of the Hindus agreed to replace the award. It was known as Poona Pact.

Ambedkar founded a party as "Free Labourers' Party" in order to protect the interests of the labourers. In 1942, he was appointed as one of the members of Executive Council of Viceroy. Later on he was appointed as the Labour Minister.

Post Second World War

After the Second World War, the British Government under Atlee decided to offer freedom to India. A constituent assembly was convened to formulate a constitution for Independent India. Dr. Ambedkar was one among those scholars in the Assembly. In the Interim Government formed after Independence, Ambedkar was offered the Ministry of Law. Further, he was entrusted with the formidable job of drafting the Constitution and the present Indian Constitution is the result of his earnest and dedicated service to the cause of the Nation.

(iii) E.V. Ramasamy

E.V. Ramasamy (1879-1973) was a great social reformer. He was an embodiment of courage, intelligence and leadership qualities. His pragmatic approach to political and social problems enabled him to become the greatest revolutionary of this country. He wanted violent and radical changes in all walks of life of the people.

Early Life

Thanthai Periyar E.V. Ramasamy Naicker was born on 17th September 1879 in Erode. His parents were Venkatappar and Chinnathayarammal alias Muthammal. He belonged to a very rich family. He also belonged to Kannada origin of the Nayakar family.

E.V. Ramasamy Naicker got married at the age of 13. He then went to many holy places. He also went to Kasi. When he noticed the ill-treatment of the non Brahmins by the Brahmins, he condemned the Brahmins vehemently and returned to Tamil Nadu. He understood the evils of Hinduism, exploitation of priests and upper class people on the poor downtrodden classes. He criticised strongly against casteism which made him to fight against social malady. As he was fighting for them, he was socially boycotted by his own caste people.

E.V.R. as a Politician

He was a Congressman in the beginning. He served as the Chairman of the Salem Municipality and earned a very good name and fame. He faithfully supported the Gandhian politics and took active role in the non-cooperation movement. He was a strong believer in prohibition and started the prohibition movement in Tamil Nadu. He cut off all the palmyrah trees in his garden and proved that he was a pioneer in exposing the evils of drinking.

Periyar was imprisoned twice at the time of Non-co-operation Movement.

In 1924 he led the famous Vaikam Satyagraha and was imprisoned by the Travancore Government thrice. Finally, the Government yielded to his demand and released him. So he earned the title of the "Hero of Vaikam" Thus, he removed the segregation there.

There was severe segregation in the Gurukulam school at Seranmahadevi in Tirunelveli District. Periyar noticed the segregation of the non-Brahmins from the Brahmins by providing drinking water and food in separate places. He protested against this and resigned the secretaryship of the Madras State Congress in 1925. In the State level conference held at Kancheepuram he moved a resolution for reservation in Government services for non-Brahmins. His resolution was not allowed and so he left the party and started the Self-Respect Movement. He advocated his ideas through 'Kudiyarasu', 'Puratchi' and 'Vaduthalai'.

He started Self-Respect Movement in 1925 because he wanted to eradicate the distinction between haves and have-nots.

In the year 1935, he fought for the abolition of Hindi as second language.

He started 'Dravida Kaghagam' in 1944. He requested his followers to wear black shirt to indicate that the Indian society is the bundle of superstitions and ignorance and it is to be enlightened and modernised through rationalism.

His Movement

The Self-Respect Movement of Thanthai Periyar is a social movement. It was started in 1925. It was intended to the non-Brahmin cause in the social sphere. In 1923 he wrote in an article the reason for the starting of the movement in the following manner. "The Self-Respect Movement came into existence only to teach the real truth of the ancients; a truth that existed where there were no differences between people and justice existed between people. It comes only to save the society. Some cheats had taken advantage of the ignorance of our people, of the poverty of our people and instilled into them so many sastras and puranas and led them that they were low caste".

The Self-Respect Movement comes to tell that God is common to all, irrespective of caste, creed, colour, sex, rank and birth. There is no low caste or high caste in the society.

In this way the followers of E.V.R. began to ridicule the social ascendancy of the Brahmins. This movement stood for abolition of untouchability and caste system.

The Brahmins constituted only 3 per cent of the total population in Tamil Nadu. But they became dominant in all walks of life. This led to commercial bitterness and sickenings in the society. A significant change took place between 1908 and 1915 amongst the non-Brahmin leaders.

In the field of education and in the field of state service the dominant minority dominated the province. They occupied many gazetted and non-gazetted posts in the Government.

Another aim of the movement was the liberation of women. They condemned child marriage and forced widowhood.

The followers of this movement welcomed Sharadha Act for better and fitter life of the marriageable girls.

They took series of steps for this, improvement of women in the society. They established Marriage Bureau and Self-Respect Substitute for women. They encouraged inter-caste marriages and remarriage of widows. They condemned the various rituals and ceremonies of the marriage. Brahmin purohitas were avoided at the time of marriages. He was against dowry system.

Due to their propaganda caste distinctions were rediculed by the people. They advocated to avoid religious festivals and the innumerable meaningless ceremonies. Periyar decided to pull down the whole edifice of Hinduism so to destroy the foundations of caste and enslavement of women.

They followed many anti-religious programmes to enlighten the people.

In 1933 he founded the Rational Book Publishing Society. Its headquarters was at Erode. Many Rationalist Forums were established throughout the length and breath of Tamilnadu. They carried the message of E.V.R.'s Self-Respect Movement to every individual in the land.

This movement published a monthly journal called 'Pakutharivu' to spread its ideas and ideologies.

This movement did a lot in the literary field also. They published the three books *viz.*, ...'Why we became enslaved?', 'Materialism' and 'Kudiarasu Kalambakam'.

Periyar E.V.R. attacked all religious minded movements like Brahminism, Muhammadanism and Christianity. He imbibed the communist ideas, but when the later was banned in 1934, he declared that his was no communist but socialist.

Periyar E.V.R. visited Singapore and Malaysia and propagated his principles of rationalism.

In 1931-32 E.V.R. visited Egypt, Russia, England, France, Germany, Portugal and Spain. Wherever he went, he studied their way of life and observed their habits. He came to a conclusion that poverty was the underlying cause for all the social evils. After his return to India he advocated the point in Socialist Manifesto. The then ruling party in Tamilnadu was Justice Party. It accepted his programme and introduced the same.

E.V.R. stood for reservation to the non-Brahmins in educational institutions and government services.

E.V.R. suggested Family Planning in order to check the growing population and to keep good health.

E.V.R. stood for partnership of the workers' management in industries.

For easy learning and writing, he encouraged reform in Tamil script.

After the decline of the Justice Party, he formed Dravida Kazhagam at Salem in 1944. A separate Dravidanad comprising the areas "where Tamil, Telugu, Kannada and Malayalam were spoken" was the demand of the party. It became an anti-Brahmin party and criticised the superstitious beliefs of the people. It attracted many people. Particularly young people came under its banner with high hopes and enthusiasm.

E.V.R. opposed caste based Varnashram-Education Scheme by Rajaji and this opposition led to the establishment of Kamaraj Ministry in 1953. E.V.R. condemned the Constitution of India and burnt copies of same. He opposed Hindi and asked his followers to tar the Hindi boards. He asked his followers to cut the holy thread of Brahmins and to break the idols worshipped by people. He served for these ideals till his death. He tried to bring change in society quickly by these unpopular methods. Thus "Periyar, the prophet of the new age, the Socrates of the South East Asia, Father of the Social Reform movement, arch enemy of ignorance, superstition, meaningless customs and base manner" is living in the heart of every one in the Tamil country,

(iv) Dr. Muthulakshmi Reddy (1886-1968)

The emergence of reform movements in the 19th century marks the beginning of new era in Indian society.

Western education and Industrial Revolution brought about a new awakening in the minds of the Indian intellectuals. The enlightened and educated Indians developed consciousness about the glory of Indian culture and realised that the existing social evils such as the sati, purdah system, untouchability, ban on widow remarriage, child marriage and infanticide, abolition of devadasi system and host of other evil practices were leading to human degradation. In such circumstances, various social and religious reformers rose to the occasion to meet the challenge of the times. Raja Ram Mohan Roy who is regarded as the Father of Indian Renaissance, is the forerunner of all reformers. In the galaxy of social reformers Dr. Muthulakshmi Reddy is considered as the first and foremost woman social reformer in India.

Dr. Muthulakshmi Reddy was born in Pudukkottai. Her father was the principal of the Maharajas College and graduated as first woman to study in the college. Then she joined Medical college. She married Dr. T. Suresh Reddy also a Doctor.

Dr. Muthulakshmi Reddy is considered as the first lady doctor of Madras Presidency. From her early days, she showed keen interest towards women's uplift. She had great sympathy towards poor and downtrodden. She always thought about the emancipation of women. Due to the efforts of women's movement she was nominated to the state legislature. In a speech before the Andhra womens' conference held at Vijayawada in 1929, Dr. Muthulakshmi Reddy, the well known social worker said. "The ancient Hindu legislators realised that both sexes were equal and said before the world that women had equal rights with men. So the laws depriving the Hindu women of her rights and privileges and assigning her an inferior place in society must be only of recent origin. I feel sorry to observe that the Hindus in particular have become creatures more of custom or habit than of reason or true religion. No enlightened women with any self-respect can put up with such one sided laws which have placed us in an inferior position even to our Mohammadan and Christian sisters, to modify such unjust laws and to make them suitable to the needs of the present day society, a reform society should be started for the uplift, protection and help of the Hindu Women".

Referring to one Andhra speech of Mahatma Gandhi, Dr. Muthulakshmi wrote a long letter to him, in 1929, drawing his attention to the various disabilities of women. 'Does not' she noted, "early marriage strike at the root of all development-physical, intellectual and even spiritual. 'Do not pangs of child wives and child mothers, and unmitigated sorrows of our widows and deserted wives, demand an immediate remedy."

Dr. Muthulakshmi expected Congressmen to shoulder responsibility for reform. Whom she became the member of the State Legislature, she moved a resolution for the abolition of 'Devadasi system' in 1929 in the Assembly. It was passed successfully in both the Houses of Legislature. But the Governor refused to give his assent. However, it was published in the bill stage itself. No wonder Muthulakshmi succeeded in her attempt of abolishing Devadasi system, a great social evil. The womenfolk suffered a lot because of this social malady for long time. Dr. Muthulakshmi Reddy gave decent good-bye to this during the rule of Justice Party in Madras Presidency.

Dr. Muthulakshmi Reddy inaugurated a new era in the history of womenfolk by starting 'Awai Illam' at Madras for deserted women, widows and orphans. They were provided food and education. Even to day the Awai Illam is rendering remarkable service for such ladies.

Another great contribution of Dr. Muthulakshmi Reddy was the starting of the Cancer Institute at Adayar. It is considered as a memorable service in the medical field. It cannot be denied that she rendered a remarkable service to the womenfolk as a great social worker. She had letter correspondence with Mahatma Gandhi regarding the uplift of womenfolk.

Dr. Muthulakshmi Reddy did a lot for the womenfolk. As a medical women, she gave free medical aid to womenfolk. As a social worker she was highly responsible for the abolition of Devadasi system, establishment of 'Awai Illam', starting of Cancer Institute and providing food, shelter and education to the abandoned women and orphans. She devoted her whole life for the sake of women and orphans. She devoted her whole life for the sake of womenfolk. She even sacrificed her life for the well-being of mankind especially womenfolk. Thus, she has earned a very good name in the social history of Modern India.

(v) Emanicipation of Women

Indian Society suffered from various social evils such as sati, child marriage, polygamy, infanticide, untouchability, purdah system, caste system and ban on widow remarriage which gnawed at the very vitals of the nation, leading to paralysing immobility of social life and economic stagnation. In Indian Society the women folk had been the most exploited class and it is fitting here to give a brief account of reforms aimed at women's movement and emancipation.

It was only in the 19th century that organised efforts towards women's emancipation started. The various socio-religious movements launched by the liberals recognised women as a distinct personality. Moreover they are considered as cradle of civilisation. They struggled to end the economic, social, political and other disabilities from which women suffered. The crusades of Raja Ram Mohan Roy against sati, the struggle of Iswar Chandra Vidyasagar, Malabari, Narmad and others for widow remarriage, the heroic fight of Karve, Dayanand and Ranade for providing to women equal access to education and the general trend of these reformers to create a psychological climate and an institutional framework for equal opportunities for women in various fields of social life are all manifestations of that basic principle of respect for women as individuals.

With the turn of the 19th century, new ideas began to sweep across the country and it was then that women's organisations and a strong women's movement took place. Women entered public life and themselves became, through their organisations, the spearhead of attack against the irrational orthodoxy, injustice, and discrimination to which women were subjected.

With the very first phase of the political movement, a new chapter had opened in the history of Indian women, even before Mahatma Gandhi came to the fore front of the national movement.

In this respect, Mrs. Annie Besant was the first and foremost woman leader who took up the cause of women in the society. Mrs. Annie Besant with her militant demand for Home Rule created deep impression on Indian women and inspired them to actively participate in the struggle for freedom. In 1916 she entered Indian politics and delivered her famous address, "Wake up India". In 1917 she was elected the first woman President of the Indian National Congress.

At this juncture in 1917 Mrs. Annie Besant with the help of Margaret Cousins, founded the Women's Association in Madras. It became a model for women's institutions elsewhere in the country.

In 1926, the All India Women's conference came into being. This organisation made sustained efforts towards social reforms affecting the position of women.

It was also during this period that a deputation of Indian women presented to the British Parliament a demand for the enfranchisement of women on the basis of equality with men.

This was a striking evidence that Indian women were rapidly becoming politically conscious.

In the national movement the status of women improved greatly under the dynamic leadership of Gandhiji. No tax campaigns, Mass satyagraha, breaking of police hand on demonstrations and meetings, picketing of liquor shops and foreign cloth shops and other items of the programmes were such that women could participate in their implementation. A large number of women enthusiastically responded to the call of Gandhiji by forming important sections of the passive resistance movement. Women courted arrests in the Non-Cooperation Movement of 1921-22. When the Civil Disobedience Movement was launched in 1929-30, women were profoundly stirred and magnificently responsive.

In 1928, for the second time, an Indian woman, Sarojini Naidu, was chosen President of the Indian National Congress. Women further consolidated their gains in 1930 when three of them — Sarojini Naidu, Jahanara Shah Nawaz and Radhabai Subbarayan were invited to take part in the Round Table Conference in London.

Because of this women's movement, they achieved a lot for womenfolk such as franchise, entry into legislature, educational opportunities, economic status etc. The constitutional provisions on the other hand, have made women equal to men. Before the eyes of law, all women are equal to men.

Besides, the movement paved the way for the establishment of Maternity Homes, Children's Hospitals, Adult Education Centres, Women Co-operative Societies and Cultural Centres.

It cannot be denied that this movement was highly responsible for the nomination of Dr. Muthulakshmi Reddy to the state legislature during this period.

This movement organised annual conference to ventilate their grievances. Moreover, the office bearers of this movements sought the help of the government to redress their grievances. Really speaking this movement was out and out responsible for the progress of womenfolk. It did a lot in a peaceful way.

The women's Association had certain short comings also. One such short coming was that the educated ladies were given due regard in the Association. The uneducated ladies were not cared for. Virtually there was no contact with those ladies.

In short this Association secured political emancipation, social equality, economic independence and opportunities for educational advancement for momenfolk.

(vi) Social Legislations

Many social legislations were brought forth by the Government between 1900 for the progress and prosperity of the society. The need and necessity of such legislations cannot be underestimated. They were immensely beneficial to them during this period; Even now they are highly helpful to the society. All legislations were enforced after enactment because to give a decent burial to all social evils in the society.

The Sharadha Act (1929) was the first and foremost social legislation of this period. In 1927 Harbilas Sharada introduced a bill before the legislature to regulate marriage among the Hindus. This Act was subsequently known as the Child Marriage Restraint Act of 1929 or popularly known as the Sharada Act. The operation of the Act extended to the whole of India. It fixed the minimum age of marriage for girls at 14 and for boys at 16 years.

During the time of the Justice Party Rule in Tamilnadu an enactment was passed to abolish 'Devadasi System' which haunted the women folk very seriously and severely in many ways.

Hindu Women's Right to Property Act (1937) was passed mainly due to the efforts of Deshmukh. The Act provided a powerful weapon in the hands of the progressive forces of Hindu society.

Untouchability, one of the ugly manifestations of the caste system, has been the cause of gross injustice and human degradation to a substantial number of Harijans in Hindu Society. The Constitution of India in the section relating to 'Fundamental Rights' declares the abolition of untouchability and forbids its practice in any kind. Later on the Act was passed in this regard.

Some sort of slavery which existed in Tamilnadu (the composite Madras Presidency) in the 19th century, by which bondsmen were sold or mortgaged by their masters was declared unlawful. Legal measures have been provided to ensure the liberty of the so called bonded labourers.

Many factory acts were passed to promote the conditions of the working classes. The acts passed in 1934 and 1938 regulated the appointment and welfare of women in factories.

Many more legislative measures were provided to eradicate all the evils which haunted the growth of a healthy society.

The Apprentices Act (1950), Juvenile Smoking Act (1946), Hindu Marriage Disabilities Removal Act (1946), Suppression of Immoral Traffic in Women and Girls Act (1950) etc are few to mention in the field of social legislations.

During this period the Bengal Tenancy Act was passed with a view to ameliorate the lot of the peasants.

In order to provide relief to the peasants, Lord Curzon passed the Punjab Alienation Act in 1902-03.

During this period labour ministries at the centre and the states took adequate measures to provide relief to the workers. Minimum wages, bonus, hours of work, medical facilities, housing and many other matters have been covered by legislative enactments.

Thus, social legislations passed during this period paved the way for the progress and prosperity of society.

8

Regeneration of Indian Society

The Varnashram system of the Hindus gradually degenerated into caste system and finally created an additional caste or group of people called the untouchables or the scheduled castes. The caste system has divided the Hindu society into thousands of groups making the task of national integration impossible. The system is not only undemocratic and unjust but positively oppressive to a fairly extensive population of India.

The ill-treatment meted out to the low caste people compelled them to launch anti-caste movements which were in the main directed against the high caste people. These movements appeared in different forms in various parts of the country. But they were very strong in Maharashtra, Kerala, Andhra and Maharashtra.

In Maharashtra the low caste people launched anti-caste movements. The Satyashodhak Samaj founded in 1873 by Jyotiba Phule, a gardener by caste played an important role in this regard. It not only launched direct attacks on the money-lenders and landlords but also challenged the ritual status of the elite. Phule asserted the worth of human being irrespective of his birth in a particular caste. He urged the non-Brahmins not to engage Brahmin priests to conduct their ritual. He also devoted attention to the education of the non-Brahmins and started a school for boys and girls in 1848. In 1851 he started a school for the untouchables in Poona. He also put forward a demand for adequate representation of number of low castes in service and local bodies. As a result of his consistent efforts. Phule succeeded in securing social representation for the non-Brahmins under Montage Chelmsford Reforms.

In September 1923 the Finance Department of the Government of Bombay passed a resolution prohibiting the recruitment of Brahmins and allied castes to the lower services till a proportion of the posts were filled by the intermediate and backward castes. Soon this policy was also adopted by the other provincial governments. As a result by 1924 the hundreds of small communities into which Indian Society was divided began to clamour for special representation in the legislature, local bodies, public services and even educational institutions.

Almost at the same time when Phule launched non-Brahmin movement in Maharashtra, an anti-Brahmin movement also started in Madras. Phule published his book 'Ghulam-giri' in 1872 to propagate his ideas. The movement led by Satyashodhak Samaj was marked by two trends. The first trend developed moderate 'sanskritizing', claimed Kshatriya origin for the Marathas and after receiving patronage of the ruler of Kolhapur from 1890 onwards, preferred to remain loyal to the British and anti-Congress. The second trend attacked the caste system itself, made use of Marathi than English for its writings and spoke in favour of Bahuja Samaj (majority association) against the Brahmans and Merchant class (Vaisyas). The second trend became widely popular particularly in villages. 'Din-Mitra' and a newspaper published by Markuntrao Patil and exhibition of Tamashas (Dramas) among villagers helped the Samaj in gaining wide popularity. From mid 1920s, Kashavarao Jedha and Dukkarrao Javalkar began providing leadership to the Samaj from Poona which proved anti-British as well as anti-Congress.

Another caste movement was led by Dr. Ambedkar in Maharashtra in 1920s. He became the leader of the untouchable community, Mahar and found 'The All India Depressed Classes Federation' and became an all India figure. He took many steps to reform the way of life of these people. He urged them to stop the dragging the dead cattle out of the village. He wanted them to give up eating carrion, alcoholic drinks and begging. He wanted them to become literates and send their children to schools. Finally, he wanted them to dress well and have self-respect for themselves. Thus, one of the chief aims was to bring about a revolution in the way of life of the untouchables and in their aspirations for themselves and for their children.

He wrote in 'Mook Nayak' (The Voice of the Dumb) which he started in 1920. "We are not yet ready to give an answer to the question of whether untouchables should have a temple of their own or attempt to enter the Hindu temple." But, on a few occasions Ambedkar made many attempts to forcibly enter the Hindu temple. The right to participate in the public Ganapathy festival was secured at least on one occasion. Ambedkar and his followers donned the sacred thread symbolizing rebirth. The abortive attempt to enter the temple at Amaravati was followed in 1930 by large scale satyagraha at the Kalaram Temple in Basik. He himself believed in idol worship. Thus, he started this programme in order to establish the rights of the untouchables. He also fought for a separate electorate for the untouchables. Several other leaders found the 'All India Depressed Classes Association' for the betterment of the lower castes. B.R. Ambedkar also founded the Independent Labour Party to link dalits, peasants in workers struggle.

Kerala

In South Tamilnadu the 'Shanars' (an untouchable community) claimed the status of Kshatriyas in the 1901 census and started calling themselves Nadar. Similarly, the Pallis of north Tamilnadu claimed Kshatriya origin and called themselves Vanniya Kula Kshatriyas. Sri Narayana Guru (1854-1928) a leader of the Izhavas, an untouchable group of Kerala led a revolt against the caste system. The Izhavas were the first people to give up the practice of untouchability with respect to the castes below them. They defied the restriction on free movement in the streets of the towns and villages based on the practice of untouchability. The upper caste Hindus found that there was no remedy in the court of law against this defiance because the law was clearly in favour of the unrestricted use of public thoroughfares.

The Izhaves also started temple entry agitation while Christians and Muslims were allowed to go up to the outer gateway of the temples, the Izhavas had to offer their prayer 50 yards or more from the gateway. Sri Narayana Guru Sanskritized and Westernised the Izhavas so that they could be classified as a backward caste rather than an exterior caste or scheduled caste.

Sri Narayan Guru established the S.N.D.P. Yogam (Sri Narayana Dharma Paripalana Yogam) in 1902 with his gospel "one caste, one religion, one God." This organisation had two important programme : one was to uplift the Izhavas, a depressed caste group of Kerala; as part of the work of Yogam. Narayana Guru started a number of schools and colleges throughout Kerala; secondly, he built a number of temples; he simplified rituals regarding worship, marriages and funerals; he made S.N.D.P. Yogam as a secular organisation with its branches throughout Kerala; he also established an order of Sanyasis to help the community regarding its religious and spiritual matters. For fifteen years he travelled widely and helped them to clear up their houses and streets and develop clean habits. He made them alter their diet and this pointed the right road to reform and prosperity.

By these two means — modern education on the one hand and Sanskritization on the other — Narayana Guru was able to transform the Izhavas from an untouchable group in Kerala to a "backward caste" community within a short period of 30 years. The temple entry programmes undertaken by some of the Izhava leaders in association with the Nayar Service Society (N.S.S.) founded by Mannath Padmanabha Pillai finally led to the temple entry proclamation in 1936. Aiyappan writes that C.P. Ramaswamy Iyer, the Dewan of Travancore State, "felt the need for consolidating the Hindus and building up the unity of the Hindus of the state as a counterpoise against the growing power and influence of the Christians." The most discontented and at the same time the best organised among the Hindu caste were the Izhavas. Nothing was dearer to the Izhavas of that generation than temple entry.

The next movement was the Vykom Satyagraha which was started in 1924 in Kerala to throw open the temple streets to the untouchables. But the people as well as the government were strongly against this movement. Gandhiji strongly opposed this view. So the government removed all barricades in the streets. But the opposition of the caste Hindus went on unabated. Afterwards radical Izhavas like K. Aiyappan and C. Kesavan were preached atheism among their followers.

Thus, All these movements fought for social reforms in Kerala.

Andhra

The anti-caste movements in various parts of the country culminated in an open revolt in Telengana in 1946-50 which was organised by the Andhra Maha Sabha an organisation constituted to the cause of social reforms and ending of dominance by the higher castes. In this revolt the 'dalits', artisans and landless as well as substantial village land-holders took part. For the first time a demand for the abolition of zamindars and distribution of excess land to the landless, with a view to meet the need of landless low castes, was made.

Despite this sustained struggle by the low castes, the higher castes continued to enjoy a dominant position in the pre-Independence period. The Congress hegemony also gave a serious set back to the anti-caste movements. However Congress under Gandhiji's leadership was able to win paternalistic sympathy for the Harijans from the caste Hindus and these ward them away from radical struggle.

(i) Peasant's Revolts

The 19th century is marked by a remarkable upsurge of agitation among the peasants who had to face the ordeal of the various natural calamities such as famines, pestilence and floods. The most excruciating had been the British policy which occasionally culminated in the over assessment of revenue and the general apathy on the part of the government to the miserable plight of the peasants. The ruthless exploitation of the peasants at the hands of the cruel zamindars assumed serious proportions, resulting in the eruption of violence and unrest. The causes for the unrest among the peasants dining the British rule are given below :

In the first place the peasant revolts were organised with a view to expel the British and revert to the previous system of government. Most of the revolts during the period 1785-1857 took place on this account. The rebels resorted to killing, looting and binning and even succeeded in expelling the British from certain areas. Even during the revolt of 1857 the armed peasants actively assisted the mutinying troops and private armies of rulers to over throw the British rule.

Secondly, some of the peasant revolts were led by religious leaders. The peasants extended blind support of these leaders, because they expected these leaders as incarnation of the supreme deity, to deliver them from British rule and establish 'dharam raj' (kingdom of virtue). This type of revolts took place mainly in the post-mutiny period and were suppressed by the British with heavy hand.

Thirdly, some of the peasant revolts were led by persons who had been dispossessed of their homelands and had taken to banditry. As they did not possess any fixed homes, they could freely roam about. It is noteworthy that these bandit leaders were not motivated by the considerations of protecting the poor against oppressors. They often served as mercenaries for landlords and princes to make money.

Fourthly, some peasant revolts were organised to strike terror in the minds of the oppressors like landlords, revenue agents money lenders and other wealthy persons with a view to secure justice. Methods like assassinations, burning of buildings and other properties were used for this purpose.

Finally, some of the mass peasant revolts were organised with a view to seek redress of particular grievances. In the main these revolts were organised as a protest against the British policy of economic exploitation and extractions by landlords.

We shall now examine the peasant revolts in detail.

Peasants' uprising in Bengal

In 1870, in Bengal tenants who suffered from object poverty refused to pay rent to their landlords. They did not honour the verdicts of the law courts and evaded eviction. However, the Government set up an Inquiry Committee to investigate into their grievances. In 1885 the Bengal Tenancy Act was passed with a view to ameliorating the lot of the peasants.

After the American Civil War (1861-65) the price of cotton fell and as a result, Indian peasants faced economic ruin and suffered much. In 1875 the riots broke out in the Deccan because of the legal steps taken by the moneylenders for the eviction of tenants from the land. The helpless but furious peasants assaulted moneylenders in their homes and seized the debt documents. However, the government came heavily on the rebellious peasants and subsequently in 1878, the Deccan Agriculturists Relief Act was enacted.

Peasants uprising in Punjab

Peasants rose in revolt in Punjab when moneylenders took legal steps to drive them out of their land holdings towards the close of the 19th century. In order to provide relief to the peasants Lord Curzon passed the Punjab Alienation Act in 1902-03.

Uprising of Peasants against European Indigo planters in Bihar

In 1917-18, Mahatma Gandhi organised a peasants satyagraha against the European indigo planters in Champran in Bihar. The Government set up an Inquiry Committee of which Gandhiji was a member. On the receipt of report of this committee the Government provided relief to the peasants. When the drought conditions prevailed in Kair, Gandhiji launched a satyagraha movement in favour of the peasants who were not in a position to pay taxes.

Peasants struggle in Bardoli

Sardar Patel led the struggles of the peasants in the Bardoli district in Gujarat during 1928-29. The main outcome of these struggles was that the peasants became conscious of their tremendous strength. Later on, in 1930-31, yet another agitation was launched by the peasants who succeeded in getting their legitimate rights.

Countrywide agrarian unrest

As a result of the great economic crisis of 1929-30, the farmers were severely hit and the country was engulfed by peasant agitations which were very intense in Andhra, Gujarat, Karnataka and U.P.

Impact of the Peasants Movements

As a result of the peasant movements, the British Government was obliged to enact legislation for the purpose of giving relief to the peasants and saving them from the tentacles of the cruel landlords and greedy moneylenders who had covetous eye on their landholdings. On the otherhand, class consciousness dawned on the peasants who began to organise themselves in their organisations. The Madras Presidency Ryots' Association, the Madras Presidency Agriculturists Association and the Provincial Kisan Sabha in the U.P. and such other associations in Bengal, Andhra, Bihar and Punjab show the organised effort of the Indian peasantry to get rid of the clutches of landlords and moneylenders and the strangle hold of bureaucracy.

(ii) Deccan riots

In 1875 the peasants of Poona and Ahmednagar organised a revolt which is popularly known as Deccan Riots. The peasants resorted to revolt because for quite sometime they had been suffering exploitation at the lands of the Marwari Sahukars who lent them money at very high rates of interest and often mortgaged their land. As a result almost one eighth of the land was actually transferred to the sahukars and moneylenders. Some of these money lenders not only charged high rates of interests but also compelled the peasants under debt to compromise the honour of their females to get relief from crushing debts. For sometime the poor peasants put up with this. But ultimately their cup of patience got exhausted and they burst out in a revolt against the money lenders. The trouble started in 1874 when a Marwari money lender seized the house of a respectable villager on the strength of the mortgage decree. This provoked the villagers and they resorted to social and economic boycott of the Marwaris. They also refused to render service as water carriers, barbers and household servants etc. This forced the Marwaris to quit the village. Soon similar movements started in their neighbouring villages.

The peasant agitation against the money lenders took a violent turn in 1875 when the mob in a village of Poona collectorate looted the houses and shops of some Gujarati money lenders and burnt one house. This was repeated in other neighbouring villages of Poona as well as Ahmedabad districts. It may be noted that the chief objective of peasants was not to kill money lenders but to obtain and destroy the bonds, decrees and other credit documents. They used personal violence against the money lenders only when they refused to handover these documents to the peasants.

The things assumed such serious dimensions that the government was obliged to use military force to suppress those uprisings though the government succeeded in bringing these riots under control, it also decided to appoint a commission to look into the nature and caused of these riots. Tire commission on the basis of its enquiry arrived at the conclusion that the poverty and consequent indebtedness of the cultivators were the real causes underlying these riots. The commission observed that "the normal condition of the riots in the disturbed areas is one of indebtedness. This had grown to an extreme point during the twenty years preceding the riots. The evil consequences of indebtedness were averted for sometime by the transient prosperity of the American war period due to the cotton boom, but returned with multiple force during the six years preceding the riots." In the light of the recommendations of the Commission the government enacted the Deccan Agriculturists Relief Act of 1879 which placed restrictions on alienation of the peasants' lands and restrained usury.

No wonder it paved the way for other similar risings in tire country.

(iii) Mopilla uprising

The Mopilla uprising or the Moplah Revolt took place in mid 1921. This revolt was organised by the Moplah (a sect of Muslims) agricultural workers and tenants against the merciless exploitation by the Nainbudris, who owned the land.

The Nambudris had been maltreating the Moplah peasants and often deprived them of their homesteads and raised rents of land at will.

As a result the Moplah revolted against them since they could not tolerate this for long. They started an agitation for reduction of rent and permanency of tenure.

Initially the movement was purely agrarian in character. However, subsequently the leaders of the agitation gave it a communal colour.

The Indian National Congress which was opposed to exploitation of peasants did not support the movement on account of fear of the damage which the movement could cause to the unity and harmony of the people.

The Madras Government suppressed the revolt with severe hand.

The Congress also condemned the cruelty of the authorities in the name of peace and order.

One of the impact of the Moplah Revolt was that the Madras Government proceeded to pass Malabar Tenancy Act and conferred permanent tenancy of land on a large section of the peasants. The Moplah Revolt was also significant in so far as contributed to the chain of anti-colonial agitation in the post-World War I period. Above all, its significance lay in the fact that it demonstrated the will of the peasantry to struggle for its rights.

(iv) Tribal Revolts in Central and Eastern India

The British expansion in India was not at all smooth and led to encounter lot of opposition from various sections of society. Even the tribal people who are spread over various parts of India, strongly resented the extension of the British rule and look at the expansion of their political and cultural influence with suspicion.

Causes of Tribal Revolts

1. In the first place they could not reconcile with the idea of presence of outsiders on their territories. So they resisted the encroachments with all tile force at their disposal.
2. Another reason for the revolt was the policy of reservation of forests by the colonial rulers with a view to extract timber and other forest products for use by railway and other industries. As the forests were the main source of livelihood for many tribals, they revolted against the colonial rule, the revolts of Garos, Koyas and Konds were chiefly on account of this factor.
3. Another cause for their revolt was the policy of dispossession of the tribals from their agricultural lands and establishment of state primary over the resources greatly undermined the importance of the community which used to serve as a cushion during the periods of crisis. This made the tribals vulnerable to exploitation by the usurious money-lenders and traders. The tribes like Santhals, Ho, Hovan, Munda Bhumij etc., resisted with full force and even resorted to violence.
4. The disruption of the traditional roles of certain tribals as a result of policy of the British Government also contributed to the tribal revolts. For example the Banjars, who used to render commissariat service to the armies during the middle ages were pushed out of their occupation due to introduction of railways. As a result they not only suffered economically not also lost many privileges which they earlier enjoyed. As a result many of them took to crime.

Khasi Revolt

One of the earliest revolt against the authority of the British was organised by the Khasis, a primitive tribe residing in the hilly region between Jaintia and Garo Hills in Assam. Like other tribal people they also greatly dreaded the idea of slow British penetration with their country and strongly resented the same. In 1765 the British granted Diwani and acquired control over Sylhot. During the times of first Burmese war the

Khasis tried to create problem for them. However, the British succeeded in bringing them under control with much difficulty.

After the war the British acquired possession of the Brahmaputra valley and appointed Scott, a civilian officer, as their Political Agent. In 1827, he made a treaty with some of the Khasi chiefs. His idea of linking the territory with Sylhot by road, did not find favour with the chiefs. But the Englishmen started their work. So the chiefs decided to overthrow them. They organised a movement under Tirut Singh.

On May 5, 1820 a party of Khasis aided by Garos raided Nunklow and massacred the European and Bengal inmates of the sanatorium. They released all the convicts employed in the construction of the road and proceeded towards Cherrapunji. This encouraged other Khasi chiefs to join in the revolt. Soon even other hill people also rose in revolt against the British and made a determined bid to throw of the British yoke.

The British tried to crush the revolt through use of force and repression. A number of Khasi villages were burnt and an economic blockade was imposed on trade and intercourse with the Khasis. The Khasis under Tirut Singh avoided open confrontation with the English and occasionally organised raids on the plains. This sent a wave of terror among the English. This kind of warfare continued for almost four years till Tirut Singh decided to surrender in January 1833 on the condition that his life would be spared and his territory resorted to his nephew under certain conditions. The other Khasi chiefs also submitted to the authority of the British.

It provided impetus to similar rising among the Singphos. In 1830 they revolted against the British authority and made open use of arms, muskets, spears and swords, However, the English Captain NeufVulle succeeded in defeating them. Similarly revolts were organised by the chief of Kapaschor Akas in 1835, the Nagas in 1849 and Kurkis between 1836-1843.

The Kol uprising

In Central India the Kolarian tribes of Chota Nagpur offered resistance to the gradual extension of the British authority over their territory and revolted against them. The Kolarian tribes were ruled by petty chieftains and had a proud record of being independent of almost fifty generations. They strongly resented occupation of Singhbhum by the British. Raja of Porahat strongly opposed reached an agreement with the British and agreed to pay an annual tribute to them. But the Hos (his subjects) could not reconcile with this and continued to harass the English. The English burnt many of their villages and as a result large number of people were put to death.

Mundas Revolt

Mundas, another tribe of Chota Nagpur revolted against the British in 1831. This revolt was a protest against the new policy of farming revenue to outsiders and the introduction of judicial and revenue regulations of the Bengal Government into the country. The revolt soon spread to areas like Ranchi. Hazaribagh, Palamau and Mambhum. The rebels resorted to violence and pillage. They were very harsh towards the foreigners and put thousands of them to death and burnt their homes. The military forces were unable to control the Mundas. So a massive military operation was undertaken by the British. The revolt was suppressed in March 1832.

In the second half of the 19th century the Mundas under the leadership of Birsa organised another serious revolt. The chief objective of this revolt was to overthrow the alien government and its supporters, the landlords because they were responsible for the social and economic ills of the people. They wanted to replace the British government by Munda self-government. This alarmed the British authorities and they decided to arrest Birsa. They arrested him when he was sleeping to avöid provocation of his followers. Birsa was tried and sentenced to two years imprisonment and fine on the charge of spreading feeling of disloyalty in the country.

On his release from jail in January 1898, Birsa resumed his former activities and raised an effective force to give a fight to the English. He provoked the people to fight against injustice and oppression. So there were number of exchanges between the Mundas and the police. But the most serious attack on the police was organised on 7 January 1900 when 300 Mundas armed with bows and arrows, battle axes and spears attacked the police station and killed one of the constables. They also set some of the houses on fire. The British government sent an army to crash the Mundas. Knowing the arrival of the army, most of the Mundas escaped into the jungles, while another 200 Mundas, mainly women and children were killed. The British succeeded in arresting Birsa in February 1900 and put him in prison where he died in cholera.

Another Munda leader Gaya Munda was shot dead by surprise.

The British also captured about 450 followers of Birsa. Out of these trials were held against eighty-seven. Out of them two were awarded capital punishment, while the rest were subjected to various terms of transportation or imprisonment. Thus, the English suppressed the Munda revolt with firmness.

The Santhal Revolt

The Santhals, a primitive tribe living in Bihar in the area adjoining to Murshidahad in Bengal, also organised a revolt in 1855-56. Firstly, this revolt was organised against the oppression of the mahajans and traders from Bengal and upper India who lent money to the Santhals and charged them excessive rate of interest.

Secondly, they were against the exactions of the police and revenue officials.

Thirdly, they raised their standard of revolt because of the dispossession of lands by the zamindars.

Fourthly, they were infuriated by the insult and indignities of the Englishmen. The Englishmen gave innumerable difficulties and indignities to the Santhals.

Finally, they were greatly irritated by the dishonour of their women by the Sahiblok.

E.G. Man who wrote about the Santhal revolt in 1867 attributed the following four causes for their outbreak :

(1) The grasping and repacious spirit of the money lenders in their transactions with the tribals.

(2) The increasing misery caused by their iniquitous system of allowing personal and hereditary bondage for debt.

(3) Unparalleled corruption and extortion of the police in aiding and abetting the Mahajans (money lenders).

(4) The impossibility of the Santhals obtaining redress from the courts.

At the initial stages the revolt was primarily economic in nature and there was no anti-British feeling. In June 1855 about ten thousand Santhals under the leadership of Sidhu and Kanshu, two brothers declared their intension to take possession of the country and set up their own government. Then they destroyed the postal and railway communications between Bhagalpur and Rajmahal, established their control over the entire area. The Santhals also proclaimed the end of the company's rule and set up their own regime. The British troops failed miserably at the hands of Santhals. But they captured some isolated posts. The Santhals followed the tactics of surprise attack and avoided open confrontation with these troops and retired to thick jungles now and then. So the British Government was forced to declare the area as disturbed area and handed over the same to the military for suppression of rebellion. In 1856 the leaders were captured and submitted to the

British authority. There after the British committed human barbarities against the Santhals and completely crushed them.

Then the Santhals launched others social movement known as Kharwar Movement. This movement aimed at reviving the golden age of the Santhals when they lived in Campa in absolute independence and had no rent or tribute to pay but only to bring a small offering to pay to their leaders in virtue of their office. This movement became prominent only in the seventies of the nineteenth century under the leadership of Bhagirath Manjhi of Godda sub-division. He appealed to the people to worship Hindu deity Ram, whom he identified with Santhal cando. He failed to restore lands to the people. So the number of his followers started fast dwindling. Then he instigated people not to pay tax on the land they cultivated. As a result Bhagirath was arrested and imprisoned by the British. His successors continued the movement for the improvement of the lot of the Santhals.

In the closing years of the nineteenth century the Kharwar movement got split into three parts *viz.*, Sapha Hor, Samra and Babajim. During times of calamity the movement became active and its members took to acts of violence and sabotage. At times the members of the movement also extended support to the national movement. This marked the transformation of the Kharwar Movement from a socio-religious movement to a political movement.

Rampa Rebellion

In 1879-80 the Rampas, a forest tribe residing in the hills bound by the Godavari valley rose in revolt against the oppressive and judicious action of the Tahsildar of Bhadrachalam. A large number of tribesmen gathered in bands and looted villages and killed some policemen. The British sent a force from Madras which suppressed the insurrection. During the next two years further disturbances took place but the revolt was completely suppressed and by 1882 the people returned to their normal activities.

On the basis of the above discussion it can be asserted that the tribals organised a number of revolts against the British and the money lenders, who were supported by the British. Though these revolts were ultimately brought under control, they certainly provided the British government some very anxious moments. The British succeeded in bringing down these revolts because they were not well organised and did not take place simultaneously. This made it possible for the British to suppress these revolts one by one and assert their supremacy.

9

The Freedom Struggle

(i) Social background to the Indian National Movement

It is accepted on all hands that it was due to the impact of the British policy of unification of the country and spread of the Western liberal ideas about liberty and nationalism which influenced the thinking of the people and promoted the spirit of nationalism. The national feeling was almost absent in India. The only unity which existed in India was the religious unity. The political outlook on national level was perhaps for the first time held by the Marathas. But the British provided all these avenues through which the approach of nation building could be undertaken. They had linked the nation with transport and communication system. They also provided one language *i.e.*, English which could be understood by the educated people all over India. No doubt the British provided a single administration for whole of the country. It may be noted here that though India was divided into British India and Native states of India, but the British India who was *de facto* ruler in the native states was the member of the civil service which controlled the whole country. All these factors contributed towards the development of a national feeling.

The first generation of the educated people as was sought by the advocates of the English language and European sciences, was much praiseworthy of the British. They considered them as the superior race. They regarded the British rule as a providential dispensation for the good of India. They believed that the social reforms over the crying need of the society rather than the political demands. The Indian National Congress which was founded in 1885, also contributed to the tune of thinking.

But the next generation was quite different. It started talking very high of India. They appealed to India's past glory. It was the beginning of nationalism. They refused to accept the British rule as a providential dispensation. They started questions of appalling poverty of the Indian people and held the foreign rule responsible for their misery. They argued that the political freedom was the essential requirement for social advancement. The Swadeshi Movement and founding of Muslim League were the consequences of this ideology.

Mahatma Gandhi belonged to the next generation. His criticism of western science and back to village was praise for Indian system. He talked for revival of cottage industries, village uplift, Harijans uddhar. He gave Indian touch to the nationalist movement in the process of his political agitations. Satyagraha, ahimsa, self-rule etc., had been pronounced by our ancient leaders. These words contained a sentimental attachment and brought the general mass in national current. In this way, the national movement was directly the result of the British rule in India. But the real contribution of this awakening was a battle against those taboos which had developed barbarous trait in the society.

Social Change

All these policies brought about a great social transformation. The missionaries not only spread European education but also forced the government to encourage knowledge of English literature and European sciences. The spread of education exercised fruitful in influences in stimulating the process of social renaissance. It was this renaissance, which caused a wave of reforms first in Bengal and then throughout the country. For women's uplift Raja Ram Mohan Roy with the help of Lord William Bentinck did a lot. He stood for the abolition of sati and advocated remarriage. He founded Brahmo Samaj to create public opinion in favour of these reforms. This task was carried further by the Arya Samaj. This dedicated work created a favourable opinion for female education. The Ramakrishna Mission, the Servants of India Society and the Viswabharati contributed virtually to the cause of female education. As a result of these reforms the outlook of the Indian society almost completely changed and the women especially in the urban centres, attained a respectable status.

Removal of Untouchability

According to 1931 census there were 5,01,92,000 untouchables or "suppressed people". Mahatma Gandhi was the greatest fighter of their causes. Prior to this many social reformers fought for the removal of untouchability. A major section of the society was treated worse than animals. Under these circumstances the leaders began the national movement. A movement against casteism was also started during this period.

During this period the state of transport and communication was bad in India. Many leaders of that time demanded greater facilities for the people. The first Railway line started working in 1858 between Bombay and Thana. Telegraph system, postal system and other means of communications were introduced during this period.

There are the social background to the Indian National Movement.

(i) Emergence of new social classes

As a result of the British policy there emerged in the agrarian sector new social classes. A.R. Desai had enumerated them as under : (i) Zamindars of British creation, (ii) absentee landlords, (iii) tenants of both of these, (iv) peasant proprietors of three grades-upper, middle and lower, (v) agricultural labourers, (vi) new class of merchants and (vii) new class of money lenders. In the urban areas also there emerged :

1. The modern class of capitalists, industrial, commercial and financial.
2. The modern working class engaged in industrial transport, mining and such other enterprises.
3. The class of petty traders and shopkeepers bound up with modern capitalist economy.
4. The professional classes such as technicians, doctors, lawyers, professors, journalists, managers, clerks and others comprising the intelligentia and the educated middle class.

   The industrial, commercial and financial people formed the so called 'bourgeoisie' of modern India. They occupied an important position in the economic and administrative spheres of India. It was this bourgeoisie which financed the nationalist movement since they found their interests were being affected by the privileged position of the British. After Independence, it was this class which reaped the minimum benefits of Independence.

Later on proletariat class emerged. With the emergence of this proletariat there emerged socialistic and community ideologies in Indian society.

Role of thinkers, Writers, Women and Youth

The first Indian in the modern period to call upon his countrymen to wake up to greatness of their spiritual heritage and mould life in the light of the spiritual principles was Raja Ram Mohan Roy. Disirkumar Mitra in his "Resurgent India" says that Mohan Roy stood for a constant quest for unity, freedom and happiness for all. His task was continued by Maharishi Devendranath Tagore and Keshav Chandra Sen.

Bankim Chatterji, the author of the national famous song, 'Bande Mataram' is rightly described as a Rishi by Sri Aurobindo. He was a Rishi in virtue of the great vision of India as the Mother he saw and the message he gave to his countrymen.

There were innumerable persons at that time who regarded India as their motherland and also recognised the desirability of national freedom, as they are at the present.

Ramakrishna awakened his country men to the supreme necessity of reviving the ancient spiritual tradition and also demonstrated the inability of reason to reveal the splendour of God.

Swami Vivekananda had the noble aim of raising the standard of life of the masses in India. He placed before them ennobling motto, "Arise, Awake and stop not till the Goal is reached". His fiery eloquence and inspiring words stirred the mind heart and soul of the nation. They lay at the back of the Indian National Movement much in the same way in which the phrases and ideas of Rousseau and Diderot prepared the soul for the French Revolution. This is the reason why Vivekananda is known as the 'Patriot Monk' as the first true evangel of Indian Nationalism. In the words of Dr. Disirkumar Mitra, Vivekananda laid the spiritual foundation of India resurgent and revolutionary nationalism which inspired and sustained the struggle for freedom by India in 1947 as the fulfilment of his prophecy made in 1897 when the Swami said : "Fifty years hence India shall be free but without bloodshed. There are great future for India after her Independence."

Swami Vivekananda inspired the national and revolutionary movement in Bengal is evident from his speeches. His famous disciple sister Niveditta, had contacts with the Bengal revolutionaries and generally gave them counsel and guidance. Swami Vivekananda though a swami was a great patriot.

Swami Dayanand and the founders of the Theosophical Society did a lot for the people to think and act for national movement. Mrs. Annie Besant proved to be a great thinker and writer to transform the mass for national movement. Mrs. Annie Besant herself helped on the propagations of nationalism in the country through the journals, the weekly *Commonweal* and the daily *New India* which were started in 1914. She advocated the cause of Home Rule of India in these journals with so much fearlessness and courage that the Madras Government took alarm and thought it necessary to intern her and her co-workers in 1917. Her internment stirred up great popular agitation in the country and all the three interned persons were soon released. Her services in the national cause were appropriately recognised by her election as the President of the Congress session in 1917. But her association with the Congress turned out to be short-lived. She did not approve of the method of non-co-operation adopted by the Congress at the suggestion of Gandhiji and, therefore, severed connections which the organisation in 1921.

The Indian National Congress set up by A.O. Hume, in 1885 attracted many thinkers, writers, women and youth. He addressed an open letter to the graduates of the Calcutta University in which he appealed to them to form an association for the moral, social and political regeneration of the Indians. In this letter he tried to impress on them that self-sacrifice and unselfishness are the only unfailing guides to "freedom and happiness." Umesh Chandra Banerjee outlined the objectives of the Congress. The prominent moderate leaders of the Congress were Dadabhai Naoroji, Surendranath Bannerji, Pherozshah Mehta, Gopal Krishna Gokhale. M.G. Ranade and Pandit Madan Mohan Malaviya. They were not only great thinkers and but also great writers of the period (1885 to 1905). They adopted the moderate policies of prayer, petition and persuation *i.e.* they believed in peaceful and constitutional methods. The extremist thinkers and writers like Bal Gangadhar Tilak, Lala Lajpat Rai, B.C. Pal and Aurobindo Ghosh did wonderful service for the cause of National Movement. They showed their discontent against the English for their failure in taking speedy action against a great famine and a bubonic plaque. Bal Gangadhar Tilak also launched a severe attack through his paper 'Kesari' on the role of the government to check the epidemic.

During the Partition of Bengal by Lord Curzan in 1905 the leaders and thinkers vehemently attacked this attitude and launched an agitation. Lord Curzon, who was the Governor-General of India from 1898 to 1905, followed very repressive and arrogant policy towards India. He passed a number of acts like the Official Secrets Act. Calcutta Corporation Act and the Indian Universities Act of 1904. Above all this he Partitioned Bengal in 1905. There by he stimulated the Indian Nationalism.

The terrorists were inspired by a high sense of patriotism and love for motherland and wanted to free it from the foreigners at the earliest. Many youths came to the fold and they tried to create a revolutionary spirit among the people by imparting necessary training to their followers. They formed a number of societies in different parts of the country. Probably strongest revolutionary movement emerged in Bengal where the educated Bengalis turned against the British. The lead was taken by Barinder Kumar Ghosh (brother of Aurobindo Ghosh) and Bhupendranath (brother of Vivekanand).

In Maharashtra, Tilak tried to infuse the young people with a sense of patriotism. He organised Akharas and Lathi clubs to make brave soldiers of the young people. Demodar, Bal Krishan, Syhamji Krishna Varma and V.D. Savarkar did a lot for freedom movement.

In Punjab the revolutionary movement was led by Sardar Ajit Singh, Lal Pindi Das and Lalchand.

The emergence of Mahatma Gandhi on the political scene of India left a deep impact on the course of Indian National Movement. He emphasised the constructive nature of nationalism and aimed to achieve Swaraj through truthful and non-violent methods. It is true that the three major movements launched by him *viz.*, Non-Co-operation Movement (1919-24), the Civil Disobedience Movement (1930-34) as well as the Quit India Movement (1942) attracted the thinkers, writers, women and youth of India during the freedom struggle. On 24 February 1919 Gandhi announced a country wide Satyagraha against the Rowlatt Act. It was a grand success. It virtually brought the whole life to a standstill. Then Gandhiji launched the Non Co-operation Movement. A large number of students left government controlled educational institutions. Complete boycott of foreign cloth was made. Picketing and public bonfires were organised. Efforts were made to popularise Swadeshi by encouraging hand spinning and hand weaving. The British administration decided to deal it with firmness. It resorted to firing and lathi-charges at a number of places and killed a number of volunteers.

During the time of salt satyagraha (12th March 1930) Gandhiji's walk (Dandi March) aroused much enthusiasm among the people. A large number of Indian women took part in public political demonstrations and courted arrest. In the Madras Presidency under the leadership of Rajaji another salt satyagraha was undertaken to Vedaranyam. Many young men and women took part in the march. Thinkers and writers of South, particularly in the Madras Presidency took a leading role in the movement. V.O. Chidambaram, Subramanya Shiva, Bharathiyar, Tiruppur Kumaran, Vanchinathan, Thiru-Vi-Ka, Rajaji, K. Kamaraj and Periyar E.V.R. suffered a lot during the movement.

The next mass movement was Quit India Movement. During this movement almost all the important Congress leaders at various levels were arrested and the movement was virtually rendered leaderless. The people organised a number of strikes, processions and mass meetings against the British Government and demanded freedom of India. They damaged railway stations, cut off telegraph wires and set a number of government buildings on fire.

With the assumption of power by Lord Wavell in 1943 the Government of India made bid to win over the Indian support in the war efforts. In this way the British attitude towards the national movement fluctuated between repression and concessions. Many constitutional changes took place and many commissions and conferences were directed to look into the demands of the Indians. Finally, Indian Independence Act of 1947 was passed to give Independence after the partition of India. Accordingly the partition of India was effected with heavy heart.

Role of Press and Literature

The Indian Press whose birth and development was inevitably connected with the spread of Western education also made a notable contribution to the growth of nationalism in the country. The rapid growth of the newspaper press accelerated the pace of the political awakening among the people. In 1853 Harish Chandra Mukerji in his paper, *Hindu Patriot* published a series of articles about the true relationship between the rulers and the ruled. During this period of National Movement every big leader had his own paper to propagate his views. For example, Raja Ram Mohan Roy and his Bengali weekly, *Samvad Kaumudi* and the *Persian weekly, Mirat-ul-Akhbar, Maharishi Devandranath Tagore's, Tattavbodhini Patrika*, Sri Aurobindo and his own papers, *Jugantra* and *Bande Mataram*; Surendranath Banerji's paper *Bangalee*, Lokamanya Tilak and his papers The *Marahatta* and *The Kesari*, Lala Lajpat Rai's *Bande Mataram*, and *The People*, Pandit Motilal Nehru and his *Independent* Mrs. Annie Besant and her *New India*; and Gandhiji's *Young India*. Maulana Mohammad Ali and Maulana Abul Kalam Azad also had their own papers. Among other papers which rendered yeoman service to the cause of nationalism and fearlessly voiced the grievances of the people and never missed an opportunity of subjecting the measures of the government to criticism, mention may be made of *The Indian Mirror* issued from Calcutta; *Bombay Samachar* and *Indian Prakash* published from Bombay, *The Hindu* of Madras and *The Tribune* from Lahore. Among monthlies, *The Madras Review, The Hindustan Review* and *The Indian Review*, stand out prominent.

These and other papers were crusaders against the foreign domination of the country. It was their mission to educate the people politically help them to assimilate progressive ideas and convey to them the doctrines of the great political thinkers of the West. Topics like liberty, democracy, self-government and nationalism were discussed and examined in their columns. It also exposed the misdeeds of the government. They made the people conscious of their rights and freedom and fearlessly advocated popular causes. The bitterly hostile attitude of some of the Indian papers greatly annoyed the government which sought to restrict the liberty of the press by passing the Vernacular Press Act of 1878.

All the early ventures in journalism in our country were made by the Britishers. The first, paper, called *Bengal Gazette* was started by one J.A. Hickey who was a great advocate of the freedom of the press. His efforts to expose corruptions, nepotism and inefficiency brought upon his head the wrath of the government and he was sent to jail. The editor of another paper was deported to England, and the government issued a rigorous Press Ordinance in March 1823. Raja Ram Mohan Roy started a vigorous agitation against the gagging of the press and a memorial was submitted to the government claiming freedom of the press. This memorial has been described as the 'Aeropagitica' of Indian History. The agitation thus started did not achieve any success; it was, however, the starting point of the method of constitutional agitations for the redress of political wrongs, and had far reaching effects.

In 1835 an act was passed to recognise the freedom of the press. Lord Canning imposed certain restrictions. The same was followed by Lord Lytton. Finally, Lord Ripon repealed those restrictions. During the time of Lord Curzon it faced some more restrictions. In 1908 an Act was passed and it was called the Indian News Papers (incitement to offences) Act of 1908 which disfigured the statue book for a long time. The press enjoyed relative freedom from 1922 to 1931, when the government armed itself with fresh powers to crush the press when Congress launched the Civil Disobedience Movement. In spite of all these difficulties, the press fought for its freedom rigorously and vigorously. The history of the struggle for the freedom of the press is an integral part of national struggle.

Literature

National literature played a prominent part in the National Movement. According to R.C. Majumdar it made the greatest contribution to it in Bengal during the last quarter of the 19th century. Literature produced in India during the first half of the last century was universal; its dominant note was nationalism and classicism. In the second half it became romantic and national. Humanity was more or less replaced by the nation. 'The call of the motherland furnished a new elan de lavie Bengal becomes a reality. India becomes a reality and a living force. Nationalism is established as a religion, as a spiritual entity'. Significant contributions in this field was made in Bengal by Bankim Chandra Chatterji the author of many books including the 'Anandmath' in which the famous national song, 'Bande Mataram' occurs; Michael Madhusudan Datta who is regarded as the father of the modern Bengali poetry; Dinaband Mitra whose 'Nila Darpan' is a scathing satire, the Indigo planters of Bengal; Ranglal Banerji whose 'Meghnath-Kavya' laid the foundation of blank verse in out country. Hemchandra Banerji who was a poet of social self-respect and sensitive patriotism and by Nabin Chandra Sen, and the great poet Rabindranath Tagore. Bharatendu Harischandra performed the same sort of service in Hindi as Subramaniya Bharathi in Tamil and G.H. Deshmukh, Vishnusastri Chiplonkar and S.M. Pranjpe in Marathi literature. Tagore's songs provide the best illustration of the tremendous influence of patriotic literature on the growth of the spirit of nationalism.

Bharatiyar's fiery and famous songs of nationalistic spirit greatly influenced the people of our century during this period. With great spirit and enthusiasm people began to sing his songs every now and then. No wonder his ideas of nationalism tremendously influenced the people.

Similarly the soul stirring poems of Hemachandra Banerji also greatly stimulated the sense of nationalism. The writings of Keshava Chandra Sen also promoted love for national freedom.

The songs of Kaviyarasu Namakkal Ramalingam Pillai too greatly stimulated the sense of nationalism.

(ii) The growth of communalism — its social and cultural base

The Muslims had occupied most of the places of profit, prestige and influence in the Muslim period. The rise of British power gave them a severe set back. The Government followed a policy of relegating them into the background. They were not given good jobs and then the Government generally preferred the Hindus to the Muslims. The Muslims had taken a leading part in the Mutinly of 1857 and the Government, distrusted them. In 1871, out of a total of 2,141 persons employed by the Bengal Government there were 92 Muslims, 711 Hindus and 1,338 Europeans.

A change took place in the attitude of the Government about the year 1870. Sir William Hunter's book, *The Indian Mussalmans* published in 1871 marked the beginning of the change. It was felt that the Muslims had become too weak for rebellion and it would be expedient to take them into alliance rather than continue to antagonise them.

Principal Beck of the Mohammedan Anglo Oriental college, Aligarh, played a very important role in winning over the Muslims. Sir Syed Ahmed Khan, the great leader of the Muslims, had been known for his tolerant views and had described the Hindus and the Muslims as 'two ways of the beautiful bride that was India.' Principal Beck convinced him that Anglo-Muslim alliance would ameliorate the condition of the Muslim community while the nationalist alignment would lead them once again to toil and tears. Under the influence of Beck, he changed his attitude towards the Hindus. The new attitude of Sir Syed Ahmed was based on the fear of permanent educational, economic and political domination of the Muslims by the Hindus. He began to say that all the people did not believe in the policy of the Congress. He laid the foundation of the Annual Muslim Education Conference in 1886 and of Mohammedan Defence Association of Upper India in 1893. Beck organised in 1889 the Muslim opposition to Bradlaugh's Bill in the British Parliament for giving representative institutions to India. The memorial sent on behalf of Indian Muslims stated that the introduction of democratic institutions was not suited to India because she was not one nation.

The Partition of Bengal by Lord Curzon in 1905 was probably another step to please the Muslims. He declared that the province of Bengal was too big to be properly administered by one person. The underlying idea of Lord Curzon was probably to create a Muslim majority province by dividing Bengal and thereby to check the rising felling of nationalism in that province.

Growth of Muslim Communalism Till 1911

Around this time the Government decided to give some more reforms to the Indians. The Muslims feared that the Hindus, being in a majority, would dominate them and they decided to put forward a demand for separate electorates. They decided to send a delegation to Lord Minto, the Viceroy and Governor-General of India. It was really done at the encouragement of the Government of India and Archibald, the Principal of Aligarh College, was made the instrument. The deputation was a communal affair. Colonel Dunlop Smith, Private Secretary to the Governor-General wrote a letter to the Principal suggesting that he should, as if on his own initiative, arrange to send a deputation of eminent Muslims of different provinces. This deputation should profess loyalty and make a request for separate of communal electorates for the

Muslims in the forthcoming reforms. The Muslims deputation headed by Sir Agha Khan met Lord Minto and placed its view point before him. Lord Minto was sympathetic to them and promised to pay due regard to their wishes.

The Muslims League was founded in December 1906 to support, whenever possible, all measures emanating from the Government, to protect and advance the interests of the Muslims in India and to controvert the growing influence of the Indian National Congress. It was an association of loyalist Muslims.

The Governor-General, Lord Minto wrote to Lord Morley, Secretary of State for India, that the Muslim request for separate electorates should be considered. The Secretary of State did not agree at first but Lord Minto told him that the Muslims would not be satisfied with anything short of communal electorates for them. He succeeded in converting the Secretary of State for India to the views. Minto-Morley Reforms of 1909 granted separate electorates to Muslims.

Hindu-Muslim Friendship and Lucknow Pact

The period from 1911 to 1922 was marked by Hindu-Muslim friendship due to several reasons. Firstly, the Muslims began to feel disgusted with the British Government due to the cancellation of the Partition of Bengal in 1911. Secondly, the Balkan wars of 1912-13 were regarded by the Muslims, a Christian conspiracy against the Muslim Turks to turn them out of Europe. In 1916 the Congress and the Muslim League held their annual sessions at Lucknow and signed the Lucknow Pact. Its causes were the following :

(i) The provinces should be free as much as possible from the control of the Central Government in matters of finance and administration.

(ii) Four-fifths of members of the Central and Provincial Legislative Councils should be elected and one-fifth should be nominated.

(iii) The Central and the Provincial Government should be bound to at according to the resolutions passed by their Legislative councils unless vetoed by Governor-General-in-Council.

(iv) The Central Legislative Council should have no power to interfere with the Government of India's conduct of military, foreign and political affairs (*e.g.*, declaration of war making of treaties).

(v) The relations of the Secretary of State for India with the Government of India should be similar to those of the Colonial Secretary with the Government of the Dominions.

The Hindu-Muslim co-operation is clear from the fact that Mahatma Gandhi and Madan Mohan Malaviya attended the sessions of the Muslim League in 1915, 1916 and 1917. The Hindus and Muslims co-operated and Satyagraha was started after the passing of the Rowlatt Act. When the Muslims decided to start agitation for the retention of the office of the Khalifa, Mahatma Gandhi took up the cause of Khilafat Movement and started Non Cooperation Movement. Later on it was called off because of Chauri Chaura incident. It was resented by the Muslims.

Mahatma Gandhi had won over the Muslims to the Non-Cooperation Movement of 1920-22 by incorporating Khilafat movements in it. The Khilafat Committee and Jamaitul-ulema-i-Hind joined the Congress in the movement and the Muslim League was forgotten. But it was a short-lived phenomenon. When Turkey was secularised, the Khilafat Movement was no more required for the Un-Islamic State of Turkey, the Muslims required their vigour of non-violence. India was full of news of communal riots between the Hindus and the Muslims. Mr. Jinnah was now trying to take the leadership of the League into his own hands, but with little success. The Muslim League suffered a split within its ranks on their attitude towards the Simon Commission. Jinnah advocated boycott of the Commission but another section of the League led by Sir Mohammad Shafi wanted co-operation with it. Strangely the two sections of the Muslim League met separately. Jinnah found himself alone. The national leaders of the Muslims, like Hakim Ajmal Khan, Dr. Ansari, Dr. Kitchlew, Maulana Azad, Syed Mohmud and Asaf Ali went against him. Jinnah was too radical to be in this nationalist group, yet too distasteful of the programme of direct action to join the Congress. But luck favoured Jinnah when within a few years, the moderate Muslim leaders like Fazal Hussain, Ajmal Khan, Mohammed Shafi, Ansari and Maulana Mohammed Ali Khan, Mohammed Shafi, Ansari and Maulana Mohammed Ali died. Jinnah returned from England to take up the reins of the League.

General Elections (1937)

On the basis of the Government of India Act of 1935, general elections were held in the provinces in the year 1937, two years after the passage of the Act. In these elections, the Muslim League did not fare well even in the Muslim majority provinces. Mr. Jinnah said, probably because he was in search for power. "There is really no substantial difference now at any rate, between the League and the Congress." He conducted negotiations in favour of coalition government, but the conditions for such government as put forward by the Congress were not acceptable to him. One example of such terms as the Congress wanted was in the United Provinces, where the coalition government, if the League as a functional group, and upon becoming part of the Congress organisation. The Muslim League naturally got "a direct rebuff' as Jinnah saw it. The League became convinced that, "the Muslims, can expect neither justice nor fair-play under Congress Government." To Jinnah, the Congress appeared as a fascist Hindu organisation. The ranks of the League were swelled by the Muslim landlords who feared the Congress agrarian policy of "land to the tillers". The middle class of the Muslim community was inefficient and unable to complete with the middle class of the Hindu society industry, professions and public services. They joined the League with the hope that in case a separate State for Muslims were to be set up, there would be no competition from the Hindus.

Hindu-Muslim Rift

The League found its principles diametrically opposed to those of the Congress. The educational policy of the Congress was professedly based on handicrafts-an essentially Hindu Policy. The Muslims thought it an attack on the very existence of their community. Brailsford in his book "Subject India" gives an account of a Muslim leader within the Congress, who deserted Congress but returned to the victorious Congress for some post in the 1937 government only to be refused bluntly and he argues that events like this swelled the number of anti-Congress Muslim adherents of the League. The principle of the Congress on mass contact was also directed at winning the poor, rulistic Mussalmans. Jinnah found it a means to death of Muslims from their professed leaders and cried 'Islam is in danger'. The League fell upon the expedient of arousing religious sentiments of the Muslims to swell its ranks and capture power. In the absence of any constructive programme it was quite logical for the League to take an attitude later on a demand for Pakistan—a demand which could only enliven the Muslim League.

Report of Raja of Pirpur

The Muslim League could not tolerate the sight of the Congress in power and charged it with tyranny over the Muslim minority. In March, 1938 the League appointed a committee of investigation under the Raja of

Pirpur. True to its spirit the Pirpur Report gave an exaggerated list of sufferings of the Muslims under the Congress regimes, though Coupland testifies that the Congress Ministries did not pursue a policy of communal injustice, still less of deliberate persecution. Yet the Muslim League did never agree to the Congress proposals of referring the charges to an impartial tribunal. When the Congress ministries reigned in 1939 as a protest against the British war policy on India, the League was very much pleased to observe the "Deliverance day". Levelling of charges against the Congress was a technique, not a truth, to influence the Muslims' loyalty towards the League, and Jinnah succeeded. Between 1937 and 1942 the League could capture 47 out of 61 Muslim seats in bye-elections whereas the Congress won only four.

Birth of Two-Nation Theory

It was not until the Allahabad Session of 1930 that the Muslim League knew of a probability of Pakistan. Sir Mohammad Iqbal nursed the idea when he said, first ever so in history, that a North West Indian Muslims State was desirable for the final destiny of the Indian Muslims. Coupland argues that Iqbal stood for a loose federation of all Indian provinces, not a separate Pakistan. But the idea once generated worked miraculously. Some Muslim students at Cambridge caught the infection, with Iqbal's suggestion. In 1933 their leader Rahmat Ali described the Indian Muslims as a separate nation, and advocated a separate Pakistan of the Punjab, Kashmir, Sindh, Baluchistan and N.W.F. Province including an Osmanistan of Hyderabad and another Bangi-Islam of Bengal and Assam. This idea which Sir Zafarulla Khan described in 1933 as chimerical did not improve upto 1938 when Jinnah came forward with a demand for the division of India. In January 1940 he advocated the thesis of Two-Nations on the Indian soil.

The Lahore session of the Muslim League of 1940 was presided over by Jinnah. In his presidential speech on March 22, Jinnah declared in an advisory way that the British Government, for the happiness of the Indians, should allow the major nations separate homelands by dividing India into two autonomous national states. In this division he saw the vision of friendliness between the Muslims and the Hindus. He argued, the Hindus and Muslims belong to two different religious philosophies, social customs, literatures, they neither inter-marry, nor interdine, and Indeed...very often the hero of one is the foe of the other, like-wise, their victories and defeats overlap. A single nation of India would, therefore mean tyranny of the majority Hindus over minority Muslims. Though this thesis was rejected by Dr. Rajendra Prasad in his book "India Undivided" yet his contradiction could not bring the Muslims around.

League Resolution on Pakistan

The Lahore Session of the Muslims League, after the Presidential speech and propaganda, passed the Pakistan resolution on March 23, 1940. This Resolution demanded the creation of a Muslim State out of geographically contiguous regions-both in the "North-Western and the Eastern Zones of India." Pakistan thus formed was to be an independent State under the rule of Muslims themselves. The resolution authorised the working committee of the League to frame a constitution for Pakistan. The Pakistan Resolution, as we have seen, was a great personal triumph of Mohammad Ali Jinnah. He in fact, had taken advantage of the British sympathy with the Muslims during the years of the World War II when the Congress was campaigning for non-cooperation with the Government.

The Viceroy who had encouraged the Muslim factionalism now discovered that the League had grown up to be a power to reckon with. As Mr. Jinnah designed it, the Muslim League henceforward challenged the sole authority of the Congress to speak on behalf of India. Before the Second World War was declared, the greatest danger to the Muslims was the possible inauguation of the federal scheme in the Central Government that had remained so far inoperative under the 1935 Act. So the League was satisfied to hear the Viceroy's statement on October 18, 1939 that the Act of 1935 would be reviewed.

Causes for the Pakistan Demand

The causes that encouraged the Muslims to formulate a demand for a separate State to Pakistan were numerous, among which the following were the important ones :

1. Refusal of the Congress to form coalition Ministries with the Muslim League after 1937 elections. Hence, the League began to accuse the ministries of oppressing the Muslims, particularly the members of the Muslim League.
2. The mass-contact movement that was started by the Indian National Congress to win the village people also led the Muslim League to press the demand for a separate Muslim State. This was because the Muslim League objected to the contact of Muslim messes by the Congress. It took the view that it alone should have the right to contact the Muslim.

3. The Muslim middle classes found themselves unable to compete win the Hindu middle classes. If India was divided and Pakistan was created these middle class Muslim would be able to procure high jobs for themselves, a state of affairs which would be impossible otherwise.
4. The Wardha Scheme of education followed by the Congress also led the League to champion the cause of Pakistan.
5. The members of the Muslim League were convinced that in case Pakistan was created their idea of Pan-Islamism would be accomplished.
6. Religious hatred of the Hindus was another factor which gave a fillip to the demand for Pakistan. The Hindus did not like to mix up with the Muslims as they thought the Muslims to be melechas. The air of superiority which was taken by the Hindus was naturally not liked by the Muslims.
7. The Hindu Mahasabha was preaching the gospel of Hindu Rashtra. Muslims felt insulted. Besides, the utterances of Hindu Mahasabha leaders also irritated the Muslims. Vinayak Damodar Savarkar openly advocated that the Hindus and the Muslims were fundamentally different and branded the Congress as an anti-Hindu and pro-Muslim organisation.
8. The influence of Sudetan Germans in Czechoslovakia for their self-determination, also encouraged the Muslims to demand Pakistan. The Student Movement had succeeded and the Muslims thought they would also succeed.
9. Encouragement of British officials to the Muslim leaders was also responsible for emboldening the Muslims. The British bureaucracy had encouraged the Muslims to demand Pakistan. The Cripps proposals of 1942 indirectly recognised the League's claim for Pakistan.

Proposals of Sir Stafford Cripps

In a way the Cripps Proposals of March, 1942 recognised the claim of the Muslim League for Pakistan. The "right of any province of British India that is not prepared to accept the new Constitution to retain its present position, provision being made for its accession if it so decides" was a right intended for the recalcitrant Muslim majority provinces. "With such non-accepting provinces should they so desire, His Majesty's Government would be prepared to agree upon a new Constitution, giving them the same full status as the Indian Union." It was natural for the unity conscuous National Congress to ridicule the Cripps Proposals as "a severe blow to the conception of Indian unity". To accept the rith of non-accession of a province, prior to the framing of a constitution would be to provide a veritable apple of discord likely to generate trouble in the provinces which may well lead to further difficulties in the way of the Indian States marging themselves in the Indian Union.

However, Mohammad Ali Jinnah could not be satisfied with a mere hint at the idea of Pakistan, and he charged the proposals of Cripps as being nebulous. On April 8, 1942 at its Allahabad session of the All India Muslim League, Mr. Jinnah declared, "The alleged power of the minority in the matter of succession suggested in the document is illusory, as Hindu India will dominate the decision in favour of one All-India Union in all the provinces and the Muslims in Bengal and the Punjab will be at the mercy of Hindu minority in those provinces, who will exert themselves to the fullest extent and length for keeping the Mussalman tied to the chariot-wheel of Hindustan."

Nevertheless the Muslim League showed some satisfaction at its working committee and resolved on April 12, 1942 that "the committee, while expressing their gratification that the possibility of Pakistan is recognised but implication by providing for the establishment of two or more independent Unions in India, regret that the proposal of His Majesty's Government, embodying the fundamentals, are not open to any modification and, therefore, no alternative proposals are invited." The Cripps proposals thus whetted the appetite of the Muslim League for an ever increasing demand for Pakistan. The League took the vow that any theme which seeks to torpedo the Pakistan demand of Muslim India will be resisted by the Muslim League and as such any political party which stands for the establishment of a democratic State in India can have no agreement with the "Muslim League". The Cripps proposals, Dr. Shyama Prasad Mukherji saw it, would made India a field of warring provinces and "interested foreign nations may find ample scope for fateful intrigues and dissensions."

Results of Cripps Proposals

The effect of Cripps Proposals on the Indian political scene is beautifully summed up by Sir Bijey Prasad Singh Roy. He says in his book entitled *The Muslim League*, the Cripps Mission led to :

1. The stiffening of the attitude of Mahatma Gandhi and the Congress;

2. The insistence of the demand by Mr. Jinnah and the Muslim League for Pakistan;
3. Dissociation of Mr. C. Rajagopalachari from the Congress with a number of his disciples in Madras;
4. The growth of a sense of frustration in the non-Congress political parties.

At least for the time being the Cripps proposals so encouraged the League as to form the strongest opposition to the Congress. In Cripps proposals, therefore, lay the germs of strained relations between the two communities of India. The years that followed saw a number of schemes in favour of the formation of Pakistan; mainly they were four, namely, (1) Dr. Latif's Scheme; (2) The Aligarh Scheme; (3) The C.R. Formula and (4) The Mountbatten plan, which ultimately partitioned India in 1947. Now we shall consider them one by one.

1. Dr. Latif's Scheme

The essence of Dr. Latif's Scheme was the assumption that India was a mosaic of different cultures and it was possible to divide India into cultural units. Dr. Latif devided his plan of a confederation of all the cultural zones of India federating together. He advocated transfer of populations on a large scale in order to foster homogeneity in the designated cultural zones. The Muslims of U.P. and Bihar were to resettle in "a block extending in line from the Eastern border of Patiala to Lucknow, rounding up Rampur on the way"—the block to be named "Delhi Lucknow State." There were, he said, twelve million Muslims "below the Vindhyas and Satpuras." For them a zone was to be carved out of the Dominion of Hyderabad and Berar. He gave vent to the idea of "the communal school of thought among the Muslims" who preferred to get a corridor to the Western Coast that is, through Bijapur. This was essential, Dr. Latif argued to settle, large Muslim mercantile and marine community living for ages on the "Coromondel and Malabar Coasts". Dr. Latif did not forget to have Calcutta port for the Muslims, but he seemed to lack logical sense, when he included Madras port in the Muslim zone.

2. Aligarh Scheme

Professor Zafrul Hassan of Aligarh University and Mohammed Afzal Hassan Qadri gave out a scheme in which Berar and Carnatic were to be restored to Hyderabad, and every Indian town with over fifty thousand population would have the status of a brought with large autonomy. In case there was a partition of India, the Muslims would be recognised as a separate nation with the two-nation theory had laid its roots deep in the minds of the confronting each other in every province, every town, every village. When Edward Thompson is reported to have remarked.

That is a very terrible solution, Mr. Jinnah", he got the reply, "But it is the only one."

3. C.R. Formula

In the background of such fanatical demands of the Muslim League Mr. Chakraverty Rajgopalachariar devised a formula for partition of India with the consent of Mahatma Gandhi. This scheme of 1944 conceded the demand of Pakistan. But the Muslim League was to support the Congress demand for Independence. During the transitional period the League would co-operate with the Congress in forming an Interim Government. After the war an independent commission was to be set up for demarcating the boundaries in the disputed North-West and North-West India to separate the Muslim majority areas from those of Hindus. A plebiscite in each region thus effected would be decisive for the region's incorporation in Pakistan. The League and the Congress were to agree on common defence, communications etc. prior to partition. In any case the C.R. Formula was to be implemented in the event the British left India. Mr. M.A. Jinnah who had earlier consented to the Formula condemned the offer as a "maimed mutilated and moth-eaten Pakistan". His Pakistan was to consist of six provinces of Sind, the Punjab, the North-West Frontier Province, Baluchistan, Bengal and Assam with necessary adjustments in the territories, but also with exclusion of non-Muslim inhabitants from the Muslim majority areas.

4. Mountbatten Plan-Cabinet Mission

The general elections were held following the end of hostilities of the World War II and in the provincial legislatures the League captured 446 out of a total 495 Muslim seats. The background was the Attlee statement of 1946 that while India would have the right of self-determination, "a minority would not be allowed to veto the progress of the Majority." Under Attlee's announcement the Cabinet Mission was sent to India in March 1946. The three member Commission produced report on March, 16, 1946, but the Plan that they gave for the solution of Indian political deadlock embodied a plea for the rejection of the demand for Pakistan. Pakistan, they argued, would not solve even the communal problem. The Cabinet Mission plan proposed a Federal Union of India with a scheme for grouping of Indian provinces into three Groups, the Groups B and C consisting of Muslim majority provinces of the North-

East India respectively. The National Congress wanted the grouping to be a voluntary affair for every province, but the Muslim League demanded it to be compulsorily imposed on the relevent provinces, so that there would be no scope for the Nationalist Muslim leaders to play into the hands of the National Congress. To avoid a deadlock on the interpretation of the Grouping clause the British Government supplied and imposed its own interpretation on December 6, 1946.

Interim Government

The formation of the Interim Government was also a veritable tangle which the Cabinet Mission could not foresee. Lord Wavell had invited on June 18, 1946 the political parties of India to form the provisional government in the ratio of six representatives for the Congress, five to the Muslim League and three to the minorities. The Congress claim to include a nationalist Muslim in its quota of was rejected. The Muslim League even demanded its right to form the provisional government with non-congress elements, but Mr. Jinnah could not succeed. Disillusioned, he attacked the British Government for its bad faith on the Muslims, and the League rejected the Cabinet Mission plan on July 29, 1946, but resolved that the Muslims would resort to Direct Action "to achieve Pakistan and to get rid of (both) the present slavery under the British and the contemplated future of Hindu domination."

On August 6, 1946 Lord Wavell could not but invite the Congress to form the interim Government. Ten days later the Muslim League was to start Direct Action, the day being declared a public holiday by the Muslim League Ministry of Bengal. The 16th August was a day of bloodshed in Calcutta and Sylhot. Noakhali and Tipperab bore testimony to the Muslim creed of violence and butchery and compulsory conversion to Islam. But the Muslim League could not give up the idea of having loaves and fishes and moreover to wreck the Congress "Caretaker" Government. The anxious League was allowed to participate in the Provisional Government in which they were allowed five representatives. The League members thereon worked in a spirit of sabotaging the Congress Government and bringing the Indian administration to a standstill.

Constituent Assembly

The plan of the Cabinet Mission on Constitution-making was going to materialise. The Constituent Assembly held its first meeting on December 9, 1946. The League denounced it as "ultra vires, invalid and illegal". Communal riots became the order of the day and the Muslim fanatics took the initiative in the butchery. The Muslim League's threatening attitude added fuel to the fire of lawlessness already obtaining in the country.

Attlee's Declaration on Independence

Mr. Clement Attlee found in intolerable to have a British Raj in India and he declared on February 20, 1947 to transfer the power to the Indians by a date not later that June 1948. But the declaration added a sinister note. The British Government "would have to consider to whom the powers of the Central Government in British India should be handed over on the due dates, whether as a whole to some form of Central Government for British India or in some areas to the existing Provincial Government or in some such other way as many seem most reasonable and in the best interest of the Indian people." This meant what the Muslim League wanted for "the happiness of the Indian."

June 3, Plan

And Lord Mountbatten, who became the new Governor-General only for the task of transferring power to the Indians, gave out his plan of June 3, 1947. The Mountbatten Plan provided for the establishment of two separate dominions of India and Pakistan, besides, the full share of the Muslim majority provinces. Pakistan would have a partition of Bengal and the Punjab. The Indian Independence Act was passed by the British Parliament and the British Government was to withdraw from the Indian soil on August 15, 1947. On August 14, Mr. M.A. Jinnah was declared to have been appointed the Governor-General of Pakistan and the world added one more new State to its list of States. Thus, Pakistan became a political reality.

Other Communal Organisations

Though the Muslim League was the first communal body organised with the object of safe guarding the political rights of a particular religious community, it was not only one of its kind in India. The Hindus, the Sikhs, the Christians and the Untouchables set up communal organisations of their own in course of time for similar purposes. India became a land of communal organisations. The differences between them were utilised by the British Government for its own purpose. A few words may be added about some of them.

1. The Hindu Mahasabha

It is the chief communal organisation of the Hindus. It was first set up in 1915 with the object of uniting the Hindus of India on a common platform for the protection and promotion of their interests and culture, but it was not before 1923 that it caught the imagination of the Hindus. Several factors contribute to its gathering strength. In the first place, it was realised that the proselytising activities of the Muslims and Christians were having a highly adverse effect on the political power of the Hindus; some steps had to be taken to counteract them. In the second place, the Hindus generally came out as the second best in the communal riots which broke out with greater frequency after the suspension of the non-violent non-cooperation movement in 1922. They suffered more losses in property and human lives than the other communities. It became necessary to organise the Hindus for self-defence. Shuddhhi and Sangathan thus became the watchwords of the Mahasabha in the early years of its life. Thirdly, the Muslim League was putting forth more and more aggressive demands and they were receiving the support of the British authorities. The Indian National Congress could not take up a strong attitude against such demands. The Hindus were thus driven to organise themselves. This is the reason why nationalists like Madan Mohan Malaviya and Lajpat Rai supported the Mahasabha. The strong and uncompromising attitude adopted by the Mahasabha towards the notorius Communal Award as compared to the neutral attitude of the Congress illustrates this aspect of the Mahasabha activities.

The Mahasabha did not achieve any success in its objectives, and for several reasons it never obtained the same backing of the Hindu masses as the League did of the Muslims. It had a great and powerful rival in the National Congress whose policies and programmes made greater appeal to the masses. The British Government also never patronised it. It, therefore, never acquired any political importance.

The advent of Mr. V.D. Savarkar wrought a great change in the character of the Mahasabha; it developed a political programme and began to give a lead to the Hindus on political questions. He came at a time when the Hindus were beginning to fell dimly that the Congress wanted to placate the League and there by might put the rights of the Hindus in jeopardy. Shri Savarkar used all his talents to impress upon the Hindus the dangerous consequences of this policy on their future. He preached the doctrine of Hindu ascendancy and asserted that the politics of India must be fashioned and tested in Hindu terms. He told the Muslims that they must be content with the status of a minority community in a democratic state which orders its life on the principle of majority rule. It would thus appear that the Mahasabha became as aggressively communal as the Muslim League. After the retirement of

Shri Savarkar. Dr. S.P. Mookerjee became its leader and gave it a more nationalist outlook.

The Mahasabha is opposed to the Congress ideal of India being a secular state, and stands for a Hindu Rashtra. Its aim is the 'maintenance, protection and promotion of the Hindu race, Hindu culture and Hindu civilization, and the advancement of the glory of the Hindu Reshtra.' Against the League demand for Pakistan it set up the solgan of Akhand Hindustan. As a protest against the Congress acceptance of the scheme of partitioning the country, the Hindu Mahasabha refused to participate in the Independence Day Celebrations on August 15, 1947. It started direct action against the policy of the Congress Government in U.P. which, however, turned out to be a dismal failure. The Government of India put a ban on this organisation as it was suspected of having a hand in the assasination of Mahatma Gandhi. But the ban was removed after some time.

In so far as it wants to make India a Hindu Rashtra and rejects the ideal of secular state, it is definitely out of tune with the spirit of the times. Though it talks of Hindu culture and highest in Hindu culture namely tolerance and forbearance.

2. Rashtriya Swayam Sevak Sangh [RSS]

A few words may be added about another Hindu communal organisation, allied to the Hindu Mahasabha but having no official connection with it. This is known as the Rashtiya Swayam Sevak Sangh. It claims to be surely cultural movement aiming at the revitalisation of the Hindu race and making it strong. It enrolls members at a comparatively early age and seeks to inculcate in them a definite ideology and outlook. Like the Mahasabha, it believes in Akhand Hindustan and stands for the establishment of a Hindu Rashtra in India. It thus rejects the conception of a secular India. Like the Mahasabha again, it was suspected of complicity in the conspiracy to kill Gandhiji, and the Government banned it. Its chief was arrested. The ban was removed after some time but restrictions were imposed upon some of its activities which had for their aim the establishment of a semi-military organisation.

The Sangh has done good work in inculcating the spirit of cohesion, social service, and discipline among its members; but it has produced a narrow and communal outlook in them. From this point of view, it is a retrograde movement. What the motherland needs is citizens with a broad vision and generous minds. Little minds and big states are incompatible.

3. Minority Communities

Minority Communities like the Sikhs, Anglo-Indians, Europeans and the Depressed Classes had their respective organisations. Each of them was anxious to get as large a share in political power under the reformed constitution as possible. The Sikhs demanded weightage in the Punjab and in the Centre similar to what was conceded to the Muslims under the Lucknow Pact. Anglo-Indians and Europeans made similar demands. The depressed Classes under the leadership of Dr. Ambedkar wanted separate electorates. Their demands could not always be harmonised. The Muslim demand for a majority in the Punjab and Bengal could not be reconciled with the Sikh demand for weightage in the Punjab, and with the European and Anglo-Indian demand for special representation in Bengal, and justice to the Hindus. Thus, arose the communal problem which proved a stumbling block during the second session of the R.T.C. and made all progress in the work of the Federal Structure Committee impossible. Mahatma Gandhi tried his best to solve it but failed. In the end the British Prime Minister was asked to give his award. The distribution of seats between the various communities and interests in the central and provincial legislatures for purposes of the Act of 1935 was determined by this Award as modified by the Poona Pact between the Caste Hindus and the Depressed Classes. It was published on the 15th of August, 1932. It is not necessary to go into its provisions.

The Abolition of Communal Representation

So long as British rule lasted in out country, communal electorates and the spirit of communalism generated by the system continued to flourish. It was with the help of the system of communal representation first introduced and applied to the Muslims only in 1909, and extended to other communities by the Acts of the 1919 and 1935, that the foreign government tried to balance and counterpoise one community against the other with a view to its own stability. Free and independent India did not stand in need of it. The New Constitution framed by the Constituent Assembly has abolished it root and branch. Seats have been reserved only for the Scheduled Classes for a limited period; common electorates have been introduced for all classes of citizens. But unfortunately the communal spirit has not been exercised; it still haunts us in a new form.

10

March of Free India

(i) Social change since Independence through constitutional safeguards

The Constitution of India provides for equality of status and the principle of social, economic and political justice to all citizens irrespective of caste, creed, sex, etc., in fact, this is put as an Article in the fundamental rights which were justifiable. Untouchability was abolished by Article 17 and Article 14 asserts that no child below 14 is to be employed in any factory. The Directive Principles of State Policy have provided for legislation on various social matters. Thus, after 1950, it has been the policy of the government to bring legislation in line with the fundamental rights enumerated in the constitution. As a consequence of this there has been considerable social legislations since Independence.

The Hindu Marriage Act of 1955 abolished all caste restrictions as a necessary requirement for a valid marriage. Thus, for the first time the Hindus of all castes have the same rights with respect to marriage; inter caste marriages are now valid.

Secondly, by not prescribing any specific form of ceremony for the solemnization of a marriage, this Act, while giving authority to the various customs, prevailing in various groups also provides for a secular outlook with respect to marriage and enables the registration of Marriage.

Thirdly, this Act enforces monogamy and this brings an equality between the two sexes. It also provides for judicial separation and divorce or dissolution of marriage so that the rights of men and women are the same.

Finally, this Act defines the term "Hindu" in the widest possible manner to include the ancient protestant groups like the Buddhists, the

Jains, the medieval protestant groups like Brahma Samajists and Arya Samajists; it also includes the Harijans (the Scheduled Castes) and the Girijans (the Scheduled Tribes). Thus, for the first time, all these various groups are treated as Hindus. It only remains for the next step to be taken according to Article 44 of the Directive Principles of State Policy, which enjoins the state to secure for all citizens uniform civil code so that the people of other creeds like the Parsis, Muslims, Christians, Jews and others could also come into operation of one secular marriage Act.

The Hindu Succession Act of 1956 confers for the first time absolute rights over the property possessed by a Hindu women. Secondly, both the sons and daughters get the right of inheritance from the property of an intestate Hindu. Thus, this act overcomes the prejudice against women getting the property of the father.

The Hindu Adoption and Maintenance Act, 1956, is also a significant departure regarding the status of woman. It permits the adoption or a son or a daughter and makes adoption more a secular act than a religious one. Further, it makes the consent of the wife necessary. Finally the widow has got the right to adopt.

Since a long time, many states had passed legislation against dowry. The government passed the Dowry Prohibition Act, 1961, making the giver as well as receiver of the dowry punishable. But this is another piece of social legislation which is absolutely ineffectives; One sees hardly any change in the situation as a consequence of this Act. The social norm, in other words, has not been affected by the law, and the society follows the social norm rather than legal not in this field.

Another very significant Act is Untouchability (Offences) Act, 1955. This is in accordance with the Article 17 of the Constitution and it replaces all the state laws in this regard which were passed earlier. This Act holds throughout the country. Offences against this Act are cognizable and compoundable. But as one has seen earlier, the status of the Harijans in the villages has hardly improved because the upper castes continue to practise untouchability.

Even with respect to labour laws there has been marked changes since independence because of the enunciation of the directive principles in the Constitution. The Factories Act of 1948 passed after independence, raises the minimum age of workers to 14 and made provision for annual medical examinations of the workers between 14 and 18. The Motor Transport Workers Act of 1961 provides for eight hours of work per day and 48 hours per week.

The Employment Exchange Act of 1959 provides for registration of the unemployed people and for training programmes. Thus, the state has taken upon itself the responsibility of helping the unemployed individuals to get jobs, but with the increase of the population, this Act is also of hardly any significance. Each five year plan sees a larger backlog of the unemployed people.

The above survey of social legislations in India after Independence clearly indicates the rapid change in the society.

(ii) Strategy for the development of S.C., S.T., B.C., & Minorities

The scheduled castes and scheduled tribes have been specified by 15 Presidential orders issued under the provisions of Article 341 and 342 of the Constitution. According to the 1981 census, about 23.51 per cent of the country's population comprised the scheduled castes and the scheduled tribes. In addition, some state governments have also specified order categories of people known as the "other backward classes" and denotified nomadic and semi-nomadic communities.

While the Constitution has prescribed protective measures and safeguards for these classes, the successive five year plans have rewarded the progress as a major objective of national policy.

I. Constitutional Safe-Guards

The Constitution prescribed safeguards for the scheduled castes and scheduled tribes and other weaker sections either specially or by way of insisting on their general rights as citizens with the object of promoting their educational and economic interests and of removing the social disabilities.

The main safe-guards are :

1. The abolition of 'untouchability' and forbidding of its practice any form (Art. 17);
2. The promotion of their educational and economic interest and their protection from social injustice and all forms of exploitation (Art. 46);
3. The throwing open by law of Hindu religious institutions of a public character to all classes and sections of Hindus (Art. 25b);
4. The removal of any disability, liability, restriction or condition with regard to access to shops, public restaurants, hotels and places of public entertainment of the use of wells, tanks, baying ghats, roads and places of public resort maintained wholly or

partially out of state funds of dedicated to the use of the general public [Art. 15(2)];

5. The curtailment by law in the interest of any scheduled tribe, of the general rights of all citizens to move freely, settle in, and acquire property [Art. 19(5)];
6. The forbidding or any denial of admission to educational institutions maintained by the state or receiving aid of state funds [Art. 29(2)];
7. Permitting the state make reservation for the backward classes in public services in case of inadequate representations and requiring the state to consider the claim of the scheduled castes and scheduled tribes in making appointments to public services (Arts. 16 and 335);
8. Special representation in the Lok Sabha and the state Vidhan Sabhas to scheduled castes and scheduled tribes till 25 January 1990 (Arts. 330, 332, and 334);
9. The setting up of tribes advisory councils and separate departments in the states and the appointments of special officers at the centre to promote their welfare and safeguard their interests. (Arts. 164 and 338 and Fifth Schedule);
10. Special provision for the administration and control of scheduled and tribal areas (Art. 241 and Fifth and Sixth Schedules, and
11. Prohibition of traffic in human being and forced labour (Art. 23).

II. Legislation against Untouchability

For enlarging the scope and making the penal provisions more stringent, the Untouchability (Offences) Act, 1955 had been comprehensively amended by the Untouchability (Offences) Amendment and Miscellaneous Provisions Act, 1976, which came into force from 19th November 1976. With this amendment, the name of the principal Act provides penalties for preventing a person, on the ground of untouchability from enjoying the rights accruing out of abolition of untouchability. Enhanced penalties/ punishment have also been provided for subsequent offences.

Under the provision of Section 8 of the Representation of the People Act, 1951, a person who is convicted of an offence under the Act is disqualified from contesting elections to Parliament and state legislatures for a period of six years commencing from the date of such conviction.

The Protection of Civil Rights Act, 1955, is administered by the state governments also from time to time. Under a provision in the Act, the Government also lays, every year, before each of House of Parliament annual report on the working of the Provisions of Section 15 A of the Act.

III. Protection of Civil Rights Act

In pursuance of the Provisions made under Section 15 A of the Protection of Civil Rights Act, central assistance is given to the state governments and union territories. Provisions for legal aid to the scheduled caste victims of Protection of Civil Rights cases have been made by 18 states. Special cells/squads have been created by 17 states for initiating and exercising supervision over prosecution for contravention of the provisions of the PCR Act. By December 1982, 18 states had set up committees at various levels to make periodical review of the problems of untouchability and cases related to it and suggest various measures for the effective implementation of the PCR Act. Necessary guidelines and instructions are issued to states from time to time for effective implementation of the provisions of PCR Act. Matching central assistance is provided to the states under the centrally sponsored scheme for implementation of PCR Act. Liberation of scavengers by conversion of existing dry-latrines has also been taken up under the centrally sponsored scheme of implementation of PCR Act. Ten states have so far been assisted under the scheme for selected towns on whole town approach with the conditions for providing alternative employment to the liberated scavengers. In Bihar, the towns of Biharshrif, Purnia, Saharsa and Deoghar with state funds have been scavenging free and the dry-latrines in these towns have been converted into waterborne. The work in selected towns of other states is in progress.

IV. Representation in Legislatures

Under Articles 330 and 332 of the Constitution, seats are reserved for scheduled castes and scheduled tribes in the Lok Sabha and state Vidhan Sabhas in proportion to their population. This concession was initially for a period of 10 years from the commencement of the constitution but has been extended, through amendments upto 25 January 1990. Parliamentary Acts provide for such reservation in the union territories having legislatures. There is no reservations in the union territories having legislatures. There is no reservation of seats on Rajya Sabha and state Vidhan Parishads. A Table gives details of their representation in the Lok Sabha and state Vidhan Sabhas.

Following the introduction of panchayati raj, safeguards have been provided for proper representation of the members of the scheduled castes and tribes by reserving seats for them in the gram panchayats and other local bodies.

V. Reservation in Services

Article 335 of the Constitution Provides that the claims of the members of scheduled castes and scheduled tribes shall be taken into consideration, consistent with the maintenance of efficiency of administration, in making appointments to posts and services, in connection with the affairs of the union or of a state. Article 16 (4) permits reservation in favour of citizens of backyard classes, who may not be adequately represented in service. In pursuance of these provisions, the Government has made reservations for scheduled castes and scheduled tribes in the services under their control.

TABLE 1 : Reservation of Seats in Legislatures

	LOK SABHA			VIDHAN SABHA		
State/Union Territory	Total No. of Seats	Seats Reserved for SC's	Seats Reserved for ST's.	Total No. of Seats	Seats Reserved for SC's.	Seats Reserved for ST's.
A.P.	42	6	2	294	39	15
Assam	14	1	2	126	8	6
Bihar	54	8	5	324	48	28
Gujarat	26	2	4	182	13	26
Haryana	10	2	-	90	17	-
HP.	4	1	-	68	16	3
J&K	6	-	-	76	6	-
Karnataka	28	4	-	224	33	2
Kerala	20	2	-	140	13	1
M.P.	40	6	9	320	44	75
Maharashtra	48	3	4	288	18	22
Manipur	2	-	1	60	1	19
Meghalaya	2	-	-	60	-	-
Nagaland	1	-	-	60	-	-
Orissa	21	3	5	147	22	34
Punjab	13	3	-	117	27	-
Rajasthan	25	4	3	200	33	24

Sikkim	1	-	-	32	2	4
Tamilnadu	39	7	-	234	42	3
Tripura	2	-	1	60	7	17
U.P.	85	18	-	425	92	1
West Bengal	42	8	2	294	57	17
Anda. & Nico.	1	-	-	-	-	-
Arunachal Pradesh	2	-	-	30	-	-
Chandigarh	1	-	-	-	-	-
Dadra N. Haveli	1	-	1	-	-	-
Delhi	7	1	-	56	-	-
Goa, Daman & Dieu	2	-	-	30	-	-
Lakshwadeep	1	-	1	-	-	-
Mizoram	1	-	-	30	-	-
Pondicherry	1	-	-	30	5	-
	542	79	40	3997	557	295

Notes :

1. Four seats are reserved for two autonomous districts. (North Cachar Hills and Mikir Hills).
2. Excluding 24 seats in the territory held by Pakistan.
3. No reservation has been made.
4. Reserved for Sikkimese of Bhutia-Lepcha origin.
5. Metropolitan Council.
6. Includes 22 seats reserved for Sikkimese of Bhutia Lepcha origin.

For the scheduled castes, reservation is 15 per cent of the vacancies or which recruitment is made by open competition on all India basis and 16-2/3 per cent of the vacancies to which recruitment is made on all India basis otherwise than by open competition. For the scheduled tribes, the reservation is 7.5 per cent in both cases, Reservation in direct recruitment to Group C and D posts, which normally attract candidates from a locality or region, is fixed in proportion to the population of the scheduled castes and tribes in the respective states and union territories.

Reservation is also made at 15 per cent of the vacancies for the scheduled castes and 7.5 per cent for the scheduled tribes in promotions on the result of the competitive examinational limited to departmental candidates in Group B, C, and D in promotion by selection in Group B,

C, and D and the lowest rung of Group A in grades or services to which direct recruitment, if any, does not exceed 66-2/3 per cent Reservation has been provided for scheduled castes and scheduled tribes in promotion on the basis of seniority subject to fitness in Group A, B, and D posts in grades or services to which direct recruitment, if any, does not exceed 66-2/3 per cent.

In promotions, by selection within Group to posts carrying an ultimate salary of Rs. 2,250 per month or less, the scheduled castes and tribes officers, who are senior enough in the Zone of consideration for promotion and are within the number of vacancies for which the select list has to be drawn, are included in that list provided they are not considered unfit for promotion.

To facilitate their adequate representation, concessions such as (1) relaxation of age limit; (2) relaxation in the standard of suitability; (3) selection, provided they are not found unfit for the posts; (4) relaxation of the qualification regarding experience in the case of direct recruitment only wherever necessary and (5) inclusion of scientific and technical posts up to the lowest grade of for research, in the scheme of reservation, have been provided for. Simultaneously, with notification to employment exchanges or advertisements in new papers, vacancies reserved for scheduled castes and scheduled tribes in Group C and D posts are announced over the stations of All India Radio located in areas having concentration of scheduled castes and scheduled tribes population, notified to the voluntary associations of scheduled casted and scheduled tribes enlisted for this purpose and to the Directors of SC/ST Welfare of the States and union territories. The scheme of reservations is all being followed by the public sector undertakings. The voluntary agencies, which are in receipt of substantial grants in aid from the Government, are also required, as a condition, to adopt certain specific features of the reservation scheme in their establishments.

To give effect to the reservations, model rosters of 40 points each have been prescribed for direct recruitment by open competition on all India basis and otherwise than open competition and promotions and 100 point roster for recruitment made on local and regional basis. If the vacancies in a service or cadre are too few for the purpose, all isolated posts are grouped together in direct recruitment. Annual statements are required to be submitted by the recruiting authorities for scrutiny by the Government. For ensuring implementation of the special representation orders, Liaison officers have been appointed in different ministries of the Union Government.

State governments have also framed rules under the power given to them by item 41 of the state list of the Seventh Schedule to the Constitution for the reservation of posts for these classes and taken steps to increase their representation in the state services. Reservation in state government services, however, is under the exclusive jurisdiction of the state governments.

The representation of Scheduled Castes and Scheduled Tribes in Central Government sendees as on 1 January 1982 in table.

TABLE 2 : S.C./S.T. Representation in Central Governments

Groups (Class)	Total No. of Employees	Scheduled Castes	Percentage of Scheduled Castes to Total	Scheduled Tribes	Percentage of Scheduled Castes to Total
A (Class I)	54,265	2980	5.49	633	1.17
B (Class II)	65,221	5,970	9.02	947	1.43
C (Class III)	19,02,805	2,55,730	13.39	66,238	3.47
D (Class IV) **(including)**	10,94,569	56,261	23.41	81,496	7.45
Total	31,24,860	5,20,941	16.67	1,49,354	4.78
IAS	4,138	417	10.01	224	5.4
IPS	2,184	219	10.02	77	3.52

All India services (As on January 1982)

Administration of Scheduled and Tribal areas

Some areas have been scheduled in Andhra Pradesh, Bihar, Gujarat, Himachal Pradesh, Madhya Pradesh, Maharashtra. Orissa and Rajasthan under Article 244 and the Fifth schedule to the Constitution. Governors of the respective states submit a report annually to the President on the administration of the scheduled areas in their states.

The tribal areas in Assam, Meghalaya and Mizoram are administered subject to the provisions of the Sixth Schedule to the Constitution. Under the schedule, they are divided into automous districts : There are eight such districts, namely, North Cachar Hills and Hikir Hills districts in Assam, United Khasi Jantia Hills, Jowai and Garo Hills districts in Meghalaya and Chakma, Lakher and Pawi districts in Mizoram. Each autonomous district has a district council consisting of not more than 30 members of whom not more that four can be nominated and the rest to be elected on the basis of adult suffrage. The councils are vested with certain administrative, legislative and judicial powers.

Welfare and Advisory Agencies

The Ministry of Home Affairs is the nodal Ministry for overall policy, planning and co-ordination of programmes of development for scheduled casted and scheduled tribes. Each central ministry and department is the noddle ministry or department concerning its sector. The Ministry of Home Affairs maintains liason with state governments and central ministries.

A commission for the scheduled casted and scheduled tribed consisting of a chairman and four members including the special officer appointed under Article 338 of the constitution known as the Commissioner for Scheduled Castes and Scheduled Tribes, was set up to constitutional safeguards, reservation in public services, to study the implementation of the Protection of Civil Rights Act, 1955, with particular reference to the objective of removal of untouchability and invicious discrimination arising thereform, and to ascertain the socio-economic and other relevant circumstances responsible for the commission of offences against persons belonging to scheduled castes and tribes with a view to recommend appropriate remedial measures.

Parliamentary Committee

Government had set up three parliamentary committees, the first in 1968, the second in 1971 and the third in 1975, to examine the implementation of the constitutional safeguards for the welfare of the scheduled castes and scheduled tribes. The committee has since been constituted as a standing committee of parliament, the tenure of the members being one year.

Welfare Department in States

The state governments and union on territory administrations have separate departments to look after the welfare of the scheduled castes and scheduled tribes and other backward classes. The administrative set up varies from state to state. In Bihar, Madhya Pradesh and Orissa separate ministers have been appointed to look after tribal welfare as prescribed in Article 164 of the constitution. Some other states have set up committees of members of state legislatures on the pattern of the parliamentary committee at the centre.

All the states having scheduled areas as also Tamil Nadu and West Bengal have constituted tribes advisory councils as per provisions in the

Fifth Schedule to the Constitution to advise on such matters pertaining to the welfare advancement of the scheduled tribes in the states.

Voluntary Organisations

A number of voluntary organisations also promote the welfare of the scheduled castes and scheduled tribes. Important organisations of all-India character are Harijan Sevak Sangh, Delhi, Bharatiya Depressed Classes League, New Delhi; Ishwar Saran Ashram, Allahabad; Indian Red Cross Society, New Delhi; Hind Sweepers Sevak Samaj, New Delhi; Ramakrishan Mission, Narendrapur, West Bengal; Bharatiya Adimjati Sevak Sangh, New Delhi, Andhra Rashtra Adimjati Sevak Sangh, Nellore; Ramakrishna Mission, Cheerapunji, Ranchi, Puri, Silchar and Shillong, Thakkar Bapa Ashram, Numakhani, Orissa; Servants of India Society, Pune; and Social Work and Research Centre, Tilloria, Rajasthan.

Government provides grants-in-aid to non-official voluntary organisations working among scheduled castes and scheduled tribes.

Welfare Schemes

The welfare of scheduled castes and scheduled tribes is given special attention by both the central and state governments. Special programmes for their welfare have been undertaken in the successive five year plans and the size of investment on these special programmes has been increasing from plan to plan as shown in table.

TABLE 3

	Period	Outlay Expenditure
First Plan	1951-56	30.04
Second Plan	1956-61	79.41
Third Plan	1961-66	100.20
Annual Plans	1966-69	68.50
Fourth Plan	1969-74	172.70
Fifth Plan	1974-78	296.19
Sixth Plan	1980-85	340.00
1.	Central Sector	240.00
2.	State Sector	720.00
3.	Sepcial central assistance for sub. plans for tribal areas	470.00
4.	Special control assistance for component plans for the developments of SCs	600.00

Plan Programmes

Some of the important centrally sponsored scheme are :

Coaching And Allied Scheme

With a view to improving the representation of scheduled castes and scheduled tribes in various posts and services under Central/ state governments and public sector undertakings, bank services, Life/ General Insurance Corporation of India, pre-examination coaching centres have been set-up in various parts of the country for preparing scheduled casted and scheduled tribes candidates for various competitive examinations held by UPSC, and State Public Service Commissions and other recruiting bodies.

The number of such centres established by the end of March 1983 was over 62.

Post Matric Scholarships

The scheme of Post Metric Scholarships for Scheduled castes was started in 1944-45 and the object of providing financial assistance to the scheduled tribes students studying at post matriculation on stages in districts throughout the course so as to enable them to complete their education. Starting with a mere 114 awards to scheduled castes students in 1944-45 and 89 for scheduled tribes in 1948-49. The years in inception of the scheme for the two categories the estimated number of awards to scheduled tribes had reached 4.90 lakhs in 1979.80, 5.65 lakhs approxilakhs in 1981-82, 7.78 lakhs in 1982-83 and 8.64 lakhs approximately in 1983-84. From 1880-81 the employed students with a total income of Rs. 75 per month are made eligible for the scholarships restricted to reimbursement of compulsory non refundable dues, fees, etc. Restrictive condition of scholarships to only two children of the same parents has also been relaxed in favour of girl students from 1980-81.

Girls Hostels

Financial assistance is given to state and union territory administrations for the construction of new hostels and to expand existing ones at any place where the facilities for girls belonging to these classes are inadequate.

Research and Training

The Government provide cent per cent financial assistance to reputed and competent organisations/institutions to undertake short duration, action-oriented studies on problems relating to the formulation, implementation and evaluation of programmes for economic, social and educational development of scheduled castes. The emphasis in such studies, however, is on the economic problems of these communities.

Book Bank Scheme

The scheme is for scheduled caste and scheduled tribe student studying in medical/engineering degree courses in the country so as to provide text books to those who can ill-afford expensive education without state support.

Pre-Matric Scholarships

This scheme, started in 1977-78, is intended for the educational development of children who are engaged in the so-called unclean occupations, scavenging of dry latrines, tanning and flying, studying in Class VI to X. A scholarship of Rs. 145 per month is given to each student under this scheme.

I. Strategy for Development of Scheduled Castes

A three-pronged strategy has been evolved to speed up the development of the scheduled castes (a) special component plans of the states and central ministries, (b) special central assistance to the special component plans for the scheduled castes of the states, (c) scheduled castes development corporations in the states.

The special component plans envisage identification of schemes under general sectors of development which would be of benefit to the scheduled castes, qualification of funds from all divisible programmes under each sector and determination of specific targets as to the number of families which are to be benefited from these provisions of basic services and facilities and of access to opportunities for social and educational development are also to be brought into the special component plans.

During the sixth plan period, an amount of Rs. 4,481.91 crore was earmarked for special component plan. This allocation was made out of the total plan outlay of Rs. 46,831.30 crore. The 1982-83 plan allocation in this sector was Rs. 675.78 crore against the total plan outlay of Rs. 9,445.59 crore and in the following year the allocation had gone up to Rs. 754.86 crore out of the total plan outlay of Rs. 11,120.80 crore.

Special Central Assistance

The Central Government provides special central assistance to the state special component plans for the scheduled castes. The special central assistance is an additive to the state plan and programmes for scheduled casted and it does not follow the systematic pattern for special schemes.

It is meant for the totality of the State efforts for the development of the scheduled castes. The additionality, according to the states, from the assistance is to be used by them only for income-generating economic development schemes in conjunction with the outlays in their special component plans so as to assist the economic advancement of the maximum possible number of scheduled caste families below the poverty line. The assistance is apportioned among the state governments and union territories taking into account facts like scheduled cast population, backwardness of the states and efforts of the state governments.

The special central assistance has helped in motivating the state governments to put in larger outlays in their special component plans as would be seen from the table below :

TABLE 3 : Central Assistance

Year	State Plan outlay	SCP outlay	Percentage central	Special assistance
1979-80	5,967.03	240.54	4.33	5
1980-81	7,140.31	547.84	7.67	100
1981-82	8.229.31	632.76	7.69	110
1982-83	9,445.49	675.76	7.15	120
1983-85	11,120.80	754.86	6.79	130

Against the allocation or Rs. 600 crore, SCA to the SCPs during the Sixth Plan, Rs.100 Crore, Rs. 110 crore, Rs. 120 crore and Rs. 130 crore were released during 1980-81, 1981-82, 1982-83 and 1983-84 respectively.

Scheduled Castes Development Corporation

The scheduled castes development corporations in the states are envisaged to interfere between scheduled caste families and financial institutions in respect of bankable schemes of economic development. The corporations provide margin money loan-an assistance to these families, thereby helping to increase the flow of funds from financial institutions to scheduled caste families.

These corporations have been set up in 17 states. Grants are given by the Central Government to the state governments for investment in the share capital of the corporation in the ratio of 49 : 51. The table shows the releases made so far.

TABLE 4 : Grants for Scheduled Castes Development Corporation

Years		State Government contribution	Amount released by the centre
1978-79	... ...	710.55	50.00
1979-80	... ...	703.16	1,224.00
1980-81	... ...	1,403.00	1,300.97
1981-82	... ...	1,367.56	1,332.87
1982-83	... ...	1,380.40	1,350.00
1983-84	... ...	1,759.93	1,400.00

Based on the experience gained by these corporations and suggestions received from the state government/central ministries certain modifications were effected in the scheme during 1981-82. The corporations can now provide margin money loan-assistance for schemes will total non-recurring cost upto Rs. 12,000 as against the earlier ceiling of Rs. 6,000. The state governments are now eligible for grants-in aid on a matching basis, for promotional activities for the staff of the corporations for loan recovery/ monitory devaluation/technical wings subject to a ceiling of a certain percentage of the cumulative central assistance.

II. Tribal Development

In the fifth Plan, a new Strategy for tribal development was evolved. Areas having 50 or more than 53 per cent of tribal concentration were delineated and tribal-sub.plans prepared in 19 states and union territories, namely Andhra Pradesh, Assam, Bihar, Gujarat, Himachal Pradesh, Karnataka, Kerala, Madhya Pradesh, Magarasgtram Manipur, Orissa, Tamil Nadu, Tripura, Uttar Pradesh, West Bengal, Andaman and Nicobar Islands and Goa, Daman and Diu. Tribal sub-plan areas were delineated in Sikkim in August 1980.

The broad objectives of the tribal sub-plan are : 1. to narrow the gap between the levels of development of tribal areas and other areas, and 2. to improve the quality of life of the tribal communities.

In order to achieve these objectives, elimination of all for exploitation of tribals particularly in land, money-lending, malpractices in the exchange of agricultural and forest produce was given high priority. During the Fifth Plan, the outlay under special central assistance was Rs. 120 crore. During the Sixth Plan, the outlay for special central assistance has been kept at Rs. 470 crore.

The tribal sub-plan areas in 19 states and union territories are grouped into 180 integrated tribal development projects as operational units.

During the Sixth Plan, tribal majority pockets, which have a total population of 10,000 and 50 per cent or more of tribal population are also to be taken up and the modified areas development approach as a part of the tribal sub-plan strategy. The concept of tribal sub-plan itself has been kept flexible and has been adopted to the local situation. Programmes undertaken include agriculture and allied sector, irrigation, marketing and co-operation, education etc. The most backward groups among tribal, primitive tribe are given special attention by preparing separate plans for them.

Tribal development has from the beginning been based on a two-pronged approach, namely, (a) promotion of development activities to raise their level of living and (b) protection of their interests through legal-administrative support.

Tribal Research Institute

Tribal research and training institutes have been functioning in Andhra Pradesh, Assam, Bihar, Gujarat, Kerala, Madhya Pradesh, Maharastra, Orissa, Rajasthan, Uttar Pradesh and West Bengal. They have played a useful role in the formulation of tribal sub-plans, projects, reports, monitoring and evaluation, research studies and training of personnel.

Backward Classes

The report of the Second Backward Classes Commission, heeded by B.P. Mandal, which was submitted to Government on, 31 December 1980 is under consideration

Through a new article 338 A, the Minority Commission has been sought to be established; It reveals :

(1) There shall be a Commission for the minorities, other than linguistic minorities, to be known as the Minorities Commission.

(2) Subject to the provisions of any law made in this behalf by Parliament, the Commission shall consist of such persons as the President may appoint and the conditions of service and tenure of office of the persons so appointed shall be such as the President may by rule determine.

(3) It shall be the duty of the Commission :

(a) to investigate all matters relating to the safe-guards provided for the minorities under tins Constitution and laws passed by the Union and State Governments;

(b) to undertake a review of the implementation of the policies pursued by the Union and the State Governments with respect to the minorities;

(c) to take into specific complaints deprivation of right and safeguards of the minorities;

(d) to conduct studies, research and an analysis on the question of avoidance of discrimination and atrocities against minorities;

(e) to serve as a national clearance house for information in respect of the conditions of the minorities;

(f) to submit to the President annually or at such other times as the Commission may deem fit, reports upon the working of those safeguards;

(g) to make in the reports the recommendations as the commission may deem fit as to the measures that should be taken by the Union or any State for the effective implementation of those safeguards;

(h) to discharge such other functions in relation to the protection and advancement of the minorities as President may by rule specify.

4. The President shall cause all such reports to be laid before each House of Parliament, within three months of their receipt along with a memorandum explaining the action taken or proposed to be taken or proposed to be taken on the recommendations relating to the Union and the reasons for the non-acceptance, if any, of any such recommendation.

5. Where any such report or any part thereof relates to any matter with which any State Government is concerned a copy of such report, immediately on its receipt, shall be forwarded to the Governor of the State who shall cause it to be laid before the Legislature of the State, within three months of its receipt by him, along with a memorandum explaining the action taken or proposed to be taken on the recommendations relating to the State and the reasons for the non-acceptance, if any, of any such recommendation.

6. For the purpose of holding any investigation, the Commission shall have the same status and powers as the Commission of Inquiry under the Commission of Inquiry Act, 1952.
7. The Union and the State Government shall consult the Commission on all major policy matters affecting the minorities.
8. In this article, references to minorities shall be treated as references other than linguistic minorities.

Commission for Scheduled Castes and Scheduled Tribes

According to Article 338 of the Constitution for which the bill was introduced in Lok Sabha on 25th January, 1985 :

1. There shall be a Commission for the Scheduled Castes and Scheduled Tribes.
2. Subject to the Provisions of any law made in this behalf by Parliament the Commission shall consist of such persons as the President may appoint and the conditions of service and tenure of the persons so appointed shall be such as the President may by rule determine.
3. It shall be the duty of the Commission,

(a) to investigate all matters relating to the safeguards provided for the Scheduled Castes and Scheduled Tribes under this Constitution and laws passed by the Union and States Governments;

(b) to undertake a review of the implementation of the policies pursued by the Union and the State Governments with respect to the Scheduled Castes and Scheduled Tribes;

(c) to look into specific complaints regarding deprivation of rights and safeguards of the Scheduled Castes and Scheduled Tribes;

(d) to conduct studies, research and analysis on the question of avoidance of discrimination and atrocities against Scheduled Castes and Scheduled Tribes;

(e) to suggest appropriate legal and Welfare measures in respect of Scheduled Castes and Scheduled Tribes to be undertaken by the Union or the State Governments;

(f) to serve as national clearance house for information in respect of the conditions of the Scheduled Castes and Scheduled Tribes;

(g) to submit to the President, annually or at such other times is the Commission may deem fit, reports upon the working of those safeguards;

(h) to make in such reports such recommendations as the commission may deem fit as to the measures that should be taken by the Union or any State for the effective implementation of those safeguards and

(i) to discharge such other functions in relation to the protection and advancement of the Scheduled Casted and Scheduled Tribes as the President may by rule specify.

4. The president shall cause all such reports to be laid before each House of Parliament, within three months of their receipt, along with a memorandum explaining the action taken or proposed to be taken on the recommendations, relating to the Union and the reasons for the non-acceptance, if any, of any such recommendation.
5. Where any such reports or any part thereof relates to any matter with which any State Government is concerned, a copy of such report, immediately on its receipt shall be forwarded to the Governor of the State who shall cause it to be laid before the Legislature of the State, within three months of its receipt by him, along with memorandum explaining the act taken or proposed to be taken on the recommendation relating to the State and the reasons for the non-acceptance, if any, of such recommendation.
6. For the purpose of holding any investigation, the Commission shall have the same status and powers as the Commission of Inquiry under the Commissions of Inquiry Act, 1952.
7. The Union and the State Government shall consult the Commission on all major policy matters affecting the Scheduled Castes and Scheduled Tribes.
8. In this article, references to the Scheduled Castes and Scheduled Tribes shall be treated as including references to such other backward classes as President may, on receipt of the report of a Commission appointed under clauses (1) of article 340, by order specify.

A bill was introduced on 25th January in the Lok Sabha for the purpose. According to it (Article 350B) :

(1) There shall be Commission for linguistic minorities to be known as the Linguistic Minorities Commission.

(2) Subject to the provisions of the law made in this behalf by Parliament the Commission shall consist of such persons as the President may appoint and the conditions of service, and

tenure of office of the persons so appointed shall be such as the President may by rule determine.

(3) It shall be the duty of the commission :

(a) to investigate all matters relating to the safeguards provided for the linguistic minorities under this Constitution and the laws were passed by the Union and State Governments,

(b) to undertake a review of the implementation of the policies pursued by the Union and the State Governments with respect to the linguistic minorities,

(c) to look into specific complaints regarding deprivation of rights and safeguards of the linguistic minorities,

(d) to conduct studies, research and analysis on the question of avoidance of discrimination and atrocities against linguistic minorities,

(e) to suggest appropriate measures in respect of any linguistic minority of any minority language to be undertaken by the Central or the State Governments,

(f) to serve as national clearance house for information in respect of the conditions of the linguistic minorities,

(g) to submit to the President, annually or at such other times as the Commission may deem fit, reports upon the working of the safeguards,

(h) to make such recommendations as the commission may deed fit as to the measures that should be taken by the Union or any State government for the effective implementation of those safeguards,

(i) to discharge such other functions in relation to the protection and advancement of the linguistic minorities as the President may be rule specify.

4. The President shall cause all such reports to be laid before each House of Parliament, within three months of their receipt along with a memorandum explaining the action taken or proposed to be taken on the recommendations relating to the Union and the reasons for the non-acceptance if any, such recommendation.

5. Where any such report or any part there of relates to any matter with which any State Government is concerned, a copy of such report immediately on its receipt, shall be forwarded to the Governor of the State who shall cause it to be laid before the

Legislature of the State, within three months of its receipts by him along with a memorandum explaining the action taken or proposed to be taken on the recommendations relating to the State and the reasons for the non-acceptance, if any, such recommendation.

6. For time purpose of holding any investigation, the Commission shall have the same status and powers as the Commission of Inquiry under the Commission of Inquiry Act, 1952.
7. The Union and the State Governments shall consult the Commission on all major policy matters affecting the linguistic minorities.

(iii) New Educational policy

India has launched a new grandiose scheme of Education for all by the year 2010. The National Policy on Education (NPE-86) aimed at making it "an effective instrument for taking the country into the 21st century" accorded a very high priority to the programme of universalisation of elementary education to ensure essential minimum education to all children upto the age of 14 years.

A modified NPE presented in Parliament on May 7, 1992 called for making the "plus two stage" part of school education throughout the country. Besides, it proposes to prepare national and state levels to ensure speedy redressal of grievances in states besides strengthening the Indira Gandhi National Open University.

Acharya Ramamurthy Committee and the Janardhana Reddy Committee have given useful recommendations for education. The new policy proposed to enlarge the scope of "Operation Blackboard" from two classrooms and two teachers to three classrooms and three teachers. It will be extended from the primary level to the upper primary stage also. Atleast 50 per cent of teachers recruited in future will be women.

The target of free and compulsory education upto 14 years have been revised. The new policy proposes to launch a national mission to achieve this goal by the turn of the century.

A phased drive called Operation Blackboard to improve the basic infrastructure of primary schools is also being pursued. Till 1989-90 a total of Rs. 383.09 crore had been spent under the scheme. A significant event in 1988 was the setting up of a National Literary Authority to manage the national literary mission aimed at achieving 80 per cent literacy in 15-35 age group in the country by 1995. (The present national literacy rate is 52.11 per cent).

The policy on Education provides for opening of residential schools for talented children. These schools are named Navodaya Vidyalayas. It is proposed to open such schools in each district in the country. Of these 275 covering 22 states and 7 Union Territories have been set up by 1991-92. Sanction for five new schools have also been accorded.

The Navodaya Vidyalayas are aimed at providing opportunities to the talented children to develop their full potentials and to promote national integration. Education in these schools is free for all students.

The central government have taken series of successful steps for the improvement of education throught this New Educational Policy. This policy has given new hope for the younger generation for their future course of education in their life. No wonder this New Education Policy is a welcoming feature for the younger generation.

(iv) Promotion of Arts and letters

(a) Lalit Kala Academy

In the wake of Independence the Government gave a fresh thought to the revival of the music and dancing and set up Sangit Natak Academy (Academy of Music, Dance and Drama) and Lalit Kala Academy (Academy of Fine Arts). The latter was inaugurated in October 1953. Its main function is to encourage and promote study and research in the fields of painting sculpture, architecture and applied arts. It will coordinate the activities of state Academies, publish literature on art, and foster national and international contacts thought exhibitions und exchange of art objects.

(b) Sangeet Natak Academy

It is an Academy of dance, drama and music. It was inaugurated in 1953. It aim at the preservation of Indian culture and promoting and developing Indian drama, music and dance. It has set up training institutions, sponsored festivals and cultural exchange in the field of dance, drama and music. Awards have been instituted to encourage these arts. The Academy renders financial assistance to various institutions and organisations of dance and music. It also encourages the talents in the various fields of music and dance by giving annual awards to the outstanding artists.

(c) National School of Drama

Besides Sangeet Natak Academy, National School of Drama has been set up for the promotion of Drama. The main objective of the institution is to faster and develop drama and to promote through them the cultural unity of the country. It gives good training and encourages the talents in the various fields of music and dance by giving annual awards to the outstanding artists.

(d) Sahitya Academy

It was inaugurated on March 12, 1954. It is a national organisation for the development of Indian letters and also to set high literary standards and to foster and co-ordinate literary activities. Since its inception in 1954 the Sahitya Academy had been propagating the idea of cultural unity by using the slogan, "Indian literature is one though written in many languages," This aphoristic statement is honestly questioned by thinkers who point out that literature is language based and hence it is intrinsically linked with the language in which it is written. The Government of India has announced annual prizes of Rs. 5000 for the most outstanding books, published since Independence in each of the 15 regional languages of India. Prizes are also awarded for printing. Twenty five foreign classics have been selected for translation into all the major Indian languages. This Academy is rendering a very good service for the promotion of language literature of India.

(e) Zonal Cultural Centres

Zonal Cultural Centres have been established for the promotion of dance, drama, music and fine arts. Classical dances like Bharat Natyam, Odissi, Kuchipudi, Manipuri, Kathakali and Kathak have been fostered not only by government bodies but also by private organisations. Their main objective is to promote through them cultural unity of the country. They encourage the talents in the various fields of music and dance by giving annual awards to the outstanding artists. Even Westerners admire and love out classical dances. Through these zonal cultural centres some of the Indian dancers visited Western countries and greatly impressed the Western audience with their performances. Madame Sumiaki popularised Kathakali in Europe as well as America and spread its tradition there. Uday Shankar, the outstanding dancer gave numerous performances of the Indian dances in Europe and America and earned great admiration of the critics.

The film industry has done a lot for the cultural unity of the country. Film festivals have been conducted periodically by zonal cultural centres and awards have been given to talented artists. In short, the zonal cultural centres have done a lot to the unity of the country and even now they are doing valuable service for the same.

Index

C

D

E

F

G

H

I

J